Prayers

of the

BIBLE

Prayers

of the
BIBLE

John McFadyen

World
REFERENCE

The Prayers of the Bible
by John E. McFadyen
© 1995 by AMG Publishers
All Rights Reserved.

Originally published in 1906
by Hodder & Stoughton in London.

ISBN 0-529-10483-0

Library of Congress Catalog Card Number: 95-83608

Printed in the United States of America

Contents

PART 4
BIBLICAL PRAYERS FOR MODERN USE

INDEXES

Foreword

"As the religion of the Bible is the source and inspiration of our own, we have much to learn from its prayers," writes John Mc-Fadyen. *The Prayers of the Bible* is an informative and enlightening collection of biblical prayers and commentary on the place of these prayers in our lives today. First published in 1906 in London by Hodder and Stoughton, *The Prayers of the Bible* discusses in detail such topics as the various styles of prayer, the themes of prayer, and forms of address used in biblical prayer. McFadyen also compares the prayers of Paul and Jesus, and presents a collection of topically arranged prayers from Scripture.

In creating this new edition of *The Prayers of the Bible,* we at AMG Publishers have made a few minor changes to the original work to help make its content more clear to modern readers. We have updated spelling in accordance with how our language has changed over the years, and in some cases, unusual forms of punctuation have been simplified.

Our hope is that this volume will enrich readers in their communion with God and encourage them to "pray without ceasing" (1 Thess. 5:17).

Preface
to the Original Edition

The Bible is richer in prayers than is commonly supposed, and it may be doubted whether they have generally received the attention which they deserve. Their interest is two-fold, scientific and practical. On the one hand, the prayers throw light upon the religion; and, on the other, as the religion of the Bible is the source and inspiration of our own, we have much to learn from its prayers. Both these interests are safe-guarded in this volume. It is an attempt to understand prayer by an examination of the prayers and allusions to prayer, and it seeks to gather up the results of this examination and to apply them to the public and private devotions of today.

In order to facilitate the study of the prayers, I have collected and arranged them topically, and in the Old Testament chronologically as well, so far as that was possible, the first period including the prayers to the exile, the second those between the exile and the New Testament. It thus becomes as easy as it is interesting to trace the development of prayer in the Bible. Following this collection is a selection of biblical prayers suitable for modern use.

The collection is, I believe, practically complete, except that I have purposely excluded from it the prayers of the Psalter. To have included them would have been to transcribe most of the Psalter, but in the selection for modern use, I have drawn from it such prayers as are of permanent interest and value. The prayers here collected might have been considerably enlarged by including the meditations—for example, Psalms 103 and 139—and the indirect prayers in the third person scattered up and down both Testaments, and especially numerous in the epistles of Paul. But I have confined the list almost exclusively to prayers addressed to God in the second person. As a specimen of the prayers of Paul, however, I have included the well-known prayer in Ephesians 3:14–19. For the sake of completeness, I have added a list of Sentences Introductory to Public Worship, though these are not all strictly prayers.

I have kept as close as possible to the Authorized Version of the English Bible, except where it is manifestly wrong, as, for example, in its rendering of Jehovah by LORD. But in the selection of prayers for modern use, I have retained the incorrect, but more familiar and not inappropriate term LORD. Sometimes, as in the Psalms, a verse has been omitted owing to the extreme difficulty of the text; at other times a reading has been adopted without discussion.

The results of recent criticism are throughout the volume presupposed. Where there is such comparative unanimity, it did not seem wise or necessary to delay the argument by discussions which were strictly extraneous to the topic in hand. In any case, the heart of the problem is not in the least affected by the findings of criticism. This may affect our view of the development, but not the essence of the prayers themselves. A prayer is a prayer, whatever be its date, and whoever composed it. Apart from all critical questions, the prayers of the Bible bring us, more than anything else can do, into the inner chamber of ancient Hebrew piety, and there we may hear how God was addressed by the men who counted Him their Friend.

JOHN E. McFADYEN.
GLASGOW.

Part 1

The Prayers of the Bible

The Naturalness of
Biblical Prayer

The Bible is the great religious classic of the world, and prayer is one of the highest exercises of religion. A study of biblical prayer must therefore be of interest alike to the student of the Bible, and to the man of religious life and temper, whether he be a student or not. We must not, of course, expect from the Bible an answer to all the questions concerning prayer which a thoughtful man of today may ask himself. But this is, perhaps, even more of a gain than a loss. Instead of controversy, we have reality, and it is always good to face reality, and to have the facts thrust upon us which are dwarfed or lost in the labyrinth of argument. Instead of discussions about the nature and value of prayer, we have perplexed and persecuted men pouring out their hearts to a God who is as real to them as their sorrow, and finding in that communion the strength that cometh in the night.

Just as the Bible assumes the existence of God, so it also assumes the naturalness of prayer. It does not answer, and, for the most part, does not even raise the problems which bear so heavily upon educated men today. What is the relation, for example, of prayer to natural law? Does it produce any effect in the world other than its effect upon the spirit of the man himself? Will prayer keep a steamer from colliding in a fog, or from foundering, when she strikes the rocks? Can a dying man be prayed away from the gates of death? Such an effect need not involve a violation of natural law, but are we to suppose that—albeit in accordance with natural law—events happen which would not have happened, and changes are effected which would not have been effected, but for prayer? If never another prayer rose from human lips and hearts, would the ordinary sequence of things be in any way affected?

Apart from the alleged inexorableness of natural law, there are other difficulties arising out of the nature of God. If He be omniscient, what, if any, is the real significance of our speech to Him? Our prayers do not instruct Him: "Your heavenly Father knows what things ye have need of." If, then, He does not need to be told, do we need to tell Him? In prayer, are we not rather making our needs plain to ourselves than to Him? But more. His will is a beneficent will. We must suppose that He wills the good of men. Does He will that good the more for their supplications and the less for their silence? And if He did, would He be such a God as reasonable men could worship?

Again, besides being beneficent, He is wise, and knows what is best for us. That is, He not only wills our good, but knows how to secure it; while we, who never foresee the remote consequences of our acts, and seldom even all their immediate consequences, may well hesitate to offer any specific petitions whatever, and may consider all these petitions most wisely expressed and included in the simple words, "Thy will be done." As we cannot inform Omniscience, neither can we make suggestions to Wisdom. Can we do better than allow our destiny to be shaped by hands of Wisdom, guided by a heart of Love?

These represent some of the difficulties felt by the modern mind in relation to prayer as commonly understood. The universality and relentlessness of natural law, the omniscience, the love, and the wisdom of God, seem to combine to render prayer little better than an idle or at most a pious exercise, whose influence is restricted to the character of the man who offers it.

It is not the purpose of this volume to discuss these problems on their intrinsic merits and in their relation to the modern view of the world, but simply to ascertain the place and meaning of prayer in the religion of the Bible. The intellectual world of the Hebrews was infinitely simpler than ours. The progress of exact science has created a scientific temper which is shared by thousands who have no technical knowledge of any particular science; and the increasing complexity of the world has been accompanied by an increasing difficulty in readjusting the ideas of an older and simpler civilization to the new situation. But, while it would be unreasonable to expect to find, in an ancient book, a final and adequate answer to modern problems, the time will never come, let us hope, when the religious thought and practice of such men as Jeremiah and Paul will be regarded as irrelevant or sterile. In religion the Hebrews are, and will remain, the masters and teachers of the world.

The problems to which we have alluded are never formally discussed in the Bible. Its world is not our world, and the Hebrews had little genius for philosophical discussion of any kind. The only really continuous discussion in the Bible—the book of Job—is rather a series of eloquently reiterated assertions than a connected argument. But here and there are traces of the skeptical mood in which such problems are born. What place would there be for prayer, for example, in that view of the world represented by the baffled thinker who regarded history as an endless and inexorable cycle, in which "that which hath been is that which shall be; and there is no new thing under the sun" (Eccl. 1:9)? No good Hebrew would have dreamt of denying that there was a God, but there were many, both among the prosperous oppressors, and their poorer victims, who had their doubts as to whether God played any real and active part in human affairs. In the latter half of the seventh century, B.C., the comfortable, easy-going plutocrats, settled upon their lees, said to themselves, "Jehovah will not do good, neither will He do evil" (Zeph. 1:12): that is, He will do neither one thing nor another; in other words, He will leave the world to run as it pleases, or rather, as they please, and can be safely trusted not to intervene. And two centuries later, men of a very different stamp are forced to the same conclusion by the cruel silence that follows their appeals to heaven. "It is useless to serve God, and what has been the good of keeping His commandments?" (Mal. 3:14). The hardships and disillusions of post-exilic times often shook faith into a temporary skepticism, and confirmed the faithless in their infidelity. "What is the Almighty that we should serve Him, and what good would we get by praying to Him?" (Job 21:15). Doubtless this skepticism is created by a too utilitarian view of religion, but, when it is entertained by pious men, it is an honest skepticism, which Malachi can only meet by assuring the disconsolate that Jehovah, to keep Himself in mind of them, is meanwhile having their sorrows recorded in a book (Mal. 3:16), and one day He will intervene in a terrible judgment of fire.

Again it might be true that God gave good things to those who asked Him (Matt. 7:11), but it was undeniable that many good things were given to men whether they asked Him or not. He caused His sun to shine, and His rain to fall no less upon the unjust than upon the just. Thus while the impartial beneficence of nature would no doubt draw a prayer of gratitude from a devout heart, it would probably confirm the indifferent in their indifference.

The Hebrew could not have been overwhelmed, as we are, by the unbroken sequence of cause and effect in the physical world. He had, of course, a keen sense of the rhythm and regularity of nature, with its seed time and harvest, summer and winter, day and night (Gen. 8:22), but he had not our sense of the sternness of law, and therefore he could not have understood the problem of prayer, as it presents itself to a modern mind. To him God was directly responsible for every phenomenon; and, so far as our problem would have had any meaning for him at all, he would have given it a summary answer: *with God all things are possible*. To any objection based on the immutability of law, he could always have replied, "Ye do err, not knowing the power of God." "Is anything too hard for the Lord?" The fleece of wool may become wet or dry, the shadow on the sundial may move forwards or backwards, the heavy prison doors, "the iron gate that leadeth into the city," may open to the prisoner of its own accord. These things may seem strange to us, but to the Hebrew they were not only possible, but natural. His God was a living God, whose ear was not heavy, whose arm was not short; and why should He be less able than man to command and control His resources? The Hebrew was in no danger of involving God in nature. Nature was not God, it was

God's. The earth was the Lord's, and the fullness thereof; might He not do with its forces what He pleased? There was no limit to the divine possibility, for God was "able to do exceeding abundantly above all that we ask or think."

These considerations must be enough to convince us that the Bible has no theoretical solutions for our modern problems. But, by the utter simplicity and naturalness with which the Hebrew heart turns to God in every conceivable situation, a conviction of the reasonableness of prayer and of its indefeasible place in religion is more powerfully borne in upon us than any that could be produced by a merely theoretical solution. "Intercourse with God," as Rothe has said, "is most natural to man as man," and it was peculiarly natural to the Hebrew, with his vivid sense of God. The common pursuits of life were hallowed by religion: the simple greetings on the harvest field between the master and his men take the form of short prayers (Ruth 4:2). The sense of the perpetual need of God and the possibility of an unbroken communion with Him is not, of course, to be expected in the earlier stages. Men could not then have said, "I need Thee every hour." But there came great hours when they were very conscious of their need, and then they turn to God as naturally as a man in difficulty turns to the friend who loves him. In moments of distress, perplexity, danger, sickness, farewell, and death, they lift up their eyes to One that is higher than they for the help which they do not find in themselves and cannot get from one another.

"What time I am in distress, I will cry to Thee." This may not be the loftiest motive of prayer, but it is the most natural and elementary. After the inexplicable defeat of Israel at Ai, Joshua takes his disappointment to his God in prayer (Josh. 7:7–9), just as David after the inexplicable famine, sought the face of Jehovah (2 Sam. 21:1). It is easy to say that Joshua's prayer is petulant, and that David seeks to ascertain the Divine will not directly, but through the oracle. That is not the point; these things were inevitable in early times. The point is that the appeal to God was natural in perplexity, and this is true, irrespective of the stage of religious development. When there are two suitable candidates to take the place left vacant by the death of Judas, the choice is only made after a prayer to the Searcher of hearts (Acts 1:24). In moments of doubt, and where a decision was important, the heart turned instinctively to God.

Face to face with danger, the appeal to God was peculiarly natural; and, as early Israel was beset more or less constantly by the obligations of warfare, prayer is often associated with the field of battle. Jonathan starts, with his armor-bearer, for his dangerous assault upon the Philistines, only after reminding himself that Jehovah may work for them—Jehovah, who can save by few as by many (1 Sam. 14:6). Before an army set out upon the march, a brief prayer, in poetical form, was offered that the enemy might be scattered (Num. 10:35), and Deuteronomy (20:2-4) prescribes that, before an assault, the priests are to encourage the soldiers and to remind them that in the battle they will not be alone, but their God will be with them, to fight for them. In a similar spirit we find Jehoshaphat, on two occasions, anxious to ascertain the will of Jehovah—once before undertaking the campaign against Ramoth-Gilead (1 Kgs. 22:5), and again before the assault on Moab (2 Kgs. 3:11). But there were other dangers than those of the battlefield. Ezra knows of the difficulties that will beset his party on their way from Babylon to Palestine; so, after proclaiming a fast, he entreated his God for a safe and prosperous journey to the home-land (Ezra 8:22). Similarly, when the lives of Daniel and his friends are in peril, because the wise men are unable to interpret Nebuchadrezzar's dream, they appeal for mercy to the God of heaven (Dan. 2:18).

In sickness, as in danger, men turned to God. He was the Lord of life, and He could heal, if He would. Hezekiah prays to Jehovah with tears, when prostrated by a sickness which seems certain to have a fatal ending (2 Kgs. 20:3), and the Chronicler takes it for granted that a pious king, when he is sick, will consult not the physicians, but his God (2 Chr. 16:12).

The beginning and the end of important enterprises were also specially committed to God in prayer. We have seen that prayer was offered when an army set out; it was also offered when the campaign was over (Num. 10:36). The unfortunate alliance of Israel with Gibeon is ascribed by the historian to the fact that Joshua acted on his own responsibility, without first "asking counsel at the mouth of Jehovah" (Josh. 9:14). A new movement must be inaugurated with prayer. Though Paul and Barnabas have had the call of the spirit, they are not sent off upon their missionary tour till the brethren have prayed (Acts 13:3). And the end must be consecrated, as the beginning. There are two very touching and picturesque farewells in the book of Acts, both of which are hallowed by prayer. At Miletus Paul prayed with the Ephesian elders before bidding them good-bye (Acts 20:36); and after a seven days' stay at Tyre, he was escorted to the shore by a large company, including the wives and children; "then we knelt on the beach and prayed and bade each other good-bye" (Acts 21:5).

Occasionally, but not often, life's last great farewell is accompanied by a simpler prayer. There are perhaps hardly half a dozen recorded instances of prayers of the dying. Samson (Judg. 16:28–30) and Zechariah (2 Chr. 24:22) die with a prayer for vengeance upon their enemies. The dying robber besought Jesus to remember him when He came into His kingdom (Luke 23:42). Jesus himself (Luke 23:34) and Stephen (Acts 7:60) die with a prayer for the forgiveness of their enemies, the former commending His spirit to the Father (Luke 23:46), and the latter calling upon the Lord Jesus to receive his spirit (Acts 7:59). The enormous difference between these Old Testament and New Testament prayers is characteristic and suggestive. The former may seen unworthy of so solemn an hour, but in truth they are little but a blunt expression of the desire to have justice vindicated. But even so, these prayers–the cry for justice and the cry for mercy–are typical of the broad difference between the two Testaments, but the prayers are alike in committing their case into the hand of God.

It would be a great mistake, however, to suppose that man considered his relations to God exhausted by offering petitions to Him in distress. Gratitude is not so natural as petition, but it has its place, even in the earlier sources. If a prayer has been answered or an unexpected favor done, the grateful heart is impelled to express itself. When, for example, in answer to the somewhat naïve prayer of Abraham's servant for a sign by which he may discover Isaac's future wife, the woman has been found, the servant "bowed his head, and prostrated himself before Jehovah and said, 'Blessed be Jehovah, the God of my master Abraham, who has not forsaken His loving-kindness and His truth towards my master.' " (Gen. 24:26, 27). Again in one aspect, the great war-ballads known as the Song of Moses (Ex. 15) and the Song of Deborah (Judg. 5) are prayers of gratitude for victory. Hezekiah, who prayed with tears for his recovery from sickness, is represented as expressing his gratitude to the God who in love had delivered his soul from the pit (Is. 38:10–20). The real date and theme of this poem are of no consequence to our present purpose: it is at any rate a proof that recovery from sickness was an occasion for gratitude. So the leper, *"when he saw that he was healed,* turned back with a loud voice glorify God" (Luke 17:15) The duty of gratitude is especially obvious after an unmistakable cure; and though it is usually forgotten—for "where are the nine?"—it is none the less obligatory. Jesus is vexed when so natural a duty is neglected. "Were there none found that returned to give glory to God save this stranger?" Once thanks is offered for the sight of kindly human faces: When Paul saw the brethren who had come from Rome to Appii Forum to meet him, he thanked God and took courage (Acts 28:15).

These illustrations—and they could be multiplied a hundredfold—are enough to show how easily and naturally prayer came, whether in the form of petition or thanksgiving, to the men who move before us on the pages of the Bible. But nothing makes so powerful an impression, or so clearly illustrates the intimacy and immediacy of this communion with God as the ease with which prayers are interpolated in the ordinary course of a historical narrative. It happens that practically all the recorded illustrations of this in the Old Testament are confined to the autobiographical memoirs of Ezra and Nehemiah, and this may possibly be explained by the growing prominence of prayer in the post-exilic period. It would be too much to say, however, that in similar circumstances such interpolations would have been impossible to pre-exilic historians, especially as they are paralleled in pre-exilic prophecy. The earlier part of the book of Jeremiah is full of such prayers, which we shall consider more fully on another occasion; and Hosea (9:14), in a moment of intense emotion, as he contemplates the depravity of Israel and its inevitable end, sends up to his God the swift wild prayer: "Give them, O Jehovah–what wilt Thou give them? give them a miscarrying womb and dry breasts."

But it is in Ezra, and especially in Nehemiah, that the phenomenon is most striking. After reciting at length the unexpectedly generous decree of Artaxerxes in favor of the Jews in their attempt to reorganize their ecclesiastical life, Ezra breaks out into an enthusiastic prayer of gratitude to "Jehovah, the God of our fathers, who hath put such a thing as this in the king's heart to beautify the house of Jehovah which is in Jerusalem, and hath extended lovingkindness unto me before the king, and his counselors and before all the king's mighty princes" (7:27, 28). The effect, upon the reader, of this bright spontaneous outburst of prayer, following the recital of a formal decree, is nothing less than startling. A somewhat similar impression is created by the doxology, "Now unto the King, immortal, invisible," following immediately upon the acknowledgment of the power of Christ "to save sinners, of whom I am the chief" (1 Tim. 1:17, cf. 1 Thess. 3:9, 10).

This phenomenon of interpolated prayer is frequent in the memoirs of Nehemiah. In the course of the narrative describing the impression made upon Sanballat and Tobiah by the efforts of the Jews to build the walls of Jerusalem, Nehemiah (4:4, 5) breaks in with the prayer, "Hear, O our God, for we are despised," etc.; and when the enemy, provoked by the rapid progress of the walls, began to consider the project of an assault upon the city, "we made our prayer unto our God" (4:9). Just as Paul often closes an argument with prayer (Rom. 11:33–36), so Nehemiah frequently ends a paragraph with prayer to his God, either to remember him for what he had done–for example, for his magnanimous conduct during his governorship (Neh. 5:19), for securing the payment of their dues to the Levites (13:4), and for preserving the Sabbath from the

encroachments of trade (13:22, cf. 29, 31); or with a prayer to punish his enemies—in one case including a woman (6:14)—for their
machinations against him and his efforts on behalf of Jerusalem
(4:4, 5). Very interesting in this connection is the brief prayer he
offers after the enemy had sought to intimidate the Jews and had
prophesied failure—"But now (O God) strengthen Thou my hands"
(6:9)—a prayer which is all the more significant as, if the text be
correct, there is no word for "O God" in the original. God was the
ever-present fact. Most interesting of all, and very significant of Nehemiah's God-ward attitude, and of the atmosphere of prayer in
which—man of action though he was—he lived and moved, is the
swift silent prayer for help he offers to the God of heaven before re-
plying, when the Persian king asks him to name his request. "The
king said to me, 'For what dost thou make request?' *So I prayed to
the God of heaven.* And I said unto the king, 'If it please the king,'
etc." (2:4). This ingenuous and altogether incidental statement
lights up, as in a flash, the whole career of Nehemiah. The coura-
geous answer that follows the unspoken appeal to heaven is the
best comment on the place and power of prayer.

Prayer, therefore, is regarded throughout the Bible as natural—
natural as the existence of need and the sense of God; and as need
is universal, prayer is the privilege of all. Out of the depths any man
may cry for himself to God. Sometimes, indeed, overwhelmed by a
sense of their own unworthiness, men felt that they needed a
prophet to intercede for them (Jer. 42:2), but, as a rule, a man confesses his own sin, and craves help for his own need. Women, too,
enjoyed the right of approach to the Deity in prayer. Naturally,
there are relatively few illustrations of women praying, because
women on the whole appear in the Bible, as in all ancient literature,
less frequently than men, but in both Testaments illustrations occur.
The allusion to Hannah's prayer for a child at Shiloh (1 Sam. 1:11)
shows that already in very early times women had the right to pray
at the sanctuaries. It is expressly mentioned that among the disciples gathered in the upper room who "continued steadfastly in
prayer," were women, with Mary the mother of Jesus (Acts 1:14). In
1 Timothy 5:5 it is the mark of a true widow to continue in suppli-

cations and prayers night and day; and the women in the Corinthian church apparently prayed, as well as prophesied, in public (1 Cor. 11:5).

Naturally, public leaders occasionally appear in prayer. Kings are not very often mentioned in this capacity. Prayers are ascribed to David and Solomon, but owing to the somewhat general nature of the historical narratives, there is little opportunity for alluding to the private prayers of the kings. In a more personal narrative, however, like that of the sickness and recovery of Hezekiah, prayer occupies a more prominent place. Nor do we hear much of the prayers of the priests. The notices are nearly all general, such as that they blessed in the name of Jehovah.* They were concerned rather with the sacrifices, and their prayers would probably be more general and formal than the prayers of individuals. Joel (2:17), however, in the distress occasioned by the locusts, represents the priests as weeping and praying. Doubtless the elders of a city, as its representatives, would pray, where its interests were specially implicated. In the case of a murder, for example, which cannot be traced, the elders of the nearest city are to confess its innocence, and to implore the divine forgiveness upon its people (Deut. 21:6–8). Very different in circumstance, yet somewhat similar in spirit, is the suggestion of James (5:14) that, when a man is sick, the elders of the Church shall pray over him.

In the Old Testament, however, the greatest masters of prayer appear to have been the prophets. With the exception of Jeremiah, their prayers are seldom recorded, but there are many incidental allusions to be referred to later, which suggest that prophecy had its roots in prayer (cf. Jer. 33:3).

In the formal worship of the congregation, alike in Old Testament and New, the congregation simply said, "Amen" (1 Chr. 16:36; Neh. 8:6). If the prayer be unintelligible, how, asks Paul, can the unlearned person be expected to say *the* Amen (1 Cor. 14:16)? The use of the article suggests that this was the customary practice.

---

* Deuteronomy 21:5. Cf. 2 Chronicles 30:27. Praise was one of the functions of the Levites; cf. 1 Chronicles 23:30.

Finally, as need is universal, prayer must be equally possible to the foreigner and the Israelite: the Roman Cornelius may pray to God as well as the Hebrew Peter (Acts 10:2). Naturally the impulse of the foreigner is to pray to his own God, but—at any rate from the exile on—the thinkers of Israel cherish the hope of a time when, under the mighty impression made in history by the God of Israel, He will be worshiped by the whole world (cf. 1 Kgs. 8:41–43). Like the foreign sailors in the book of Jonah, they begin by crying each man to his own God, and end by praying to Jehovah (Jon. 1:5, 14). Hints of this universal worship of Jehovah, of the time when "many peoples and strong nations shall come to seek Jehovah of hosts in Jerusalem, and to entreat the favor of Jehovah" (Zech. 8:22), are already found in pre-exilic sources, where occasionally prayers are offered to Jehovah by foreigners.

It is probably no accident, however, that these prayers do not usually take the form of petition, but are rather a recognition of something that Jehovah has done for Israel. The marvelous deliverance of Israel from Egypt, for example, draws from Jethro the following prayer: "Blessed be Jehovah, who hath delivered you out of the hand of the Egyptians, and out of the hand of Pharaoh; who hath delivered the people from under the hand of the Egyptians. Now I know that Jehovah is greater than all gods" (Ex. 18:10, 11). A similar ascription of praise to Jehovah is offered by the Tyrian Hiram, when Solomon approaches him with a request for timber to build the temple (1 Kgs. 8:3). Again, the queen of Sheba when she saw the marvelous glory and wisdom of Solomon, said, "Blessed be Jehovah thy God who delighted in thee, to set thee on the throne of Israel" (1 Kgs. 10:9). It is singular and significant that these prayers should all begin in the same way, and should celebrate circumstances or events distinctively Israelitic—the deliverance from Egypt, the founding of the temple, the wisdom of Solomon. Exactly similar both in form and spirit is the post-exilic prayer in Daniel 3:28, where Nebuchadnezzar is represented as thanking the God of Israel for delivering Daniel's three friends from the fiery furnace into which they had been cast (cf. Dan. 4:34). Similar in spirit, though not in form, is the prayer of Darius, embodied in a decree, that the God of Israel should confound all who put forth their hands to destroy His temple in Jerusalem (Ezra 6:12).

The triumph of the gospel of Jesus dealt the death blow to this particularistic view of religion. He taught men to pray not to the God of Israel, but to "our Father in heaven," and that true prayer was that which offered "neither in this mountain nor yet in Jerusalem" (John 4:21), but anywhere the wide world over that men worshiped God in spirit and in truth.

The Speech of God to Man
and Man to God

Prayer implies reciprocity. It is more than meditation, it is communion. It is a dialogue, not a monologue. It is not enough that man speak to God; he must believe that God can hear and, in some way, speak to him again. And one of the most welcome and surprising features of the Bible is that it is even more full of God's speech to men than of man's to God. In the very early stages of a national literature, this is to be expected. In Homer, the gods are on easy and familiar terms with men; and, generally speaking, the ancient mind, which has a keen appreciation of the mystery and poetry of things, but no power of philosophical analysis, instinctively peoples its world with supernatural beings who sustain direct and real relations to men.

But the peculiar thing about the Bible is that this phenomenon persists through every stage of the literary and religious development. The prophetic parts of the Pentateuch are full of tales of the meeting and converse of God with men. There we might expect them; for these tales are among the oldest prose narratives in the Bible, and they represent a tradition older still. But such converse is not confined to the Mosaic or pre-Mosaic period: it occurs also in the books of Samuel and Kings, in Isaiah, Jeremiah, and Ezekiel, prophets who stand in the full blaze of history; it occurs even in the New Testament. It may be difficult enough to form any clear or adequate idea to our own minds of the way in which Deity thus impinged upon human experience, but summarily to brand all the recitals as legendary is impossible. In any case, this description could only apply to the earlier narratives, while the phenomenon itself persists throughout the whole development. Doubtless the men who, in later times, so clearly heard the voice of God were men of special spiritual capacity; it is also possible that there were peculiarities in their mental, spiritual, and even physical constitution, which increased their native susceptibility to impressions of the divine. But, however we explain it, the Bible is saturated throughout with the idea that God can speak as well as man.

In later and more reflective times, the divine voice could be detected in the processes of nature, and in the large movements of history. There was no speech nor language, but the voice was heard clearly enough by the attentive ear. Often the later psalmists heard it sounding across the centuries from "the days of old," on which they love to meditate (Ps. 78; 95:7; 105); it was heard in the roar of the thunder (Ps. 29), in the solemn inexplicable processes of nature (Job 38, 39) in the measured westward tramp of the Assyrian hosts (Amos 3:8). But the voice of God of which we hear most in Scripture was more definite and particular than that. It was a still small voice, which fell upon the inward ear almost like the voice of a man.

In the earlier narratives, God speaks much and man comparatively little. Promises are made (Gen. 13:14–18) and commands are given (Gen. 12:1), and the patriarchs have little to do but believe the one and execute the other. Abraham is silent when he hears the voice bidding him take his son, his only son, and offer him in sacrifice upon a mountain (Gen. 12:2). Sometimes, indeed, a divine speech is nothing but a palpable device on the part of the historian to summarize a situation graphically, as, for example, the *résumé* of Israel's earlier history with which Joshua introduces his farewell speech to the people (Josh. 24:2–13); and occasionally there is a certain stiffness or formality in the dialogue which suggests that the historian has a didactic aim in view, as in the intercession of Abraham for Sodom (Gen. 18:23–32), or in the choice of David and the rejection of his brethren for the kingship (1 Sam. 16:6–12).

But, as a rule, the dialogues are full of life, psychological interest and literary beauty. So much is Jehovah like the men to whom He speaks that they can even argue with one another. " 'Come now, and I will send thee to Pharaoh,' says Jehovah to Moses; and Moses said, 'Who am I that I should go?' and He said, 'Certainly I will be with thee.' " (Ex. 3:10–12). Later on, Moses demurs. "Oh, Lord, I am not eloquent, I am slow of speech and of a slow tongue. And Jehovah said to him, 'Who hath made man's mouth? or who maketh a man dumb, or deaf, or seeing, or blind? is it not I, Jehovah? Now therefore go, and I will be with thy mouth, and teach thee what thou shalt speak.' And he said, 'Oh, Lord, send, I pray thee, by the hand of him whom Thou wilt send,' " (Ex. 4:10–13) and very naturally the anger of Jehovah was kindled against him. There is a somewhat similar discussion in the late book of Jonah. "God said to Jonah, 'Doest thou well to be angry for the gourd?' and he said, 'I do well to be angry, even unto death.' " And Jehovah is represented as reasoning with the narrow-hearted prophet, and seeking, as it were, to appeal to his common sense. *"You* care for a little plant, on which you have spent no thought or effort, and am *I* not to care for the great city of Nineveh?" (Jon. 4:9–11).

Even in the earliest narratives, the divine speech is always serious and worthy. Often, as was to be expected, its theme is the future greatness of the Hebrew people;* but it is often, indeed, usually inspired by moral and religious motives. The voice that came to Adam and Cain was a voice that carried conviction of sin, and throughout the historical narratives religious motives are implicated with the political. That voice addresses itself especially to those who are called to prominent service among the people of Israel, as in the Old Testament, or in the kingdom of God, as in the New. It may be heard by children, by warriors, by kings, but most of all by prophets. It comes to Samuel in the sanctuary (1 Sam. 3:4), it reassures Joshua repeatedly with the promise of victory and in the words, "Be not afraid" (Josh. 8:1, 2; 10:8; 11:6), it sends

---

* Cf. also the Balaam story in Numbers 23.

Gideon forth with cheer upon his perilous task (Judg. 6:14, 23), and tells him the precise moment when he is to strike the blow (Judg. 7:9), it speaks to Solomon in the sanctuary at Gibeon (1 Kgs. 3:5–14), its imperious tones ring in the ears of Elijah, impelling him to face the king (1 Kgs. 18:1), and again forcing him away from the desert retreat to which he had fled from the wrath of Jezebel (1 Kgs. 19:9, 13).

To the great prophets that voice is the realest of all realities. "When Jehovah has spoken, who can help prophesying?" (Amos 3:8). So deeply have its notes sunk into their soul that it is not so much they that speak as the voice that speaks in them. When they appear before the great audiences gathered on festal occasions at the country sanctuaries, or in the Jerusalem temple, they are conscious of a direct commission from above, and they preface their brave and searching speeches with the words, "Thus saith Jehovah." The people may resent and deny their claims, but at the risk of their lives they unflinchingly assert the divine authority of their message. "You may put me to death, if you please, but if you do, know that you are putting to death an innocent man, and my blood will be upon you and your city, for it is really Jehovah who has sent me to speak these words in your ears" (Jer. 26:14, 15).

The supernatural voice is usually that of God, or rather, in the Old Testament, of Israel's God, Jehovah. Another mode of representation regards it as an angel's voice (Judg. 2:1–3; 13). The angel of Jehovah is practically identical with Jehovah Himself—in Judges 6:12 it is the angel of Jehovah who speaks, and in verse 14 Jehovah Himself, but in later times, when the sense of the transcendence of God is beginning to produce a more elaborate angelology, divine messages are mediated to men by angels (Zech. 1, 2, 4, 5, 6), who are so far personalized that even their names are sometimes mentioned (Dan. 9:21; Luke 1:19, 26). Frequently also in the New Testament, important messages of warning or comfort are brought to men by angels. An angel of the Lord appears repeatedly to Joseph with messages concerning the birth of Jesus, the flight into Egypt, and the return from Egypt (Matt. 1, 2). Gabriel announces to Zacharias the birth of John the Baptist, and the birth of Jesus to

Mary (Luke 1, 2). An angel appears to the apostles in prison with the command to preach in the temple (Acts 5:19, 20). An angel directs Philip on the way on which he is destined to meet the Ethiopian eunuch (Acts 7:26). An angel urges Cornelius to send for Peter (Acts 10:3). An angel appears to the shipwrecked Paul with words of encouragement (Acts 27:23, 24). It is worthy of note that most of these angelic appearances are expressly connected with dreams or trances (Acts 18:9; 23:11).

Sometimes the voice is said to proceed from the spirit. It was the spirit that told Philip to approach the Ethiopian chariot (Acts 8:29), and that indicated to Peter the presence of the three men who had come from Cornelius to seek him (Acts 10:19). Sometimes the voice is more mysterious still, as in the eerie specter that came at midnight upon the sleeping Eliphaz, and made all his bones to shake (Job 4:12–17), or that epoch-making voice that smote upon the ears of Saul as he hasted away to Damascus (Acts 9:4). This was the voice of "the Lord"; and it is not without significance that "the Lord (that is) Jesus" (Acts 9:17) occasionally speaks in the book of Acts, to Paul, just as Jehovah speaks in the Old Testament to a patriarch or prophet. It is He who commissions Paul to his great task among the Gentiles (Acts 22:18–21), and who sustains him in that task by words of cheer (Acts 18:9; 23:11; cf. 2 Cor. 12:8, 9).

Thus, in one way or another, voices from beyond were borne upon the ears of men. Now it was the voice of Jehovah, now of an angel, and again of the risen Jesus. The Hebrews were very sensitive to the divine speech, and their history is one long dialogue between this world and the world above.

In ancient times, prayers were directed by "every man to his own God" (Jon. 1:5), by the Hebrews therefore to Jehovah, but in later times there are traces of the idea that they may be offered to angels, or at least that the angels can intercede for men,[*] and the rich man in the parable cries to father Abraham to have mercy upon him (Luke 16:24, 27).

---

[*] Job 5:1. The "holy ones" here are the angels.

We have seen how God spoke to man, let us now see how man spoke to God; and as the prayers of the New Testament will receive special consideration in two subsequent chapters, we shall confine our attention here chiefly to the Old Testament.

Throughout the Bible, God is the Friend of man (2 Chr. 20:7); and, especially in the earlier books, man speaks to God as a man to his friend. A growing sense of the distance of God and of the reverence due to Him inspires the later speech with a becoming humility, but many of the older addresses are marked by an ease, a candor, a bluntness even, which are peculiarly welcome as showing how real to the speakers, and how human, was the God they thus boldly addressed. Goethe remarks somewhere that the speech of a man to his friend may be more deadly than to a stranger. To his friend he is less careful of the proprieties and conventions. He lets himself go; and, in a moment of provocation, he may stab with a word the friend he loves. A similarly dangerous familiarity, occasionally degenerating into something very like impertinence, marks some of the speeches in the patriarchal narratives.

After an unsuccessful visit to Pharaoh, Moses thus addresses Jehovah: "Lord, wherefore hast Thou dealt ill with this people? why is it that Thou hast sent me? For since I came to Pharaoh to speak in Thy name, he hath dealt ill with this people; neither hast Thou delivered Thy people at all" (Ex. 5:22, 23). Even more extraordinary is the temper displayed in the speech made by Moses when the people, tired of the manna, begin to clamor for meat. "Why hast Thou dealt ill with Thy servant? and why have I not found favor in Thy sight, that Thou layest the burden of all this people upon me? Have I conceived all this people? Have I brought them forth, that Thou shouldest say unto me, Carry them in Thy bosom as a nursing father carrieth the sucking child, unto the land which Thou swarest unto their fathers? Whence should I have flesh to give unto all this people? For they weep unto me, saying, 'Give us flesh, that we may eat.' I am not able to bear all this people alone, because it is too heavy for me. And if Thou deal thus with me, kill me, I pray thee, out of hand, if I have found favor in Thy sight, and let me not see my wretchedness" (Num. 11:11–15). Two other disappointed prophets beseech, in their petulance, Jehovah to kill them.* Jacob once addresses God almost in the spirit of a man who is driving a bargain (Gen. 28:20–22); and the skeptical Gideon, after putting the word of God to one test which issued in a way that should have satisfied his misgivings, immediately proceeds to demand another test (Judg. 6:36–40).

The primitive nature of ancient religion and the familiarity of men in their relations to God are often quaintly illustrated by the motives with which they urge their prayer upon Him. Sometimes the divine sense of justice is appealed to: "Shall one man sin and wilt Thou be angry with all the congregation?" (Num. 16:22). Or the divine mercy is besought for the guilty people because of Jehovah's special relations with the patriarchs (Deut. 9:27), or because of the redemption which He wrought for them in ancient times (Deut. 9:29; 1 Kgs. 8:51–53), or because they are called by His name (Dan. 9:19).

But the most characteristically primitive appeal is the appeal to Him to consider His reputation. If He fails to help Israel, what will the nations think (Joel 2:17)? They will be more inclined to say that He was unable than that He was unwilling. So, to save His reputation, as it were, He is bound to interpose; otherwise not only Israel's name, but His name will be cut off (Josh. 7:9). This reminds us of the practice of Müller of Bristol who, it is said, "used to employ arguments in prayer, giving eleven reasons why God should do a certain thing: He could not suffer His own glory to be dimmed or His promise to be dishonored," etc. Perhaps the most delightfully naïve illustration of this type of appeal is in the memoirs of Ezra (8:21–23). He had already told Artaxerxes that God protected those who trusted Him, and so he was ashamed, he tells us, to ask him for a guard of soldiers to protect his company on the way to Palestine. Consequently they prayed very earnestly to God that He would Himself guide them safely. God was thus, if we may say so, put upon His honor; "and He was entreated of us, and He delivered us from the hand of the enemy and the ambush by the way" (8:23, 31).

---

* Elijah (1 Kgs. 19:4) and Jonah (4:3). Cf. Job 6:8, 9.

These easy relations of men with God bordered, as we have seen, sometimes on irreverence, but they have also a very attractive side. Just because He stands so near them, can be spoken to and reasoned with, as a man speaks to and reasons with his friend, so they can introduce into their requests details of the most concrete kind. Very charming, for example, is the prayer of Abraham's servant for guidance. "Behold, I am standing by the fountain of water, and the daughters of the men of the city are coming out to draw water; and let it come to pass that the damsel to whom I shall say, 'Let down thy pitcher, I pray thee, that I may drink,' and she shall say, 'Drink, and I will give thy camels drink also': let the same be she that Thou hast appointed for Thy servant Isaac, and thereby shall I know that Thou hast showed kindness unto my master" (Gen. 24:13, 14). The precision with which the details are arranged is very naïve, and the trust which inspires the prayer is beautiful.

So practical is the spirit of biblical prayer that proper names, elaborate descriptions of the speaker's situation, and historical and geographical allusions are of frequent occurrence. When David, pursued by Saul, is at a loss to know which move to make next, he prays, "Will Saul come down as Thy servant has heard? O Jehovah, the God of Israel, I beseech Thee, tell Thy servant." And —when an affirmative answer is given—"Will the men of Keilah deliver me and my men up into the hand of Saul?" (1 Sam. 23:11, 12). The tearful prayer in Lamentations 2:20–22 contains a vivid catalogue of the horrors of the siege of Jerusalem, and Lamentations 5, in form a prayer, is really an elaborate description of the people's distress. Other prayers give a glimpse of the temple, "our holy and beautiful house where our fathers praised Thee," trodden under foot of the adversary and burned with fire (Is. 63:18; 64:11).

Another proof of the extreme ease and naturalness of biblical prayer lies in the fact that, but for the context one would often suppose that a petition, which is in reality addressed to men, was a prayer to God. Take, for example, Aaron's intercession to Moses for Miriam: "Oh, my lord, lay not, I pray thee, sin upon us, for that we have done foolishly, and for that we have sinned. Let her not, I pray thee, be as one dead" (Num. 12:11, 12). Or take Shimei's confession to the king whom he had cursed: "Let not my lord impute iniquity unto me, neither do thou remember that which thy servant did perversely; for thy servant doth know that I have sinned" (2 Sam. 19:19, 20). No hard and fast line was drawn between the vocabulary of religion and that of daily life. Words like "grace" (Ruth 1:8) and "blessing"* were equally applicable to God and man.

Perhaps there is no part of the Old Testament from which we learn so clearly the fearlessness and candor with which men who felt their awful need of God could pray to Him, as the book of Job. The appeals of Job, until he is humbled by the marvelous panorama of God's mighty wisdom and love (Job 38–42), are always brave, often bold, and occasionally all but blasphemous, so that we cannot wonder that his conventional friends were shocked or that the oldest of them should reproach him with forgetting that spirit of humble devotion which becomes men in the presence of God (15:4). The boldness of Job even in prayer–if such his desperate appeals can be called–is the boldness of conscious integrity, intensified a thousandfold by his intolerable and unmerited suffering. Repeatedly he asserts that he would not be afraid to appear before God, and he clamors for an audience with Him, if only the conditions of the audience be fair, and such that he will be able to do his own case justice: that is, God must, on the one hand, remove his leprosy from him, and, on the other, He must not overwhelm him by His terrible majesty (9:34, 35; 13:20, 21). If these conditions be fulfilled, then Job is ready to appear, not as a coward with hanging head, nor yet as a penitent suppliant, but with head erect "as a prince would I go near unto Him" (31:37). Why should God torment him so? "Am I a sea-monster, that Thou settest a watch over me? Granted that I have sinned, what harm can I do unto Thee, O Thou who watchest men only too terribly well. Why hast Thou set me as a mark for Thee? Granted that I have sinned, why then dost Thou not pardon my transgressions and take away mine iniquity?" (7:12, 20, 21). He refuses to be condemned unjustly, and

---

* A blessing (2 Kgs. 5:15) is a very tangible thing. It may be a present of two talents of silver and two suits of clothes (2 Kgs. 5:23).

demands that God should show him why He condemns him (10:2). "Thou knowest that I am not guilty" (10:7). What good does God get by crushing him, by despising the work of His own hands (10:3)? He parodies the eighth Psalm: "What is man, that Thou shouldest count him so great and set Thy mind upon him, and visit him every morning"—only to torment him (7:17, 18)? He denies that the world is governed on moral principles: "It is all the same: He destroys the innocent and the guilty alike" (9:22). And in a terrible moment he utters the audacious thought that God has made him only to destroy him (10:7–13).

Such utterances are not perhaps prayer in the common sense of the word. They are rather a volley of angry bitter questions, and of agonized appeals. But through the audacious form breathes a spirit which is the condition of all prayer—the overwhelming recognition of the fact of God. These bold speeches remind us again of Goethe's remark: they suggest the liberty, the thoughtless liberty, that a man in a passion will take with him friend. They are very different from the sweet humility of Psalm 131.

> Jehovah, my heart is not haughty, nor mine eyes lofty,
> Neither do I exercise myself in great matters,
> Or in things too wonderful for me.
> Surely I have stilled and quieted my soul;
> Like a weaned child with his mother,
> Like a weaned child is my soul within me.

The temper is very different, but both are inspired by the same passion for the friendship of God. It has, of course, to be remembered that the book of Job is poetry and not history, though probably it correctly enough mirrors the struggles through which perplexed souls passed in the political and intellectual confusion of post-exilic times.

There is perhaps no Old Testament character, certainly no Old Testament prophet, whom we know so intimately as Jeremiah. He is the most intensely human of all the prophets, "bone of our bone and flesh of our flesh." He has nothing of the transcendentalism of Ezekiel, nothing of the serenity of Isaiah. His eyes are so blinded with tears that he cannot see the King upon His throne high and lifted up. The religion of such a man must be of peculiar interest to us, and it is a matter of great good fortune that so many of his prayers have been preserved. Most of his recorded prayers, however, are wrung from him by the treachery and heartlessness of his people, and together they give a very inadequate and perhaps totally misleading impression of the man.

He "rolled his cause upon Jehovah"—that is the phrase in which he describes his recourse to God in time of persecution (Jer. 20:12); and often enough, in the course of his checkered and heartbreaking career would he have occasion to turn to the God whom he calls "my strength and my stronghold and my refuge in the day of affliction" (16:19). The siege of Jerusalem, when "the city was being given into the hand of the Chaldeans that fought against it" (32:24), would bring him many a sorrowful moment, and at least two allusions to prayer come from that time. After purchasing the field of his cousin in Anathoth, though humanly speaking the prospects are that the land will be permanently alienated, he seeks in prayer for the guarantee of the hope of ultimate restoration that seems to be belied by the existing situation (32:16–25). And again comes the impulse to pray when he is imprisoned in the court of the guard (33:3).

But more than by the doubt and misery of the siege was Jeremiah distressed by the depravity of his fellow-countrymen, who hated and feared him so much that they plotted against his life; and some of the most appalling prayers in the Bible are offered by him that the divine vengeance may fall upon these base and treacherous men. "Let their wives become childless and widows, and let their men be slain" (18:21). "Bring upon them the day of evil, and destroy them with double destruction" (17:18). "Pull them out like sheep for the slaughter, and prepare them for the day of slaughter" (12:3), and "let me see Thy vengeance upon them" (20:12).

These are singular prayers, but prayer has to be interpreted, like prophecy, in its historical context. On Jeremiah's view of the world, such prayers were inevitable. Generally speaking, the ancient Hebrew belief was that God rewarded men according to their works;

their material fortune was therefore the key to their character. This creed seems to be palpably belied by the facts. Jeremiah is perplexed and confounded by what he sees. He does not doubt the justice of God, and yet he would fain discuss with Him the principles on which He governs the world (12:1). He had meant the best and suffered the worst; if he fails in the end, and his enemies succeed, he is discredited, and with him the character of God and His government of the world. It is this that accounts for the temper of Jeremiah's prayers. Without any sure outlook upon immortality, if the moral order is to be vindicated at all, it must be here and now. Jeremiah, therefore, repeatedly protests his own innocence, as well as his persecutors' guilt. With transparent sincerity, he fearlessly appeals to God's knowledge of his heart. "Thou that triest the righteous, that seest the heart and the mind [20:12], Thou knowest me, Thou seest me and triest my heart toward Thee" (12:3).

Jeremiah's contemporary Habakkuk was equally perplexed, but he meets his doubts more serenely. He takes his stand upon the watch-tower of faith and listens for an answer (Hab. 2:1; cf. Ps. 85:8). Jeremiah remains down below upon the plain in the din and confusion of the battle, with the footman and the horsemen and his own hot heart (Jer. 12:5). His temperament, his tragic experience, his sensitive religious nature, all combine to inspire his prayers with a passion and familiarity which have no parallel anywhere. He addresses God as one who is behaving like a man who has lost his head, and who cannot save (14:9); he compares Him even in prayer to a deceitful brook and to waters that fail (15:18). He charges Him with beguiling him into his prophetic mission (20:7). He, the mighty Jehovah, had overmastered the tender-hearted Jeremiah, who was but a child (1:6), and thrust him upon a career in which he had become a laughing stock all the day (20:7).

Yet nothing in the world is so precious to Jeremiah as the God who tries and perplexes him so. He stands alone, without wife or child (16:2) or any of the human joys that lift men over trouble or console them within it; he has no seat in the gatherings of men who meet to make merry and rejoice (15:17). All the more real to him, therefore, is God. God is all that he has, and He must be everything. He is his refuge in the day of evil (17:17), and His words are the joy and the rejoicing of his heart (15:16). Jeremiah is, in some ways, the most religious spirit in the Old Testament, and it is significant that among historical characters—for Job is not historical—his prayers are the boldest. He speaks with all the fearlessness and passion of a man to his friend.

No book dealing with historical times is so replete with dialogue between God and man as Jeremiah. His ear is very sensitive to the divine voice; he can both speak and listen. For himself, he beseeches help and healing (17:14); upon his enemies he calls for vengeance. But that is not all. Again and again we find him in the capacity of intercessor. It is unfortunate that none of his intercessory prayers have been preserved, but it is plain from a few stray references that they must have been habitual and earnest (11:14; 14:11). "Remember how I stood before Thee to speak good for them" (18:20). Such a man as Jeremiah, even when his message was rejected, must have produced, like Jesus, a tremendous impression upon the people. He is universally recognized as a man whose intercession is powerful. Even when his fortunes are at their lowest, Zedekiah the king recognizes the power of his prayer (37:3), and no less the people (42:2).

The greatness of Jeremiah both in prophecy and prayer is all the more striking when we contrast him with Ezekiel. To Ezekiel God is also very real, but He is girt about with a mysterious glory which renders Him all but inaccessible, and it is significant of this remoteness of God that dialogue and prayer are very rare in the book of Ezekiel. The dialogue in Ezekiel 4:14–16 turns upon ceremonial cleanness, and though "the hand of Jehovah" was often upon him, there are only two brief prayers in the book. Ezekiel's characteristic address is "Ah Lord Jehovah" (Ezek. 4:14; 9:8; 11:13). There is, if you like, a profounder reverence than in Jeremiah, but he lacks that prophet's terrible passion and his overwhelming sense of the need of God as his friend.

It now remains to discuss how the answer to prayer was mediated. In early times the methods were primitive. An answer might, of course, come directly, without any other mediation than that of circumstance. Abraham's servant prays for a specific sign to guide him to the woman of whom he is in search, and the sign comes to pass (Gen. 24:15). Such prayers, in their naïveté, often come perilously near dictation. The speaker needs definite guidance, and he can be most sure of it when the conditions are pre-arranged by himself. Sometimes, as in the case of Gideon, the circumstance through which the divine will is declared is miraculous.

But in early times, as a rule, it had to be professionally interpreted. How elaborate was the apparatus of Oriental peoples for ascertaining the divine will, we may see from the very earnest protest raised against all but prophetic mediation in Deuteronomy 18:9–16. There were diviners, augurs, enchanters, sorcerers, necromancers, etc.; and though as early as the reign of Saul, there was an energetic attempt to remove these influences from Israel (1 Sam. 28:9), they continued to flourish more or less openly for centuries. Saul himself tried to pierce the secrets of the future by the aid of necromancy; the practice is attested for Isaiah's (8:19) time, and persisted at any rate a century longer (Deut. 18). There is a curious reference in 2 Kings 16:15 to an altar which Ahaz used "to inquire by." The common methods of ascertaining the divine will are summarized in the story of Saul, who, it is said, inquired of Jehovah but received no answer, "either by dreams or by Urim or by prophets" (1 Sam. 28:6; cf. 15).

We have already seen how both in the Old and New Testaments God is represented as speaking to men in dreams and visions. From this early notice, therefore, we may conclude that, apart from a revelation which might come directly in a dream, the divine answer was usually conceived as mediated by priests and prophets. It was an Israelitish priest who was sent from Assyria to teach the way of the God of Israel (2 Kgs. 17:27, 28)—in this case the way in which He should be worshiped; and the Urim just mentioned were part of the paraphernalia of the priest. Precisely what they were we do not know, but an interesting notice, preserved in the Greek version of 1 Samuel 14:41, but suppressed in the Masoretic text, suggests that they were a means of casting lots. Instructive, too, is the notice in 1 Samuel 30:7, 8. When David is in doubt as to whether or not he should pursue the Amalekites who had raided his camp, he "inquired of Jehovah." But in order to do this, "he said to Abiathar the priest, 'I pray thee, bring me hither the ephod,' and Abiathar brought thither the ephod to David." And, now that the priest is present with his oracular instruments, "David inquired of Jehovah, saying, etc."

The priest had control of the oracle,* and it was by the oracle that the divine will was ascertained. Especially were affairs of tribal and national importance submitted to it. It is consulted, for example, before the assault of Israel upon Canaan (Judg. 1:1), it is repeatedly referred to in the book of Samuel, and it is an interesting fact that these references nearly all occur in the life of David, who determines, in particular, the movements of his military career by it (1 Sam. 23:10; 30:8; 2 Sam. 2:1; 5:19). The answer of the oracle is not confined to Yes and No. It can give specific guidance (Judg. 1:1; 20:18; 1 Sam. 10:22; 2 Sam. 2:1). Possibly alternative questions were put and the answer determined by lot (1 Sam. 23:10–12). The last illustration of the casting of lots in the Bible is in connection with the appointment of a successor to Judas (Acts 1:26). Possibly it was felt that such methods were no longer worthy or compatible with absolute reliance upon the guidance of the spirit.

But far more important for the development of religion than the oracle of the priests was the prophetic interpretation of the divine will; and it is with a true instinct that in Deuteronomy 18:15 prophecy is singled out as that which is distinctive of and essential to Israel's religion. "Jehovah Thy God will raise up unto Thee a prophet: unto *him* ye shall hearken." It was to them that Jehovah revealed His secret (Amos 3:7), and though multitudes of the professional prophets were time-servers (1 Kgs. 22:6; Amos 7:12; Jer. 23:9–24), it was they more than any others who were felt to be repositories of the purpose of God. When the divine will has to be ascertained on the eve of a campaign, on two occasions Jehoshaphat is anxious to hear what a true prophet has to say (1 Kgs. 22:7; 2 Kgs. 3:11).

---

* 1 Samuel 22:10. For peoples outside of Israel, cf. 1 Samuel 6:2, 3.

Hezekiah, distressed by the blasphemous insolence of the Assyrians, and their menace of Jerusalem, appeals to the prophet Isaiah, and receives a divine answer through him (2 Kgs. 19:1–6), just as, more than a century afterwards, Zedekiah receives an answer through Jeremiah (Jer. 21:1–4). The prophetess Huldah was also consulted by the deputation of Josiah, whom the discovery of the book of the covenant had thrown into consternation (2 Kgs. 22:14).

How the prophets themselves reached their lonely pre-eminence as interpreters of the divine will is a mystery to the depths of which we cannot altogether penetrate. But it is plain that the knowledge they won of the purpose of God was conditioned, in very large measure, by their sympathy with that purpose. It is the pure in heart who see God, and it is they who hear Him too. The prophets who uttered false messages were those who cared less for the truth than for the bite that was put into their mouths (Micah 3:5). Intercourse of the highest kind was possible only to one who was cleansed of all mercenary motives and whose sole ambition was to see the people turn to purity and God. But even to such men the answer did not always come quickly. The will of God could only be revealed to those who could possess their souls in patience. Twice we find Jeremiah reaching certainty only through a period of watching and waiting. Once, as he lies in prison, he hears a voice telling him to buy the field in Anathoth which his cousin will come to offer him for sale; and, when the cousin comes, "then I knew that this was the word of Jehovah" (Jer. 32:6–8). Another time, Hananiah promises complete deliverance from Babylon within two years (Jer. 28:1–5). At first Jeremiah does not know how to deal with the prophecy, and contents himself with pointing out that, according to the teaching of history, prophecies of peace are less likely to be fulfilled than prophecies of evil: "and he went his way." But afterwards the conviction that Hananiah was wrong grew upon him till it became a certainty. Then he appeared, denounced Hananiah's message as a lie, and prophesied his death within the year—a prophecy which seems to have been literally fulfilled.

The pause before the answer comes is not always so obvious as in these two cases, but it is usually plain enough for those who can read between the lines. Jeremiah, perplexed by the anomalies of the moral world, appeals to the God who sees him and knows his heart, to pull his enemies out like sheep for the slaughter (12:3). But no bolt from heaven falls. Then after the silence and agonized meditation of days and it may be of months, a voice articulates itself, and answers his prayer, but only by assuring him that more terrible things are in store. "If thou hast run with the footmen and they have wearied thee, then how canst thou contend with horses? and if in a peaceful land thou fleest, how wilt thou do in the jungles of Jordan?" (12:5). So it was with Paul. In a matter that concerned him very closely the answer came only after he had besought the Lord three times; and when at last it came, it seemed, as did the answer to Jeremiah, stern and hard. The desire of his heart was not granted, but there came to him an assurance which was better still—the assurance of the grace of Christ, and that was sufficient (2 Cor. 12:9).

Themes of Prayer

If proof were wanted that the religion of Israel underwent development, it could be secured in abundance from an examination of the prayers of the Bible. Not that the later prayers are universally finer or profounder than the earlier; prayers for vengeance, for example, are among the latest as well as the earliest in the Bible. But, generally speaking, there is an advance from the material to the spiritual. In the earlier times, God was seen only, or at least most clearly, in His gifts. Men longed for them, partly because in them they found Him. But in course of time they learned to love Him apart from them, and, even without them, to be content with Him. The descendants of the men who had prayed for abundance of corn and wine and oil learned to pray for the nearer presence of God and for the spread of the gospel of Christ.

We shall consider, first, the *petitions* of the Bible. More or less throughout the Old Testament, but especially throughout the earlier period, they gather round things material. Food, drink, and raiment—after these things the Gentiles seek, said Jesus; and the same might have been said of the average Hebrew. A perusal of Deuteronomy 28 or Leviticus 26 illustrates the things which even to the later Hebrews constituted a blessing and a curse, and there is much truth in Bacon's aphorism that "prosperity is the blessing of the Old Testament." "The dew of heaven, the fatness of the earth, and plenty of corn and wine"—these words of an ancient blessing (Gen. 27:28) find an echo very late in Hebrew religion. "Thy great goodness" to

35

which Ezra refers in his prayer of confession was represented by "a fat land, houses full of all good things, cisterns hewn out, vineyards and oliveyards, and fruit trees in abundance" (Neh. 9:25). In the prayer associated in 1 Kings 8 with the dedication of the temple by Solomon, petitions are offered for deliverance from pestilence, famine, drought, siege, exile, but not for spiritual things as we understand them; though it is only fair to note that these prayers are to be offered in a spirit of true penitence—the worshipers are to turn to their God "with all their heart and with all their soul" (1 Kgs. 8:48)—and in a sense they are prayers for forgiveness. A later writer prays indeed that he may have neither poverty nor riches, but only such food as was needful for him (Prov. 30:8), but, broadly speaking, the object of petition and the ideal of blessing is "the fruit of the body and the fruit of the ground, grain and wine and oil, increase of cattle, victory over enemies and immunity from sickness" (Deut. 7:13–16).

And as a land without people is worthless, the blessing which is entreated and promised takes the form of an increase of numbers in the family, the tribe, or the nation (Gen. 28:3; Deut. 1:11; 13:17); so that to "bless" practically means to "multiply" (Gen. 1:22; 28:3). This was very natural to a people whose existence and prosperity were being continually menaced by foes on the right hand and on the left. The more numerous were the defenders of the city, the more confidently could they speak with their enemies in the gate (Ps. 127:5). Thus prayers for children are of very frequent occurrence: they are offered sometimes by the man (Gen. 25:21), sometimes by the woman (Gen. 30:17; 1 Sam. 1:11), and invariably by those who wish a family well (Ruth 4:11). There is a beautiful prayer of a father for guidance in the training of his yet unborn child [Judg. 13:8 (cf. v. 14)], though the context suggests that the prayer has in view material rather than spiritual things. Riches, honor, and long life were no doubt the theme of many a petition (1 Kgs. 3:13); and a somewhat sinister light is cast upon the possibilities of early Hebrew prayer by the circumstance that even the life of one's enemies is conceived as a possible object of petition (1 Kgs. 3:11).

Petition might be negative as well as positive: it might express the desire of the heart for certain gifts or the desire to be delivered from certain evils or dangers. It is most of all when men's souls faint within them that they remember and cry to Jehovah (Jon. 2:7). The conscience-smitten Jacob, on the eve of facing the brother whom he had wronged, prays earnestly that God may deliver him from his hand (Gen. 32:11). So Hezekiah, in mortal terror of the Assyrians, who "have laid waste the nations and their lands," prays the God of Israel to save him from the hand of Sennacherib (2 Kgs. 19:19). Jeremiah reproaches his contemporaries with worshiping stocks and stones, and turning their back upon the living God; "but in the time of their trouble they will say, 'Arise and save us' " (Jer. 2:27).

"Save us." This might be said to be the most characteristic prayer of the Bible, but, in the Old Testament, the deliverance besought is not usually from sin, but from enemies of a more tangible sort. The Psalter is haunted by the cruel faces of scheming men, and it is from them that the psalmists pray for deliverance. Then, as ever, distress drove men to God. "Is any suffering, let him pray" (James 5:13). When tender women, maddened by hunger, were eating the bodies of the children they loved (Lam. 2:20); when Zion had become a wilderness and Jerusalem a desolation; when Jehovah's holy and beautiful house had been burned with fire (Is. 64:10, 11); then men were constrained to "pour out their heart like water before the face of the Lord" (Lam. 2:19), and to "lift up their heart with their hands unto God in the heavens" (Lam. 3:41).

As we have already seen, the need of God, acutely felt in all times of danger, was felt with special acuteness before the very obvious dangers of battle; and from every period of Israel's history prayers rise from the battlefield. One of the oldest prayers in the Bible is Joshua's apostrophe to the sun and moon during the battle of Gibeon (Josh. 10:12). Samuel prays for Israel before the battle of Ebenezer (1 Sam. 7:5). Between these periods the union of piety and heroism is illustrated by Nehemiah, one of whose weapons in battle is prayer. He urges his men not only to fight with all their might for their wives and children, but to "remember the Lord, who is great and terrible" (Neh. 4:14).

There are several characteristic references to prayer before battle in the book of Chronicles. Abijah delivers a long religious ha-
rangue before the battle with Jeroboam I (2 Chr. 13:4–12), and Asa
prays to Jehovah before his assault upon the Ethopians (2 Chr.
14:11). Most interesting, however, and most characteristic of all is
the Chronicler's description of the preparations for the attack upon
the combined forces of Moab and Ammon (2 Chr. 20). The king
Jehoshaphat offers a very earnest prayer to save Judah from the
great army opposed to them; and, as if that were not enough, an
exhortation is delivered the day before the battle by a Levite, after
which they all fall down before Jehovah. The next morning Jehoshaphat again heartens them: "Believe in Jehovah, your God, so
shall ye be established"; and after that singers are appointed to go
before the army singing, "Give thanks to Jehovah; for His loving-
kindness endureth forever." It seems natural to suppose that the
Chronicler has imported into his battle scenes that peculiar type of
ecclesiastical piety which colors his whole history. The speech of
Abijah is replete with ceremonial allusions, and Jehoshaphat concludes his prayer with the words: "We have no might against the
great company that cometh against us, neither know we what to
do, but our eyes are upon Thee" (2 Chr. 20:12). It can hardly be
denied that there is a certain unreality about this, when we consider
that, according to the Chronicler's own account, he had nearly a
million and a quarter fighting men (2 Chr. 17:14–18). But whatever
the historical value of such narratives may be, they are at least significant for the piety of the period: it was incredible that Israel
should enter a battle without committing her cause to God.

But even within the Old Testament there are prayers for other
things than bread and victory. The seers of Israel knew that men
did not live by bread alone (Deut. 8:3), and prayers rise for wisdom and forgiveness, for guidance and a closer walk with God.
The noble prayer of Solomon for wisdom is regarded in the narrative as touching unusual heights (1 Kgs. 3:11; cf. James 1:5) in its
deliberate rejection of riches and honor. Ezra acknowledges that
along with the manna which fed Israel "Thou gavest also Thy
good spirit to instruct them" (Neh. 9:20). One of the most fervent

prayers in the Bible is for the presence of the spirit, and for the cleansing and renewing of the heart.

> Create in me a clean heart, O God,
> And renew a right spirit within me.
> Cast me not away from Thy presence,
> And take not Thy holy spirit from me
> (Ps. 51:10, 11).

There were men who longed for the light of God's face, and to whom that light was better than corn and wine (Ps. 4:6, 7), men whose heart's desire was to be delivered from every crooked way, and led in the way everlasting (Ps. 139:24), men who felt that a man was nothing profited, if he gained the world and lost God and his soul.

The supreme longing of the profounder souls of Israel was for God, not His gifts but Himself. This passion receives everlasting expression in the words of a later psalmist: "If I have but Thee, I ask for nothing in heaven or earth. Though flesh and heart fail, yet God is my portion forever. . . . My happiness lies in being near my God" (Ps. 73:25–28). Such men felt that God held them by the hand, and guided them through this world, and they were sure that He would afterwards receive them to glory (Ps. 73:24). When, after the anguish of doubt, they had found him, they were content with Him, and they could dispense with all the visible and customary proofs of His goodness.

> For though the fig-tree shall not flourish,
> And there be no fruit in the vines,
> Though the labor of the olive fail
> And the fields yield no food,
> Though the flock be cut off from the fold,
> And there be no herd in the stalls;
> Yet will I rejoice in Jehovah,
> I will joy in the God of my salvation
> (Hab. 3:17, 18).

The defects of the Old Testament prayer are associated with the defects of the Old Testament religion generally. To one who forgets that the biblical religion was in every stage historically conditioned, nothing can be more disappointing than the frequent cries for vengeance which are heard more or less loudly in every stage of its development. One of the very oldest poems in the Bible–the so-called Song of Lamech (Gen. 4:23, 24)–is a song in glorification of revenge, and one of the oldest prayers–Samson's–is a prayer for vengeance (Judg. 16:28); and the note struck thus early reverberates throughout the centuries. Each of the first four elegies in the book of Lamentations concentrates its passion in a concluding cry for vengeance–Do to them as Thou hast done unto me. We have already seen how the torn heart of Jeremiah utters itself in wild appeals to Jehovah to "bring upon his enemies the day of evil and destroy them with a double destruction" (Jer. 17:18; 11:20; 15:15); and Nehemiah prays that God will remember his enemies according to their works (Neh. 6:14), frustrate their plans, carry them to a foreign land, and refuse to pardon their sin (Neh. 4:4, 5).

It is somewhat remarkable that the two historical characters whose prayer life we know best and whose piety was of the intensest, should have repeatedly prayed in this strain. It is equally remarkable that some of the tenderest and most beautiful voices in the Psalter occasionally break into imprecation (Ps. 137). It is the man who expressed in language of unapproachable simplicity and beauty his sense of the mysterious omnipresence of God, that confesses to hating his enemies with implacable hatred, and prays for their destruction (Ps. 139:19–22). Two men die with prayers for vengeance upon their lips (Judg. 16:28; 2 Chr. 24:22); and in the book of Revelation (6:10) the martyred souls beneath the altar are represented as crying aloud to God for vengeance on those who had slain them.

It has to be remembered that these imprecations are seldom or never the utterance of a selfish passion. The enemies denounced are enemies of the moral order (Ps. 94:5, 6). They are the men who plotted against the innocent Jeremiah, who sought to frustrate the patriotic work of Nehemiah, who longed to see Jerusalem razed to the ground (Ps. 137:7). Further, there was for long no outlook upon immortality, no certainty of a judgment beyond. If God was to interpose to vindicate the violated order of the moral world, He must do so speedily. Of the Old Testament saints it could seldom be said, "believing where they did not see." Seeing was believing; and, without sight, faith was difficult, sometimes impossible. Very seldom does the Old Testament religion shake itself completely free of this materialism. The skeptics are not convinced, and the pious are not content, till they see something. "Let him make speed, let Him hasten His work, *that we may see it"* (Is. 5:19), say the former. They taunt Jeremiah with the challenge, "Where is the word of Jehovah? Let it come now" (Jer. 17:15); and it is this challenge that drives the prophet to his passionate prayers. The disconsolate who cry, "Where is the God of justice?" (Mal. 2:18) Malachi points to a coming judgment in which the righteous shall be spared and the wicked consumed; and then "ye shall *see* the difference between the righteous and the wicked, between him that serveth God and him that serveth Him not" (Mal. 3:18).

The weakness of Old Testament religion is its materialism, but this is also its strength. Deprived for centuries of the hope of another world, it threw itself with passion upon the world that now is, and claimed it in its every part for God. Without the splendid range and versatility of the Greek, the Hebrew had an almost Greek interest in this world. There is an occasional mysticism about Hebrew poetry: every man walketh in a vain show, and life is but a pilgrimage and a dream (Ps. 39). But that is not the dominant note of the older religion. It did not lose itself in the distant heavens. The earth was the Lord's, and He had given it to men; and there, if at all, they were determined, and even bound, to find Him. If He moved upon it, was it unreasonable to expect that His footprints would be visible? And so all the treasures of field and vineyard, all the delights of home and country were regarded as blessings from His good hand. History was but the march of the Divine purpose; and when virtue seemed to be defeated and vice triumphant, faith was put to a terrible strain. It seemed as if God had left His world. But though Old Testament religion was limited, within its limitations it was intensely and passionately real. Its healthy materialism was one manifestation of its faith. It expected and found God in the world, because it claimed the world for God.

In the New Testament, prayer is, as we might expect, predominantly for things spiritual. Doubtless material things could not be altogether ignored or forgotten; had not the Master Himself taught His disciples to pray for bread, and had He not made upon them the impression that any request they made in His name would be answered? But requests by such men and in such a name would be overwhelmingly for things spiritual. Those whose ambition was to "abide in Him" would not be sorely troubled by ambitions of a worldly kind.

All requests were to be made in accordance with the Divine will, and as that will was the salvation of all men through the gospel of Jesus, many of the New Testament prayers are for the success of that gospel among those to whom it is preached, for boldness in proclaiming it, and for the further strengthening and establishing of those who have already accepted it. One of the earliest prayers in the book of Acts (4:29, 30) is that the servants of the Lord may be enabled to speak His word with all boldness, and that signs and wonders be done through the name of Jesus. Paul, like his Master (John 17:15), prayed that his converts should be preserved from all that was evil and perfected in all that was good, that they should be filled with the knowledge of the Divine will (Col. 1:9), and with the desire to do the same. In the early church, this spiritual note is the dominant one. Epaphras prays earnestly that the Colossians "may stand perfect and fully assured in all the will of God" (Col. 4:12), and in almost the same words the author of the Epistle to the Hebrews (13:21) prays that those whom he addresses may be made perfect in every good thing to do His will.

One of the most eloquent proofs of the profound seriousness of Israel's religion, despite its materialistic bias, is to be found in the prayers of *confession*. She needed forgiveness as well as bread. Her creed was, "there is no man that sinneth not" (1 Kgs. 8:46); and although the conception of sin included breaches of the ceremonial no less than of the moral law, all the formal confessions of the Old

Testament fall within the latter category. It is very significant that, with probably only one real exception, these prayers are collective, not individual, confessions, that is, of national and not of personal sin. The exception is the confession which David makes after numbering the people, where he prays that the punishment may fall, not upon his innocent people, but upon himself and his father's house (2 Sam. 24:17). This last phrase throws light upon the comparative absence of individual confessions. In reality, the father's house should have been no more entitled to pay the penalty than the innocent people, but in earlier times, the whole family of the sinner was involved in his doom.* This, of course, was due to a defective sense of the absolute value of the individual soul. Relatively speaking, at least till the time of Jeremiah, and more or less till the time of Jesus, the individual was lost in the community. The religious unit was the nation, not the man; the individual had not yet fully come to his own.

A striking feature of these public confessions is that almost invariably the worshipers acknowledge the sin of the fathers as well as their own. The ages are felt to be linked each to each by a chain of sin. "We have sinned against Jehovah our God, we *and our fathers*" (Jer. 3:25). "We acknowledge, O Jehovah, our wickedness *and the iniquity of our fathers*" (Jer. 14:20). "Since the days of our fathers," prays Ezra, "we have been exceedingly guilty unto this day" (Ezra 9:7). Another confession led by him is introduced with the words, "they stood and confessed their sins *and the iniquities of their fathers*" (Neh. 9:2; cf. Lev. 26:40); and a much later prayer runs: "For our sins *and for the iniquities of our fathers,* Jerusalem and Thy people are become a reproach to all that are round about us" (Dan. 9:16). Sometimes the speaker acknowledges his own personal guilt in the general confession—"my sin and the sin of my people Israel"†—and sometimes the various classes of the community, especially the leading classes, are expressly mentioned—"kings, princes, priests" (Neh. 9:33; cf. Dan. 9:8)—as if to include all under the same condemnation.

---

* Cf. Achan in Joshua 7.
† Daniel 9:20; cf. Nehemiah 1:6, "I and my father's house have sinned."

Usually in the Old Testament confession is connected with calamity: suffering is the impulse to self-examination. It was when Israel was "sore distressed," that she "cried unto Jehovah, saying, 'We have sinned against Thee' " (Judg. 10:9, 10). The sins confessed are usually general rather than specific. As the grace of God was most typically manifested in the deliverance of Israel from Egypt, so the sins of that early period are typical of the sins of Israel's subsequent career: obstinacy, disobedience, rebellion, ingratitude, incredulity, forgetfulness, indifference, idolatry (Neh. 9; Ps. 106; Is. 64:5, 6). Since to later times, the religion of Israel was supremely embodied in Moses and the prophets, the worshipers confess in general terms that they "have not kept the commandments, nor the statutes, nor the ordinances, which Thou didst command Thy servant Moses" (Neh. 1:7; cf. Dan. 9:5), that they had cast the divine law behind their back (Neh. 9:26). In particular, Ezra confesses the breach of the law which forbade intermarriage with their heathen neighbors (Ezra 9:12). Again it is said that they had not walked according to the laws which Jehovah had set before them by His servants the prophets (Dan. 9:10); they had even gone the length of slaying the prophets who had testified against them (Neh. 9:26).

The climax of the confession is usually solemn and impressive, and it conforms to a certain simple type. In two Hebrew words (Dan. 9:15), or three (1 Kgs. 8:47), or four—"we have sinned, we have dealt perversely, we have done wickedly, we have rebelled" (Dan. 9:5)—the penitents pour out their hearts. It is more like a series of sobs than a prayer. The simple brevity[*] of the Hebrew is very solemn and impressive, and is altogether lost in the diffuse language of the English translation. Prayers of confession are more frequent and elaborate in post-exilic than in pre-exilic times, partly because the church, as a whole, is more highly organized, and partly because, as the religion advances, under the strain of sorrowful experience, it is led to take on a more somber color.

The formal confessions of later times always acknowledge the justice of God. "Thou hast punished us less than our iniquities de-

---

[*] Cf. the confession of the prodigal son in Luke 15:21.

serve" (Ezra 9:13), and "Thou art just in all that has come upon us" (Neh. 9:33). So the worshipers can do nothing but throw themselves upon the marvelous mercy of God. "To the Lord our God belong mercies and forgiveness" (Dan. 9:9). He is ready to blot out as a thick cloud their transgressions (Is. 44:22). He is a God that pardons iniquity (Mic. 7:18, 19). True, it is this persistent goodness of God—what Ezra twice calls His "manifold mercies" (Neh. 9:19, 27)—that makes their wickedness so heinous. They had sinned against a light that had shone as the noon-day. But as that mercy was the deepest thing in the divine nature, it could always be depended upon by those who turned to it in sincerity and truth. So they confess in hope (Mic. 7:9). "For we do not present our supplications before Thee for our righteousness, but for Thy great mercies' sake" (Dan. 9:18); and a passionate earnestness rings through the words with which this prayer concludes: "O Lord, hear; O Lord forgive; O Lord hearken and do. Defer not, for Thine own sake, O my God" (Dan. 9:19).

We shall now consider the *intercessory prayers*. They are not very numerous, but they are of great significance. It would not be unfair to estimate a man's religion by the earnestness with which he longs for the welfare of others; and love of the brethren will express itself, in normal circumstances, in prayer for them. Those who love them most and those who are most responsible for their spiritual welfare will be likely to pray most for them. It is, therefore, very fitting that the prophets, who in a special sense were charged with the religious welfare of Israel, should so often appear as intercessors. We think of them pre-eminently as preachers, but they had first pled with God for the men to whom they afterwards appealed in His name. Most of them must have been powerful, or at least, impressive speakers. Their gifts and temperaments differed widely, but the passionate sincerity of such men as Elijah and Jeremiah must have produced a stupendous impression even upon audiences that were not disposed to accept their message; and we can well believe that a special efficacy was supposed to attach to their prayers.

Twice, in moments of danger, the people beseech Samuel to cry to their God for them (1 Sam. 7:8; 12:19), and Samuel seems to regard intercession as part of his official duty, the neglect of which is a sin. "Far be it from me that I should sin against Jehovah in ceasing to pray for you" (1 Sam. 12:23; cf. 7:5). A similar sense of the duty and power of prophetic prayer shines through the words of Jeremiah: "Though Moses and Samuel stood before me, yet my mind would not be toward this people."* Moses is regarded as the incomparable prophet whose like had not arisen since in Israel (Deut. 34:10), and it is worthy of note that nearly all the prayers ascribed to him are intercessory. Repeatedly he prays that the plagues be removed from Pharaoh. He prays for his apostate people in language that reaches almost unparalleled heights of self-sacrificing devotion (Ex. 32:31, 32). He prays that the leprosy be removed from Miriam (Num. 12:13). And, in his case, as in Samuel's, the people recognize his intercessory power (Num. 21:7). The date of these narratives is immaterial: they are at any rate a proof of the power which later ages conceived to accompany the prophet's speech with God no less than his speech to men.

Practically all the intercessory prayers of the Old Testament are offered either by prophets or by men—such as Abraham (Gen. 20:7) and Job—whom later ages idealized as prophets. Abraham's intercession for Sodom (Gen. 18:22–25) and for King Abimelech (Gen. 20:17), and Job's intercession for his friends are characteristic; and their prayers are efficacious. "Abraham is a prophet, and he shall pray for thee, and thou shalt live" (Gen. 20:7). "My servant Job shall pray for you" (Job 42:8), that is, for the "orthodox" friends, who had not spoken of God the thing that was right.

The historical prophets from Elijah† on appear frequently in the role of intercessors. Elijah prays for the restoration of the widow's

---

* Jeremiah 15:1. There may also be here the feeling that the prayers of the ancient prophets were more efficacious than the modern. Ezekiel (14:14, 16, 18, 20), in a similar connection, mentions the names of Noah, Daniel and Job.

† Cf. the late story in 1 Kings 13:6, where Jeroboam I entreats the man of God to pray for the restoration of his withered hand.

son (1 Kgs. 17:21). Amos the stern, from whom one would expect little pity, pleaded twice that the blow should not fall upon Israel (Amos 7:2, 5). King Hezekiah, after the insulting message of the Rabshakeh, entreats Isaiah through the priests and two court officials to "lift up his prayer for the remnant that is left" (2 Kgs. 19:4); and the Chronicler puts into the mouth of Hezekiah himself a very beautiful prayer to "Jehovah the good" for pardon for those who had earnestly sought their God, even though their conduct had not been ceremonially correct (2 Chr. 30:18, 19).

Most instructive, however, is the intercession of Jeremiah. From several allusions in the course of the prophecy we may conclude that Jeremiah habitually prayed for the people (Jer. 7:16; 11:14; 14:11), and we have his own express statement, "I stood before Thee to speak good for them, to turn away Thy wrath from them" (Jer. 18:20). People and king alike request his prayers. During a temporary respite in the siege of Jerusalem, Zedekiah sent two men to Jeremiah with such a request (Jer. 37:3); and, in the confusion that followed the assassination of Gedaliah, the governor of Judah, a great crowd visited Jeremiah with a similar request. "Pray for us unto Jehovah thy God . . . that Jehovah thy God may show us the way wherein we should walk and the thing we should do" (Jer. 42:2, 3). The double recognition of Jehovah as Jeremiah's God is very striking. They may indeed have besought his prayers, because of the acknowledged and peculiar efficacy of a prophet's prayer, but they may also have felt that their sin (Jer. 7:9) had rendered their approach impossible or their prayers unavailing. Twice, too, Ezekiel is moved to a brief intercessory prayer for the remnant of Israel (Ezek. 9:8; 11:13). Prayers are occasionally offered for foreigners, but here, as everywhere in the Old Testament, the national note is heard. Jeremiah, for example, urges the exiles to pray to Jehovah for Babylon and to seek her welfare, *"for in the peace thereof ye shall have peace"* (Jer. 29:7); and Darius, in his decree, desires the prayers of the Jews for himself and his dynasty (Ezra 6:10).

In the Old Testament, intercessory prayer is usually offered for forfeited or imperiled lives; in the New Testament, its object is usually the spiritual welfare of those for whom it is offered, as when

Jesus prays that Peter's faith fail not (Luke 22:32), or Paul, that his converts be strengthened with power in the inward man (Eph. 3:16–19), or that the Philippians may abound more and more in love (Phil. 1:9). There are occasional prayers for blessings of a more material sort. The elders of the church are to pray for a sick member (James 5:14) and Peter prays for the restoration of the dead Tabitha (Acts 9:40). The "great Prophet that should come into the world," like the ancient prophets, was great in intercession. He poured out his heart not only for his disciples (John 17:6–19), but for His murderers (Luke 23:34).

A reminiscence of the ancient belief in the power of prophetic prayer is to be seen in the request of Simon Magus that Peter should pray to the Lord for him (Acts 8:24), but, with the progress of the gospel which proclaimed the equality of all men, this belief would tend to disappear, especially after the last of the disciples had passed away. The prayer of any righteous man should avail as much as the prayer of an apostle; and, in accordance with the belief that, irrespective of rank, men need the prayers of one another (James 5:16), we find Paul not only praying for his converts, but equally earnest in his requests that they should pray for him (1 Thess. 5:25, etc.; cf. Heb. 13:18). The Lord's prayer had taught men that spiritual interests were paramount, and the lesson was deeply written upon the mind of the early church. The apostles pray that the Samaritans should receive the Holy Spirit (Acts 8:15): and elsewhere it is recommended that intercession be offered for all men, especially for those in positions of authority, "that we may lead a tranquil and quiet life in all godliness and gravity" (1 Tim. 2:1, 2). The "welfare of Jerusalem" was still, as of old, the object of fervent prayer, but it was now no more the old Jerusalem, but the unseen city not built with hands.

We shall consider in conclusion *the prayers of thanksgiving.* It is characteristic of the difference between the Old Testament and the New that such prayers are relatively far fewer in the former book than in the latter. For one thing, gratitude is less natural than petition; besides, fullness of joy was possible only to those who were partakers of the salvation proclaimed and wrought by Jesus. But even in the Old Testament there is a deep undercurrent of joy. The religious festivals of pre-exilic times were happy gatherings at which men rejoiced and were glad, as they looked at the produce of the field and vine-clad hillside, and reminded themselves of the divine goodness; and even post-exilic religion, though in many ways somber, is also glad. Worship was solemn, but happy.

> Enter into His gates with thanksgiving,
> And into His courts with praise.
> Give thanks unto Him, and bless His name;
> For Jehovah is good, His love is everlasting
> (Ps. 100:4, 5).

These last words—the summary confession of Israel's faith—are repeatedly echoed, especially throughout the writings of the priestly school; for example, in the ideal descriptions of the founding of the first and second temples.[*] They form the burden of one of the most beautiful of the later psalms (Ps. 107; cf. Ps. 145–150), and they doubtless incarnate an important element in the temple worship. One of the principal functions of the Levites was "to thank and praise Jehovah" (1 Chr. 23:30; cf. 2 Chr. 8:14), and the book of Daniel represents him as "kneeling on his knees three times a day, and praying, and *giving thanks* before God" (Dan. 6:10).

In spite, however, of this pervasive joy, there are few recorded prayers of thanksgiving in the Old Testament, and those that occur usually express gratitude for things material—for land (Deut. 8:10), and food (Deut. 26:6–10), and victory (Ps. 149:5, 6). Just as the Philistines praise Dagon for their victory over Samson (Judg. 16:23, 24), so Jephthah vows and offers a sacrifice for his victory over the Ammonites (Judg. 11:30, 31), and much of Israel's war-poetry was simply a poetic tribute to Jehovah, their great "man of war" (Ex. 15:3). The only prayer that is formally prescribed in the Old Testament is a prayer of thanksgiving to be offered by the worshiper after he has set down the basket of firstfruits before the altar

---

[*] 2 Chronicles 5:13; Ezra 3:11; cf. Jeremiah 33:11 at the restoration.

(Deut. 26:6–10). He thus expressed his gratitude–not in word only, but in deed and truth. As we may infer from many a Hebrew proper name, prayers of thanksgiving were no doubt offered for the birth of a child (cf. 1 Sam. 2); also for the recovery from sickness (Is. 38:10–20). David, in accordance with the rough spirit of a primitive time, blesses his God, when death has removed Nabal out of his way (1 Sam. 25:39).

In the New Testament, though the incomparable joy is that which comes through Jesus, gratitude for material things is not forgotten. Both Jesus and Paul are recorded as having prayed before meat; and, although the occasions on which these prayers are alluded to are always remarkable for other reasons–Jesus' prayers being associated with his miracles of feeding the multitude (Matt. 15:36; Mark 8:6, 7; Matt. 14:19; Mark 6:41; Luke 9:16; John 6:11), with the institution of the supper (Matt. 26:26, 27; Mark 14:23; Luke 22:19), and with the evening meal at Emmaus after the resurrection (Luke 24:30), and Paul's with his shipwreck (Acts 27:35)–there is every reason to believe that they did this habitually in accordance with Jewish custom. Recovery from sickness is often acknowledged in the New Testament by prayer, the gratitude being sometimes expressed by the man who is healed (Luke 18:43; Acts 3:8), and sometimes by the multitudes that witnessed the cure (Matt. 9:8; Mark 2:12; Luke 5:26; 7:16; 18:43).

But most characteristic of the New Testament are the prayers of thanksgiving offered to God for the gift of Jesus, and for the triumph of His gospel. Two of the earliest prayers in the gospel of Luke–those of Simeon and Anna (Luke 2:29–32, 38)–are prayers of thanks to God for Jesus, and this reflects faithfully the spirit of the early church (Acts 4:25–30). The triumph of His gospel among the Gentiles is also a source of the profoundest gratitude. The Jerusalem church, a little inclined to be narrow-hearted, is led by the marvelous stories of Peter (Acts 11:18) and Paul (Acts 21:20) to glorify God, because that to the Gentiles also He had granted repentance unto life. One offers thanks for being called to the ministry of Jesus (1 Tim. 1:12), and another for the hope of immortality which is inspired by the resurrection of Jesus (1 Pet. 1:3–5).

Songs of praise are unusually abundant in the book of Revelation. Day and night they rise from the lips of the four living creatures to Him that sitteth upon the throne (Rev. 4:8). And the reason why the great multitude in heaven rejoices and gives the glory to God (19:6) is because Christ has conquered the world, and He shall reign forever and ever (11:15). The scene is set in heaven, and the vision is a vision of faith, not of reality; yet, though of faith, it is intensely real. The writer sees, if only with the eye of faith, what Jeremiah had longed to see, and was perplexed and grieved because he could not see the manifest vindication of the moral order, the indisputable triumph of the Kingdom of God. "We give Thee thanks, O Lord God, the Almighty, because Thou hast taken Thy great power and didst reign" (11:16). He had proved Himself more than a match in the struggle with the cruel powers of evil. Salvation and power belonged to Him, because "He had judged the great harlot and avenged the blood of His servants" (19:2). They had poured out the blood of the saints and prophets, "and blood hast Thou given them to drink: they deserve it" (16:6). Therefore Hallelujah, and again Hallelujah (19:1, 3). Yes, "righteous art Thou, true and righteous are Thy judgments" (16:5, 7; 19:2). It is the contemplation of the divine justice, of the thoroughness and terribleness of the divine judgment upon the gigantic forces of evil, of the victory of right and good and God, it is these things that stir the writer's blood. In its longing for a vindication of the moral order by the divine vengeance (Rev. 6:10) upon all opposed to that order, this great literary witness to the spirit of Jewish Christianity stands very near the Old Testament.

But the book, though intensely Jewish, is also intensely Christian. It draws its inspiration, if not always from the spirit of Jesus, at any rate from an absolute faith in Him, an immovable confidence in His power and ultimate victory. This confidence is enthusiastically shared by all the writers of the New Testament; and so it is fitting that although the New Testament doxologies are usually offered to God (1 Pet. 1:3, 4; 5:11), there is at least one undisputed doxology to Christ. "To Him be the glory both now and forever. Amen" (2 Pet. 3:18).

The Relation of Faith
and Prayer

Apart from the Psalter, the Bible contains fewer prayers than we should be inclined to expect in a religious literature of so great compass; and although the incidental allusions to prayer are numerous enough, the question forces itself upon us whether prayer—at least in the sense in which it is recommended by Paul—formed so vital and essential a part of practical religion as we are accustomed to suppose. Prayers are often absent where we should naturally expect them.

There is, of course, a view of the world to which prayer is impossible, if not absurd. It is stifled, for example, in such an atmosphere as that of Ecclesiastes. If one event happened to us all (Eccl. 2:14), "to the righteous and to the wicked, to the clean and to the unclean, to him that sacrificeth and to him that sacrificeth not" (Eccl. 9:2), what would be the meaning of prayer? Would the faith in such a blessed immortality as is anticipated in Psalm 73:24 not be a delusion, and was the baffled thinker who wrote Ecclesiastes not right when he refused to console himself with a beatific vision, but after the dust returned to the earth as it was and the breath to the God who gave it, pronounced his monotonous and melancholy verdict, "Vanity of vanities; all is vanity" (Eccl. 12:7, 8)? With such an outlook upon life prayer would lose most of its meaning, and we need not be surprised at its absence from such a book.

But what is, at first sight, really surprising, is its absence on occasions where it would seem most natural and appropriate. Abraham offers no prayer of gratitude when the angel voice delivers

53

him from his frightful obligation to sacrifice his son (Gen. 22:13, 14). Jacob mourns, but he does not pray, when he learns of the calamity that had befallen Joseph (Gen. 37:34, 35); he faints for joy, but he does not pray, when he learns that that son is yet alive (Gen. 45:28). Joseph himself is a man of the most profound and beautiful piety, but there is no record of a single prayer. The reformations of Hezekiah and Josiah, though both were dictated by a sense of sin, were, so far as the records go, unaccompanied by prayer, even in the Chronicler's account (2 Chr. 29, 35), which is all the more remarkable, as he frequently embellishes his narratives with prayer. Much is said of sacrifice and music, but nothing of prayer. It is not mentioned in Romans 12:6–8, or in 1 Corinthians 12:28, among the gifts which distinguish the members of Christ's body from one another, nor among the fruits of the spirit in Galatians 5:22, 23 It is incidentally mentioned in Paul's description of the Christian warrior, but not as part of his armor (Eph. 6:18).

More remarkable still is the way in which prayer is ignored in the books which deal with the worship of the sanctuary and the duty of its ministers. There is no mention of it even in connection with the consecration of the priests (Ex. 40:13–15; Lev. 8:10–36) or the Levites (Num. 8), or in connection with the offerings prescribed for the various festivals in Numbers 28, 29. In a chapter which describes a service of peculiar solemnity, there is only the briefest allusion to it–"Aaron lifted up his hands toward the people and blessed them" (Lev. 9:22)–and an equally brief allusion to the confession of sin in the imposing ceremonies connected with the great day of atonement (Lev. 16:21).

Most of the casual references to the priests and Levites occur in connection with the sacrificial and musical arrangements of the temple–with the offering of burnt-offering, incense, thanks, and praise (1 Chr. 16:4; 23:13, 30; 2 Chr. 29:11; 31:2; Luke 1:9; Heb. 8:3). The priests also exercised judicial functions (Deut. 17:9; 21:5; Ezek. 44:14), and had the duty of teaching the people the ritual distinction "between the holy and the common, the clean and the unclean" (Ezek. 44:23; Hag. 2:2–13). The casual allusions to thanks and praise no doubt give us a glimpse into a musical service which, judging by the musical superscriptions of the psalms, may have been tolerably elaborate; and, in one aspect, these hymns of thanksgiving may be regarded as prayers. In a description of such a service two lengthy fragments of Psalms 96 and 105 are incorporated (1 Chr. 16:8–22=Ps. 105:1–15; 1 Chr. 16:23–33=Ps. 96:1–13; 1 Chr. 16:34–36=Ps. 106:1, 47, 48). Nevertheless, it is striking that in the distinctively ritual books or sections (Ex., Lev., Num., Ezek. 40–48), there should be hardly any mention of prayer in the sense of petition. It would be absurd, of course, to infer from this silence that petitions were not offered in the temple worship. Sacrifice even in earlier times was accompanied by prayer (Gen. 12:8). In the calamity described by Joel, the priests are urged to pray Jehovah to spare His people (Joel 2:17), and what they did in a crisis they no doubt did, if with more formality, always. The fact that the priestly legislation deals all but exclusively with ceremonial goes a long way to explain its almost unbroken silence on prayer; still that silence cannot but be regarded as striking.

In estimating, however, the frequent omission of references to prayer where they might naturally have been expected, the scantiness of our records should never be forgotten. Because, on a certain occasion, a prayer is not recorded, we have no right to infer that none was offered. No historian is bound to record everything; and the Bible historian, in particular, exercises sovereign liberty in his choice of what he shall record and omit. He often depicts the religious mood so graphically that the prayers which are unrecorded may be taken for granted. David refuses to curse Shimei, because "it may be that Jehovah will look on the wrong done unto me, and that Jehovah will requite me good for his cursing of me this day" (2 Sam. 16:12). Without doubt such a hope would express itself in prayer. So Jehovah-jireh, the name said to be given by Abraham to the place where he was delivered from his dilemma (Gen. 22:14), is an expression of faith which is almost equivalent to a prayer.

Often, again, where no prayer is expressly recorded, an incidental remark or a parallel passage raises a strong presumption that one was offered. In Leviticus 23:10, 11 no mention is made of any prayer of gratitude in connection with the offering of the firstfruits, but in Deuteronomy 26, on a similar occasion, not only does prayer accompany the offering but a definite prayer is prescribed. After the prayer (vv. 5–10) occur the words, "and thou shalt rejoice." It would not be unnatural to infer from this that all the other numerous references to rejoicing at the festivals in the sanctuaries were accompanied by prayer, even though it is not explicitly mentioned.

Further, a stray word in the course of the narrative sometimes suggests an unrecorded prayer. Important, for example, as was the Jerusalem council in Acts 15, there is no mention of prayer, but its presence is strongly suggested by the words, "It seemed good *to the Holy Spirit* and to us" (Acts 15:28). Again, though the heathen sailors in the Book of Jonah (1:5) pray when overtaken by a storm, no prayer is ascribed to Paul during the storm which wrecked his ship, but when, in the night, he hears an angel saying to him, "Fear not, God hath granted thee all them that sail with thee" (Acts 27:24), it is most natural to infer that the message comes in response to earnest prayer for himself and his company.

It is further to be remembered that the Hebrew, like the God he worshiped, revealed his inmost nature in deeds rather than in words: consequently we may find an act where we expect a prayer. The feast of booths, for example, according to the later view of its origin, recalled the deliverance of Israel from Egypt: it is the pictorial embodiment of gratitude (Lev. 23:42, 43). Another aspect of that deliverance is supposed to be commemorated by the Passover. These and other festivals "remind" Israel (Deut. 16:3, cf. 12) of the ancient goodness of her God, and so, by the celebration, she keeps her gratitude fresh; she may also well have expressed it in the formal language of prayer, though none is recorded. Similarly, no formal prayer of thanksgiving is recorded when Israel crosses the Jordan, but memorial stones are erected (Josh. 4). The mood which dictates these memorials is the same as that which expresses itself in prayer. Indeed, it is perhaps more earnest and religiously valuable; for it expresses not only a momentary gratitude, but also the deep determination to perpetuate the memory of the love of God.

A living faith is bound to express itself. It may do so in words of prayer, but it is at least conceivable that it could do so in the general attitude and direction of the life, without formally expressing itself in language. This may partly explain the absence of prayer in the story of such a life as Joseph's, and on other occasions where it would be natural. Of course we must never forget, as we have already said, how extremely meager our sources are and to what injustice and absurdity the argument from silence could lead in such a case. Still, the absence of all mention of prayer from the story of Joseph is somewhat remarkable. Occasions enough there were for it. For long he trod a path of sorrow. He was destitute, afflicted, tormented. It was through a hard discipline of misunderstanding, persecution, and imprisonment, that he reached his seat beside the king. Besides, he was a man of noble piety; yet it is never said that he prayed.

Such a life, we may suppose, must have expressed itself in prayer, but it is significant, at any rate for the standpoint of the historian, that he says nothing of it. In its place, however, is an overwhelming sense of the presence and providence of God. "It is not in me," says Joseph; "God shall give Pharaoh an answer of peace" (Gen. 41:16, cf. 28, 32). Joseph gives the answer (Gen. 41:25) at once without any recorded prayer for help, such as is sent up by Nehemiah (Neh. 2:4), but he recognizes here, as elsewhere (Gen. 40:8), that the answer comes to him from God, and Pharaoh himself admits this (Gen. 41:39). Joseph believes in a gracious providence, guiding both the past and the future. "It was not you that sent me to Egypt," he says to his brothers, "but God" (Gen. 45:5, 7, 8). "Ye meant evil against me, but God meant it for good" (Gen. 50:20), and the God who has graciously guided my life "will surely visit you" (Gen. 50:24). The controlling power that the thought of God exercised over him receives its most brilliant illustration in his memorable answer to the woman who tempted him: "How can I do this great wickedness and sin against God?" (Gen. 39:9). Here is a man of the most splendid piety, but it is interwoven with his life. It is not—at least in the record—expressed in the formal language of prayer.

With Joseph it is very interesting to compare the story of Daniel. In the later book, prayer and allusions to prayer are frequent. Daniel offers a prayer of gratitude after the revelation of Nebuchadnezzar's dream (Dan. 2:20–23), and an elaborate prayer of entreaty for the forgiveness and restoration of Jerusalem (Dan. 9:4–19). He requests his companions to pray that God would mercifully reveal the secret of the dream (Dan. 2:18): he himself prayed three times a day (Dan. 6:10), and there are other references to prayer in the book. Now this difference in the emphasis on prayer in the two narratives of Joseph and Daniel is all the more striking when we consider how very similar were the careers of the men. An element of romance attaches to both stories. Both are full of dreams and interpretations, the heroes of both were captives, and they both rose in the land of their captivity to positions of exceptional honor and influence.

The one story comes from the ninth century B.C., and the other from the second. In this simple fact lies no doubt the real explanation of the difference in their attitude to prayer. The same great faith in God animates both narratives, but the one expresses itself in prayer and the other does not; and this, together with many other facts, leads to the conclusion that prayer shared in the development which characterized the religion generally. We cannot too often or too earnestly repeat that from silence we are not entitled to infer indifference; and yet the relative prominence of prayer in post-exilic as compared with pre-exilic literature is no accident. The prayers are at once more numerous, more elaborate and more formal. This may be partly due to the need and desire of the Church to organize her religious life, but it is also due to a growing sense of the place of prayer in religion. Even more than to the compilation of history and prophecy must the exile have given the impulse to prayer. The men who were sinking in the horrible pit and the miry clay would cry to be set upon a rock. Sorrow would impart to prayer a seriousness it had never known before; and the exigencies of political and ecclesiastical life after the return would necessitate a more formal regulation of public worship than had hitherto been customary. The exile seriously affected both the spirit and the form of Hebrew prayer.

This could be abundantly proved by an examination of the Book of Chronicles. The Chronicler inserts prayers for which there is no warrant in Samuel and Kings, his principal sources, and a very slender pretext suffices him for such an insertion. Jehoshaphat, for example, cried out, when the charioteers turned upon him, mistaking him for the king of Israel; and Jehovah helped him (2 Chr. 18:31). There the implication is that the cry is a prayer, but this presumption is not raised by the narrative in 1 Kings 22:32. When David built his altar upon Araunah's threshing-floor and offered sacrifice (2 Sam. 24:25), the Chronicler adds, "and he called upon Jehovah, and He answered him from heaven by fire" (1 Chr. 21:26). Doubtless the sacrifice was accompanied by prayer, but it is significant that the Chronicler should elaborate the point. The very beautiful prayer put into the mouth of David after the presentation of the free-will offering for the temple (1 Chr. 29:10–19) has no support in the Book of Samuel and is altogether in the later style. Jehovah is directly addressed in almost every verse, twice in one verse (v. 11), also as "our God" (v. 16), "my God" (v. 17), and more elaborately in the last appeal as "O Jehovah, the God of Abraham, of Isaac and of Israel."* The tendency to multiply addresses is illustrated by David's prayer in 1 Chronicles 21:17, where, in the middle of the prayer, "Let Thy hand, I pray Thee, be against me and against my father's house" (2 Sam. 24:17), the Chronicler inserts "O Jehovah, my God."

We have already dealt with the prayers which the Chronicler inserts before a battle (2 Chr. 14:11; 20), and commented upon their occasional unreality. A Levite encourages the men of Judah before a battle with the words, "The battle is not yours, but God's. *Ye shall not need to fight. Set yourselves, stand still, and see the salvation of Jehovah*" (2 Chr. 20:15, 17). This is completely out of touch with the world of reality, and altogether unlike the vivid battle scenes of the Judges or the Maccabees, but it goes to explain the exclusive emphasis on prayer, which a cloistered piety supposed was the only weapon needed in a fight. This pietistic and impossible view

---

* Verse 18. The multiplication of addresses and titles is very common, but not an invariable feature of later prayer; in Jehoshaphat's prayer (2 Chr. 20) the Deity is addressed only three times (vv. 6, 7, 12).

of war could not, of course, be shared by a practical man like Nehemiah, who, not content with prayer, first saw that his men were supplied with swords and spears and bows, and then addressed them with the words, "Don't be afraid. Remember the Lord, *and fight"* (Neh. 4:13, 14).

The Book of Kings (2 Kgs. 21) has much to say of Manasseh's wickedness, but nothing of his prayer. The Chronicler, however, relates that when he had been carried into exile by the king of Assyria, "he besought Jehovah his God and humbled himself greatly before the God of his fathers. And he prayed unto Him, and He was entreated of him, and heard his supplication, and brought him again to Jerusalem into his kingdom" (2 Chr. 33:12, 13). And, as if that were not enough, the prayer is subsequently twice mentioned in two consecutive verses (2 Chr. 33:18, 19). Indeed, it is said to be extant in one, if not two, already existing histories (vv. 18, 19), and therefore presumably a prayer purporting to be Manasseh's was in circulation probably as early as 400 B.C.

The half-theoretic, half-practical interest that continued to gather even in New Testament times round the prayers of Old Testament worthies may be seen from James's allusions to the prayers of Elijah, which he adduces as illustrating the efficacy of the prayers of a righteous man (James 5:17, 18). But the allusions to Elijah's prayers for drought and rain are not supported by the Book of Kings, unless the posture in 1 Kings 18:42 is intended to indicate prayer for rain. Besides the three years of Kings have become three years and six months (Luke 4:25). In the time of James there may have been prayers of Elijah in existence, or, at any rate, narratives expanded from the Book of Kings and illustrating the power of his prayer.

In the light of all these facts it is very plain that prayer underwent development, and this, no doubt, accounts for its simplicity and comparative infrequency in the earlier records of the Old Testament. But it is also possible that faith did not always express itself in prayer. It is by no means inconceivable, though it would hardly be normal, that faith should take the form of a steady confidence to which prayer would be superfluous. The God whose goodness was so manifest in the past, is the same yesterday, today, and forever;

and that goodness could be trusted without being entreated. The constancy of the Divine love and law, as proved by history, is a great fact, in which men of a certain religious temperament will quietly and confidently rest.

"Rejoice and remember" (Deut. 16:11, 12): that is the motto of the Hebrew festivals. "Beware lest thou forget Jehovah, who brought thee forth out of the land of Egypt" (Deut. 6:12). The people rekindled their faith in Jehovah by rehearsing His righteous acts (Judg. 5:11), that is, the deeds by which He had vindicated them against their enemies. This appeal to the past is one of the most characteristic things of the Old Testament. Inspiration often seems to come rather from memory than from prayer. The thought of the past and the Divine goodness which crowded it, strengthened in the present crisis and nerved for the future; for what God had been He would ever prove Himself to be to the souls that trusted Him. The mood in which, according to the late story, David approaches Goliath, is a thoroughly religious mood: "Thou comest to me with the sword, but I come to thee in the name of Jehovah" (1 Sam. 17:45–47). But David does not pray. He says: "Jehovah that delivered me out of the paw of the lion and out of the paw of the bear, He will deliver me out of the hand of this Philistine" (1 Sam. 17:37). There is no recorded prayer, but there is a steady confidence, determined by past experience of God's goodness.

The Hebrew people had an altogether unique sense of the presence of God. "What great nation is there that hath a God so nigh unto them as Jehovah our God is, whenever we call upon Him?" (Deut. 4:7). And the later poets felt that, not only when in the definite attitude of prayer, but uninterruptedly and persistently, He beset them behind and before (Ps. 139). Heaven was not far from any one of them. Its doors were open wide; and, without knocking, they could go in and walk about as men who were at home. Thus it comes that many of the Psalms, though they take the form of speech to God, are almost more meditation than prayer. Their writers are so sure of God and so satisfied with Him that they are content to rest in Him without assailing Him with petition. The one hundred and thirty-ninth Psalm, with the exception of the last two verses, expresses communion without request. In the twenty-third Psalm, the writer does not pray that the Lord be his shepherd, to lead him beside the waters of rest, and guide him through the valley of the deep shadow. He knows that the Lord has been this to him already, and he is sure that He will continue to be this to the end. The Psalm is not a prayer, but a confession of faith. This accounts for the rapid transitions of the Psalter—as in this very Psalm—from the third person to the second, and vice versa: "*He* restoreth my soul: *Thou* art with me." They are not due to inattention. They are due to the fact that to the Psalmists God was the ever-present fact. Whether they prayed to Him or thought of Him, He was ever with them, as real to them in meditation as in petition.

The motto of the Bible is "Immanuel," that is, "with us is God." Whatever else may totter or disappear, He abides; and His mercy endureth forever. Amid life's innumerable uncertainties He is the great certainty, therefore it is wisdom to "rely on Jehovah thy God, so shalt thou be established" (2 Chr. 20:20; 16:7; Is. 7:9). By the man of faith every issue may be faced with confidence, for he knows that God doeth all things well. Nehemiah advances to the task of building the walls of Jerusalem, sure that the God of heaven will prosper him (Neh. 2:20), and the three Hebrews face the furnace not with any spoken prayer, but in the confidence that God will deliver them from it (Dan. 3:17).

Prayer is an attitude as well as a practice. It is the sense—at once cleansing and inspiring—that "my times are in Thy hand" (Ps. 31:15). And, if the spoken prayers of the Bible are not so numerous as we might have anticipated, all the more abundantly clear is the steadfastness with which the true Hebrew life was rooted in God and set towards God. This attitude is known in the Old Testament as "the fear of Jehovah." It is this that keeps Joseph pure in the hour of temptation, and that preserves Nehemiah from taking dishonorable advantage of his official position (Neh. 5:15). This fear is the basis of all wisdom (Prov. 9:10), the condition of all true success, and the guarantee of inward peace.

When thou liest down, thou shalt not be afraid,
Yea, thou shalt lie down, and thy sleep shall be sweet
(Prov. 3:24).

In peace will I both lay me down and sleep (Ps. 4:8).

The practical effect of this controlling fear of God is to drive out the fear of man. The number and variety of occasions on which men hear a Divine voice saying, "Fear not," makes a very interesting study.* "Fear not, for I am with thee": and the human response is:

Jehovah is on my side, I will not fear;
What can man do unto me (Ps. 118:6)?

How this fearlessness which issues from the fear of God, and sometimes more particularly from the consciousness of a Divine call, affects practical life may be strikingly seen in Amos's brave answer to the insinuations of the courtier-priest Amaziah (Amos 7:12–17; cf. Jer. 42:11). But if "fear not" means much in the Old Testament, how much more does it mean in the New, after the "good news" has found eternal expression in the words and in the life of Jesus! "Be of good cheer. It is I, be not afraid." This superiority to all fear rests in the last resort on the recognition of God as Father; for we have received the spirit, not of bondservants unto fear, but of sons (Rom. 8:15; Gal. 4:6).

"Be not anxious." This is one of the great watchwords of Jesus. Be not anxious for food or drink or raiment (Matt. 6:25; Luke 12:22), be not anxious for the morrow (Matt. 6:34), be not anxious when, for My sake, ye are brought before tribunals (Matt. 10:19; Luke 12:11). Depend upon the love of God. But the whole teaching and practice of Jesus go to show, not only that that immovable confidence in God which we call faith is thoroughly compatible with prayer,

---

* Joshua 8:1; 10:8; 11:6; Isaiah 41:10, 13, 14; 44:2, 8; Jeremiah 1:7; 30:10, 11; Lamentations 3:57; Ezekiel 2:6; Daniel 10:19; Joel 2:21; Zephaniah 3:16; Zechariah 8:15; Matthew 10:26; 17:7; 28:5; Mark 6:50; Luke 1:13, 30; 2:10; 5:10; 12:4, 7, 32; Acts 18:9; 23:11; 27:24; Revelation 1:17.

but that it demands it as its natural and necessary expression. "Your Father knoweth what things ye have need of, before ye ask Him. Nevertheless after this manner pray ye" (Matt. 6:8, 9). Quite in the spirit of the Master, Paul says, "In nothing be anxious, but let your requests be made known" (Phil. 4:6). So James (James 1:6): "Let him *ask* in faith." A prayerless believer would be no less of a monstrosity than a child who never spoke to his father. According to one account, the disciples were unable to cure the epileptic boy, because of their little faith (Matt. 17:19, 20); according to another (Mark 9:29), it is implied that they failed through lack of prayer. Faith and prayer are correlate: their interrelation is suggested by the phrase "in prayer believing" (Matt. 21:22). Faith is the inspiration of prayer, as prayer is one expression of faith. The twelve, it is said, resolved to continue "in prayer and in the ministry of the word" (Acts 6:4). The prayer was the fountain of the ministry, coordinate in the importance with preaching and the source of its power. The whole practice of the New Testament and the implications of the Old justify the remark of a French writer that "the ideal of the Christian life is a perpetual communion with God, sustained by prayer as frequent as possible."

Who is then the God to whom the men of the Bible pray? He is spirit, invisible (Deut. 4:12) and absolute: there is none beside Him (Deut. 4:35). He is in heaven above and upon earth beneath, there is none else (Deut. 4:39). He is unlike man (Hos. 11:9), yet He is like him. He is not a force, but a Person. He has the pity of a father (Ps. 103:13; Deut. 1:31). Yet He is infinitely kinder than the kindest of fathers; for, if earthly fathers give gifts to their children, how much more will the heavenly Father give gifts to His (Matt. 7:11)! He will listen to the cry of poor men whose wages have been withheld; and He can not only listen, but help. All nature is His (Ex. 8–10), so that His arm can never wax short (Num. 11:23; Is. 59:1).

He is so great that the heaven of heavens cannot contain Him (1 Kgs. 8:27), and He sits above the centuries (Lam. 5:19; Ps. 102:26; Dan. 6:26). He is the King of kings and Lord of lords, dwelling in light inaccessible, whom no man hath seen or can see

(1 Tim. 6:15, 16). Yet He is not remote from the world. He is the Life of men, and the Lord of history. His eyes run to and fro throughout the whole earth (2 Chr. 16:9). He sees in secret (Matt. 6:6) and searches the hearts of men (1 Kgs. 8:39; 1 Chr. 28:9; Luke 6:15; Acts 1:24). But more marvelous than His power or His wisdom is His love. The central message of the Bible is that He "is merciful and gracious, slow to anger, and abundant in loving-kindness and truth" (Ex. 34:6; Deut. 4:31; Neh. 9:17; Ps. 86:15; 103:8; 145:8), and it is this that makes prayer worthwhile. To Him belong mercies and forgiveness (Dan. 9:9), and whosoever comes to Him in penitence and sincerity will be in no wise cast out.

With such a God, then—one who is not imprisoned within the walls of the world which His own fingers framed, nor indifferent to the men who live and move upon it, but Himself like unto a man, with an ear open to the cry of men, and a love that goes out with the strength of omnipotence to those "that are broken in their heart and grieved in their mind"—with such a God prayer becomes a necessity and an inspiration.

> O Thou that hearest prayer,
> All flesh shall come to Thee (Ps. 65:2)

—not only all the tribes of men, but all that can call itself flesh, all that is conscious of its weakness.

The attitude of the worshiper and the character of the God whom he addressed in prayer may also be appropriately studied in the names by which He is called, and the epithets by which He is described. As a rule, the mode of address is the very essence of simplicity. Sometimes it is simply "O God" (Num. 12:13). A personal touch is given to the name in the address "my God," which seems to have been a favorite with Nehemiah (cf. Neh. 5:19). This is amplified in the Korahitic psalms to "My King and my God" (Ps. 44:4; 84:3). Here the "my" may be collective rather than individual, but the practical difference is not great.

As Israel's God is Jehovah, this name naturally occurs with very great frequency in prayer; and even in prayers of great intensity, these simple names, God and Jehovah, unadorned by any epithet,

are felt to be enough. There is no more passionate prayer in the
Old Testament than Isaiah 63:7–64:12, yet throughout the mode
of address is simply "O Jehovah." So usually in the Book of
Lamentations. But Jehovah's special relation to Israel and the fathers of the Hebrew people is frequently emphasized in the address. Jacob, for example, prays to the "God of my father Abraham
and the God of my father Isaac" (Gen. 32:9), and Elijah to the
"God of Abraham, Isaac, and Israel" (1 Kgs. 18:36). This feature is
peculiarly common in the later prayers, and served to remind the
worshipers of the continuity of their national history, and of the
gracious links that bound them to the great men of the past.

Jehovah is therefore addressed as the "God of our fathers"
(2 Chr. 20:6; cf. Dan. 2:23), or the "God of Israel" (Ezra 9:15) our
father (1 Chr. 29:10), or as the "God of Abraham, Isaac, and Israel
our fathers" (1 Chr. 29:18), but it is worthy of note that in these
very prayers which emphasize the national aspect of worship and
the presence of God in the days of old, the worshipers also—and
almost in the same breath—address God as *"our* God" (1 Chr.
29:16; 2 Chr. 20:7, 12; Ezra 9:10, 13; Dan. 10:1), and even as *"my*
God" (1 Chr. 29:17; Ezra 9:6; Dan. 9:18). The address "my God"
seems to be peculiarly characteristic of post-exilic prayer. In pre-exilic times, the individual's right to approach Jehovah was conditioned by his membership in Israel, the people of Jehovah; he
could not so easily have thought of himself as having an indefeasible and unmediated right of his own to approach Jehovah and
call Him "my God."* Jehovah was the God of Israel, rather than
his God. But, speaking broadly, religious individualism was born
with Jeremiah. Jehovah is to him no more only the God of Israel,
but "my strength and my stronghold and my refuge in the day of
affliction" (Jer. 16:19). Post-exilic Israel felt itself to be a religious
unit as much as pre-exilic Israel had ever done, but the collective
aspect of religious life was now accompanied by an individualism
which had never been possible, in the same measure, before. The
lesson burned by his fiery experiences into the soul of Jeremiah

* 1 Kings 3:7 is probably affected by the redaction.

was written by him indelibly upon the religion of Israel; and the worshipers who still addressed Jehovah as the God of Israel could address Him with equal ease and sincerity as our God and my God.

The term "Jehovah" suggests intimate historical relations with Israel, and consequently usually carries an atmosphere of grace about it, whereas "Lord"* suggests possession and power. The combination therefore "O Lord Jehovah" is a peculiarly impressive one, and usually occurs in prayers of special earnestness, whether of intercession of entreaty. It is found, for example, in Moses' prayer to be permitted to enter the promised land (Deut. 3:24), and in his intercession for the guilty people (Deut. 9:26), in Joshua's prayer after Israel's defeat at Ai (Josh. 7:7), in Samson's dying prayer for strength (Judg. 16:28), repeatedly in David's prayer of gratitude for the brilliant future foretold for his kingdom by Nathan (2 Sam. 7:18–29), in Amos' intercession for guilty Israel (Amos 7:2, 5), and in two similar intercessions of Ezekiel (Ezek. 9:8; 11:13, cf. Jer. 4:10).

The effect of the term "Lord" is heightened where it stands alone unaccompanied by Jehovah, and such contexts are always worthy of special considerations. God is addressed as Lord, for example, throughout Abraham's intercession for Sodom (Gen. 18:23–32), and Daniel's intercession for Jerusalem,† and in the remonstrances of Moses (Ex. 4:10, 13; 5:22).

It is possible that Jehovah was directly addressed by the Hebrews as Father oftener than the records of the Old Testament would lead us to suppose. Israel was Jehovah's son (Ex. 4:22), and it would be natural for Israel to acknowledge Jehovah as Father. Indeed this is actually done twice in one prayer (Is. 63:16; 64:8; cf.

---

* Daniel 9:4–19. "Jehovah" occurs in the course of the prayer (cf. vv. 10, 14), but not as a direct address. Very instructive is the introduction: "I prayed unto Jehovah my God"–that is narrative–"and made *confession,* and said, O *Lord.*"

† To appreciate this distinction, the English reader must use the American Revised Version. In the other English versions, the Hebrew word for Jehovah is nearly always erroneously represented by the word Lord.

Mal. 2:10), and Jeremiah represents Israel in her distress appealing directly to her God as "my Father" (Jer. 3:4).

Attributes are not common in the earlier prayers: the name of God was held to be sufficient. Epithets and adjectival clauses are usually a sign of lateness. Jeremiah addresses God as "Jehovah of hosts, who judgest righteously, and triest the heart and the mind" (Jer. 11:20), and this style of address is greatly developed in post-exilic times. Nehemiah (Neh. 1:5), for example, begins a prayer thus: "I beseech Thee, O Jehovah, the God of heaven, the great and terrible God, that keepeth covenant and loving-kindness with them that love Him and keep His commandments." This seems to have been a favorite mode of address (Neh. 9:32; Dan. 9:4). He is also the "God of the spirits of all flesh" (Num. 16:22; 27:16). In an imprecatory Psalm (Ps. 94:1), He is addressed as the "God of vengeance," and once He is called "Jehovah the good" (2 Chr. 30:18).

From all this we may infer that the God addressed by the later Hebrews was felt, in the moment of prayer, to be at once the God of the national* and the individual life, of the past and of the present, of the existing church as a whole, and of each of the members of which that church was composed—Israel's God and our God and my God. He is Lord, but He is also Jehovah: great and terrible, but also just and faithful; Sovereign, but also Father; and indeed—in spirit, if not in name—Father most of all.

In the New Testament, with one remarkable exception, there is little that is really new in the mode of address to God, but the difference—which is profound—between the two Testaments, lies in a change of emphasis. There He was often God, seldom Father; here He is usually Father, and seldom God alone. In the Apocalypse,

---

* Of course it must not be forgotten that most of the extant prayers of later times are public prayers. The private prayers of Nehemiah are usually addressed to "my God" without any specific allusion to the God of Israel. Cf. even in the narrative "my God" 7:5. But his work was essentially a national work, and he would naturally commit it and himself to the tutelage of the national God; cf. *our* God, 4:4, 9; 6:16; and the long opening prayer of the book is addressed substantially, though not formally, to the God of Israel (1:5–11).

which is intensely Jewish, echoes of the Old Testament are unmistakable. He is the Lord God, the Almighty (Rev. 4:8; 16:7). He is the *Despotēs*–a difficult word to translate (6:10)–but significant and occurring also in the prayer of Simeon (Luke 2:29). Elsewhere He is the King eternal, immortal, invisible (1 Tim. 1:17). There is, in some quarters, the same tendency towards the use of epithets betrayed by the later books of the Old Testament; for example, "O Lord *who knowest the hearts** of all men" (Acts 1:24)–perhaps a customary epithet, or it may have been a favorite phrase of Peter's (cf. Acts 15:8). Sometimes the epithets seem to be otiose, as in the prayer for boldness in preaching, which begins: "O Lord, *Thou that didst make the heavens and the earth and the sea and all that in them is*" (Acts 4:24). Such a phrase, which also seems to have been a favorite (cf. Acts 14:15), may have formed part of the general vocabulary of prayer and preaching. A frequent address of Paul's seems to have been "my God" (cf. Phil. 1:3)–which recalls the practice of Nehemiah.

But that which is new, not in fact, but in emphasis, is the use of the word Father; and this is directly due to Jesus. His own prayers are addressed to God simply as Father: not our Father, or my Father,† but Father. Probably this simple address was seldom amplified, but, in moments of more than usual exaltation, the title is expanded by an adjective or a clause. The unique prayer in Matthew 11:25 begins, "O Father, *Lord of heaven and earth*," and in the high-priestly prayer of John 17. He calls God holy (John 17:11) and righteous (John 17:25) Father, as well as Father (John 17:1, 5, 21, 24). The atmosphere of Fatherhood hangs about most of the New Testament prayers. God is addressed as the Father of mercies (2 Cor. 1:3); and He may also have been addressed as the Father of spirits (Heb. 12:9; cf. Num. 16:22) and the Father of lights (James 1:17), though it happens that these words occur not in prayer, but in narrative.

---

* One word in the Greek.

† "My Father" in Gethsemane, according to Matthew 26:39, 42.

The exception, to which allusion was made above, is the address—so familiar in the epistles of Paul—to the "God and Father of our Lord Jesus Christ" (2 Cor. 1:3). It may be considered to have a remote parallel in the Old Testament addresses to the God of Abraham, Isaac and Jacob, at least insofar as it contemplates God in relation to a historical personality; yet it is something widely different and deeper. It is a subtle reminiscence of Jesus' own method of prayer; was it not He preeminently who had called God Father? It is further a most remarkable tribute to His uniqueness that Paul calls Him the Father of Jesus. It suggests that his new relation to God, which involved nothing less than a spiritual revolution, had been created and mediated by Jesus. It suggests the infinite obligation of him and of all men to Jesus. Prayer is now surer of itself than ever it could have been before, because it is prayer to the Father of Jesus.

Inward and Outward Conditions

Having examined the contents of biblical prayer, and its relations to the faith which creates it, but does not supersede it, we shall now consider the mode of the worshiper's approach to God, the spirit in which he offers his prayer, the other religious exercises or practices which occasionally accompany it, the place in which and the time at which prayer was wont to be made.

In earlier times, as we have seen, the man who prays is often on surprisingly familiar terms with his God. A penalty had to be paid for that anthropomorphic view of God which makes biblical religion so attractive to us. God was much like man himself. Like a man, He had to leave His home to acquaint Himself with facts which he was anxious to ascertain (Gen. 18:21; cf. 11:5); like a man, He worked and rested from His labors; like a man, He walked in the garden in the cool of the day. It is not surprising, therefore, that the language addressed to Him by men was occasionally lacking in that reverence which was His due, that it was sometimes defiant (Gen. 4:9; cf. 3:12), and sometimes familiar even to the point of impertinence. Many of the early prayers are beautiful (Gen. 24:12–14), but on the whole it is true, here as elsewhere, that when Israel was a child, he spoke as a child.

But it is also true that when Israel became a man he put away—by no means all, but many—of his childish things. Some of the latest prayers in the Old Testament breathe a spirit which shows how much Israel had yet to learn (Ps. 149:6, 7), but, speaking broadly, experience had wrought wisdom, and wisdom reverence. Men approached God with the knowledge that He was the high and lofty One that inhabiteth eternity (Is. 57:15), that life was a mystery before which it was wisdom to bow, that, as we receive good at the hand of God, we should also unmurmuringly receive evil (Job 2:10). Such a God must be approached in a spirit of humility, as by servants who come into the presence of their lord. In prayers of every age, the speakers call themselves "thy servant" and "thy handmaid,"* and even a very early worshiper acknowledges that he is not "worthy of the least of all the love and of all the faithfulness that God had shown him" (Gen. 32:10).

Sometimes, as in the case of Job, men might be tempted to address God in words of bitter and almost irreverent audacity, but it must not be forgotten that the daring and awful speeches of Job are spoken "in the anguish of his spirit and in the bitterness of his soul" (Job 7:11; 10:1). Such prayers may be models of intensity, but not of devotion. Jonah's foolish and impudent prayer has a somewhat similar excuse. "Was this not just what I told Thee, while I was yet in my own country?" he prays in the petulance of his disappointment. "So kill me, for I would rather die than live" (Jon. 4:2, 3). This was a prayer offered by the prophet when he was "exceedingly displeased and angry" (Jon. 4:1). That is not the mood in which to pray. Besides, men could only pray thus who had not had an adequate vision of God. After Job had truly seen Him, and not merely heard of Him with the hearing of the ear (Job 42:5), humbled and overwhelmed he laid his hand upon his mouth and would proceed no further (Job 40:4, 5). Without the humility inspired by such a vision, one may pray, like the Pharisee, a prayer of gratitude, when one ought to cry, like the publican, for mercy (Luke 18:11, 13). When a mortal comes before the heavenly throne, he will pray as a man who remembers that he has need to be forgiven (Mark 11:25), and whatever else his prayer contains, it is likely to be, like the publican's, for mercy, and for grace to help in time of need (Heb. 4:16).

The throne is a throne of grace (Heb. 4:16), and the holy mountain is not a mountain that burns with fire and blackness and storm

---

* 2 Samuel 7:25, 26, 27, etc.; in 1 Samuel 1:2, three times in one verse.

and tempest. The God whom man approaches in prayer is not, as Job imagined in his despair, a God of devastating and unscrupulous omnipotence (Job 9). He is one whose tender mercies are over all His works; and though in His presence man may, in certain moods, consider himself but "dust and ashes" (Gen. 18:27), yet it is not forgotten that He pities His children like a father; and, rejoicing in that loving kindness which endureth forever, His worshipers may enter His gates with thanksgiving and His courts with praise— not only the gates and courts of His spacious house where brethren meet together to worship Him in unity, but also the door of the quiet inner chamber where the spirit is alone with Him. The man whose heart has been searched by Christ, will never indeed, like Job, with loud declaration of innocence, approach his God with the proud bearing of a prince (Job 31:37), but, though reverent and humble, he will be unafraid. God is the Lord of men, but He is also their Father. They are His servants, but they are also His sons; and as sons, they are not bondmen, but free. How well the lesson of the Fatherhood had been learned may be seen from the frequency of the word "boldness" in the New Testament allusions to prayer. It was men of unimpeachable reverence who urged that we should "draw near with boldness unto the throne of grace" (Heb. 4:16) and enter with boldness into the holy place (Heb. 10:19), and who spoke of the boldness which those may have towards Him (1 John 5:14), whose hearts condemn them not (1 John 3:21).

Another condition of prayer is sincerity. It is "with a true heart" that we are to draw near with boldness (Heb. 10:2). Men must not only honor God with their lips (Is. 29:13; Matt. 15:8), they must cry unto Him with their hearts (Hos. 7:14; Jer. 29:13). It is the prayer of the upright that is His delight (Prov. 15:8), the prayer of the righteous that He hears (Prov. 15:29). "If I regard iniquity in my heart, the Lord will not hear" (Ps. 66:18). "No evil man can be a guest of Thine" (Ps. 5:4). The prayer at the festival that Jehovah should look down from heaven and bless the people and the land was only to be offered after the tithes had been reserved for the fatherless and the widow (Deut. 26:12–15), and it contains an explicit confession that the divine commandments had been kept and all the obligations met (Deut. 26:13, 14). It is significant of the difference made by Jesus that a very similar confession is used to pillory the Pharisee in the parable (Luke 18:12).

It is a singular and very interesting feature of the Old Testament that confessions of integrity are nearly as common as confessions of sin. Doubtless this is largely due to the fact that religion is conceived somewhat externally. Where it is supposed to consist in the outward observance of laws, the man who observes them is free to count himself innocent. Of course, Old Testament religion is a much profounder thing than that, but there was a great deal, especially in the elaborate ecclesiastical regulations of post-exilic life, to encourage this view (Ps. 44:18, 19; 119). Even apart from this, however, a certain rugged honesty led men to assert their innocence before God in a way no longer possible, when religion has learned to make the infinite demand which it makes in Christianity. Alongside of the beautiful prayer of Jacob that he is unworthy of all the love God has shown him, is Hezekiah's appeal to God to remember how he had walked before Him in truth and with a perfect heart, and had done that which was good in his sight (2 Kgs. 20:3), Jeremiah's appeal to God's knowledge of His heart (Jer. 11:20; 12:3), and Job's violent and repeated protestations of his innocence (cf. Job 10:7; 13:23). Whatever objections theology might make to statements of this kind, they are indicative of a rare and splendid sincerity. We may not imitate these prayers, but we may well imitate the lives which made such prayers possible.

But sincerity will also show itself in its willingness to confess the sins of which it is conscious and to translate penitence into action. On behalf of the people Ezra confesses, "Thou, O Jehovah, art righteous; we are before Thee in our guiltiness. None can stand before Thee because of this" (Ezra 9:15); and the prayer is followed by an attempt to remove the cause of guilt (Ezra 10). The promise made by the people to Jeremiah that they would obey the will of God as soon as he made it clear to them was easier to make than to keep (Jer. 42:3, 20, 21). Without sincerity, it is impossible to pray.

Besides humility towards God, there must, in prayer, be love towards man. The link that binds us to Him binds us also to each other, and the deepest interests of men lie among the things that all can pray for. The temple is *the house of prayer for all nations*. Whatever may be their political differences, in the interests represented by the house of prayer all nations are one. And this sense of community, of brotherhood in the deepest things, ought to be implied, if not expressed in prayer. It is to *our* Father that we pray. The opening word of the Lord's prayer compels us to acknowledge our brotherhood. This is one of the permanent lessons of the Old Testament, that the individual is not the only unit. He lives and moves and has his being in the nation of which he is a member, and his prayer is to the God of Israel. True, He is also *my* God (Ezra 9:6; Neh. 5:19; Dan. 9:8), but the men who address Him with the understanding as well as with the heart, also call Him *our* God (Ezra 9:10, 13; Dan. 9:17).

Further, God must be approached in a spirit of absolute and implicit confidence. The earth is full of His glory, and the past of His mercy; and, though man cannot by searching fully find Him out, he knows enough to trust Him. On the lower levels of biblical religion, men doubt—for example, Gideon and Hezekiah (Judg. 6:36–39; 2 Kgs. 20:9; 2 Chr. 32:24)—and have, as the stories go, to be reassured by a sign, but the best need no sign, and the bad need look for none (Matt. 12:39). Job, as his heart is torn by the dreadful conflict between the God of tradition and the God of his conscience, has, in one of his profounder moments, the clear assurance of a vindication somewhere, somehow; for "my Witness is in heaven and my Sponsor is on high" (Job 16:19). In one of the sayings of Jesus, prayer is compared to the knocking at a closed door, behind which is a Person—a Person with a gracious will—who can and will open. But that will must be trusted: the heavenly Father knows what the kingdom and its subjects need. A sublime illustration of this confidence in God is Elijah's command to drench the bullock and the wood upon the altar, before calling down upon it fire from heaven (1 Kgs. 18:33, 34). Isaiah's offer to the skeptical Ahaz of any sign in the height above or in the depth beneath, though not in a prayer context, is another illustration of the same daring—one had almost said reckless—faith (Is. 7:10). Very beautiful is the confidence, on which we have already commented, of Ezra, before starting for Palestine, that his God would protect him from the perils of the way (Ezra 8:21–23).

This leads us to ask what is meant by an answer to prayer, what sort of prayers are answered, and what is the condition of an answer to prayer. These problems begin to find an approximate solution, as soon as it begins to be understood that man's chief end is to discover the will of God, and to learn to do it gladly. In prayer, the heart's desire is turned into a supplication to God (Rom. 10:1), and is purified of all selfishness and worldliness, by having His white and searching light thrown upon it. The only true prayers are those that can live in His presence. The moment prayer is realized as contact with a holy God, all merely selfish desires are burnt up; and if "ye ask and receive not," it is "because ye ask amiss, that ye may spend it in your pleasures" (James 4:3).

If then, the desire to have the will of God fulfilled in us and by us be the sovereign impulse of our lives, on the one hand, our petitions, whatever their concrete contents may be, will always be controlled and inspired by a passion for the will of God, and will always, in their essence, be a prayer that that will be done; and on the other hand, the answer to that prayer will be conditioned by a sincere and earnest desire to have that will fulfilled. This is the great circle from which there is no escape. In other words, the man who would pray with the hope of an answer must love the will of God, and that for which he prays must ultimately be the realization of the will of God. God must be an end and not a means. The place which the desire for the glory of God should occupy in prayer is illustrated, in a way that is somewhat superficial, but here adequate for our purpose, by Hezekiah's prayer for deliverance from Sennacherib. "Incline Thine ear, O Jehovah, and hear; open Thine eyes, O Jehovah, and see; and hear the words of Sennacherib. . . . Save us, I beseech Thee, out of his hand, *that all the kingdoms of the earth may know that Thou, Jehovah, art God alone*" (2 Kgs. 19:16, 19; cf. 1 Kgs 8:60). Jerusalem was to be delivered, and through that deliverance the God of Israel was to be glorified.

It will always be with a humbling consciousness of the infinite complexity of life and of our own infinite foolishness, that we approach God with specific petitions affecting the concrete details of our life; for though our Father knows the things that we have need of, we do not. Therefore specific petitions must be begun, continued, and ended with the prayer, "Thy will be done." The answer to this prayer, at least, is, in one sense, inevitable. If we ask anything *according to His will,* then assuredly in some sense He heareth us (1 John 5:14). Ask, and—in the asking—ye receive; for the prayer, if it be sincere, is itself a sign that the human will is, in its deepest depths, in harmony with the divine. True prayer is not the desire to determine the divine will, but to be at one with it; and the eternal answer to all true prayer is, "Be not afraid, for I am with thee."

The question might even be raised whether, in view of our pathetic and inevitable ignorance, specific petitions are worthwhile, and whether the simple prayer, "Thy will be done," does not more wisely and safely express the ultimate and only real longing of the devout soul. But the examples of Jesus and Paul would seem to justify a negative answer to this question. Jesus said, "Take away this cup from me: yet Thy will be done"; and he said it again and again (Matt. 26:44). And Paul, like his Master, also prayed three times, that the thorn be removed from his flesh (2 Cor. 12:8). It is of the profoundest religious interest and importance to note that, in the ordinary sense, neither of these prayers was answered. The cup had to be drained to the dregs—*My God, why hast Thou forsaken me?*—and the thorn was not removed. But it is of equal interest and importance to note that, in the profoundest sense, these prayers were both answered. The will of God was done. With fine insight, the author of the Epistle to the Hebrews remarks that Jesus "in the days of his flesh, having offered up prayers and supplications with strong crying and tears unto Him that was able to save Him from death, *was heard* for His godly fear" (Heb. 5:7); and Paul was so strengthened by the grace of Christ that he actually learned to glory in his weakness, because in it he was conscious that the power of Christ rested upon him (2 Cor. 12:9).

The prayers that are answered are prayers for the fulfillment of the will of God, though, as we have seen, the answer may come in a form very different from that entreated by the speaker. Jeremiah prays for deliverance from one distress, and for answer he learns that he has to face another. Wearied in his race with the footmen, he is divinely summoned to contend with the horses (Jer. 12:5). Sometimes, indeed, the answer may come at once, *before he had done speaking* (Gen. 24:15); sometimes only after many days, and sometimes, to all seeming, not at all. Habakkuk thought he had found an answer in his own day (Hab. 1:5) to his prayer for divine intervention, but, after years of disappointment, he begins to learn that the purpose of God, though sure, may be slow. The will of God is ultimately done in history, but not as and when we will; therefore "though it tarry, wait for it" (Hab. 2:3). But if it is slow, it is sure. It has its appointed time. "It is sure to come, it will not lag behind" (Hab. 2:3).

The most comprehensive petition is "Thy will be done." But how may this will be known, and where is it expressed? Contrary to the genius of the Christian religion, the ordinary man longs for definite statements. Like the perplexed people who came to consult Jeremiah, his prayer is, "Show us the way wherein we should walk and the thing that we should do" (Jer. 42:3). It is astonishing how often in the Old Testament the will of God is identified with social justice, and how often this is made a condition of answered prayer. This is the whole burden of the Book of Amos, but all prophecy is weighty with the message that the only man to whom God listens is the man whose dealings with his fellows are governed by principles of justice and mercy. Seeking God is equivalent to seeking good (Amos 5:4, 6, 14; cf. Zeph. 2:3), and the good is the "establishing of justice in the gate" (Amos 5:14). He who would be a friend of God must be a friend of the poor. Those who "eat the flesh of My people and flay their skin from off them, when they cry to Jehovah He will not answer them" (Mic. 3:3, 4). If thou feed the hungry, and shelter the poor and cover the naked, "then thou shalt call and Jehovah will answer; thou shalt cry, and He will say, 'Here I am' " (Is. 58:7, 9). Those who crush the widow, the fatherless and the poor, and make their hearts like an adamant stone, "when they cry, I will not hear" (Zech. 7:10, 12, 13). The iniquities which separated the people from their God, so that He would not hear, were cruelty, treachery, and in general, social injustice (Is. 59:2, 3, 12–15). And just as, for the men of wealth and influence, the will of God would have been fulfilled in the discharge of social obligations in a spirit of justice and mercy, so, for the poor, it lay in that meekness and humility which the hard discipline of life was calculated to produce in pious natures. The poor in this world's resources were very often, in the nature of the case, the poor in spirit (Matt. 5:3; Luke 6:20), and theirs was the kingdom of heaven.

It is very significant for the post-exilic period that a discharge of ceremonial obligation is sometimes regarded as a condition of the presence of God. The apathy of the people towards the rebuilding of the temple (Hag. 1:4), and their contemptible offerings after it was built (Mal. 1:13), had hindered a blessing. When the tithes were paid, the blessing would pour down from the windows of heaven (Mal. 3:10). This view is not without relative justification. Indifference to the formal ordinances and obligations of religion, meant for those days, and very frequently means for these, indifference to religion itself.

And as the will of God in the Old Testament expressed itself chiefly in the commandment to love the brethren,[*] so it is also essentially in the New. The conscience is infinitely searched and quickened by the royal words of Jesus, but the new commandment, no less than the old, is that we should love one another. This is the demand alike of James (James 2:15, 16) and John (1 John 3:17), as well as of Jesus. He who dwelleth in love dwelleth in God, and "he prayeth best who loveth best."

We shall now consider briefly a few illustrations of answers to prayers for external things. After the previous discussion, it will be no surprise to find that these cases are much more numerous in the

---

[*] Cf. Deuteronomy, *passim.*

Old Testament than in the New. It has to be remembered, of course, that the former literature is much more extensive than the latter, and further that, in the nature of the case, the tone of the latter is much more severely spiritual, and its literary records much more exclusively and intimately related to the kingdom of God. The more private and personal prayers of the early Church remain, for the most part, unrecorded. But even so, the difference is striking and suggestive.

The prayers of prophets, or of men who were regarded as prophets, were believed, as we have seen, to be peculiarly efficacious (Jer. 42:2–6), though Moses' request to cross the Jordan was not granted (Deut. 3:26). Abraham's prayer for Abimelech (Gen. 20:17) and Moses' for Miriam (Num. 12:13) were heard. But no continuous section so thoroughly illustrates the efficacy of prophetic prayer as the career of Elijah and Elisha, especially the latter. Elijah's prayer for the dead child (1 Kgs. 17:21, 22) and for fire from heaven upon the altar on Mount Carmel (1 Kgs. 18), Elisha's curse in the name of Jehovah upon the youths who mocked him (2 Kgs. 2:24), his prayer for the Shunammite's dead son (2 Kgs. 4:35), his prayer that his servant's eyes should be opened to see the horses and chariots of fire upon the mountain (2 Kgs. 6:17), his prayer that the Aramean army should be smitten with blindness (2 Kgs. 6:18) and afterwards recover their sight (2 Kgs. 6:20)—these prayers, according to the historian, were all answered; and all this goes to illustrate the idea that the prophets were believed to speak as powerfully with God as with man. Their note of authority they probably owed in large measure to prayer.

But the prayers heard are as various as the worshipers who offer them: witness Isaac's (Gen. 25:21) and Hannah's prayer for a child (1 Sam. 1:27), Hezekiah's prayer for recovery from illness (2 Kgs. 20:5), and Paul's for the father of Publius (Acts 28:8)—for the prayer of faith shall save the sick (James 5:15)—Hezekiah's prayer for deliverance from Sennacherib (2 Kgs. 19:20), Ezra's for safe conduct to Palestine (Ezra 8:23), the prayer of the Church for Peter in prison (Acts 12:5–7). Answered prayers for the restoration of the dead are naturally rare: note the prayer of Elijah (1 Kgs. 17:21) and the similar prayer of Elisha (2 Kgs. 4:35) for a dead child, and that of Peter for Tabitha (Acts 9:40). Most of the miraculous answers to prayer, however, occur in documents or sections which are either late, or whose historicity has, with more or less justice, been doubted. To this class belongs the story of Gideon's fleece (Judg. 6:36–40) and of the sundial on which the shadow went backward (2 Kgs. 20:11). The story of the healing of Jeroboam's hand by a prophet occurs in a chapter which is demonstrably very late (1 Kgs. 13:6), and the interpretation put upon Joshua's appeal to the sun and moon (Josh. 10:13, 14) rests on a misunderstanding of the poem cited.

The spirit of worship is infinitely more important than the rules by which it is hedged about, and the ceremonies that accompany it, but this is a lesson that is learned late in religion and seldom learned perfectly. The inward attitude of the man who approaches God in prayer has already been considered: we shall now discuss the concomitants, the place, and the time of prayer.

Throughout the Old Testament, sacrifice is very frequently and naturally associated with prayer. One of the ideas underlying the practice was that God, like a human lord, had to be approached by His suppliants with gifts as well as words. At the festivals celebrated in the various sanctuaries scattered throughout the land, and afterwards in the Temple exclusively (Ezra 6:21, 22), sacrifice played an important part, and was accompanied by prayer. In the exile, sacrifice was not possible, and men learned then that it was not indispensable: "the lifting up of the hands" in prayer could be "as the evening sacrifice" (Ps. 141:2). But the close connection between seeking God and sacrifice is indicated in the request of the "people of the land" to be allowed to share with the returned Jews in the work of rebuilding the Temple; for "we seek your God as ye do, and we sacrifice unto Him" (Ezra 4:2). The intimate relation between sacrifice and prayer must have been of very ancient origin. Abraham called upon the name of Jehovah, after building an altar (Gen. 12:18; cf. 26:25). The practice was shared by the sister religions. The Philistines accompanied their song of praise to

Dagon for the capture of Samson with a sacrifice (Judg. 16:23, 24). Sacrifice is also mentioned in connection with intercessory prayer. Job's intercession for his friends (Job 42:8) and Samuel's for the people (1 Sam. 7:9) were accompanied by sacrifice, the latter also by a libation (1 Sam. 7:6). In Revelation 8:4 the smoke of incense ascends with the prayers of the saints unto God. In prison, Paul and Silas sang hymns as well as prayed (Acts 16:25).

Fasting is also a frequent accompaniment of prayer, especially, though not exclusively, in later times. It is mentioned in connection with the prayer of Samuel just alluded to (1 Sam. 7:6), but its importance increased after the exile. Ezra proclaims a fast before his prayer for the Divine protection on the way home (Ezra 8:21), and Nehemiah (Neh. 1:4) and Daniel (Dan. 9:3) before their intercession for the desolate Jerusalem. The custom lasted into New Testament times—"the disciples of John fast and make supplications, likewise also the disciples of the Pharisees" (Luke 5:33)—and was adopted by Christians (Acts 13:3; 14:23). The earliest disciples of Jesus, however, had not fasted (Mark 2:18), and the best texts in Mark 9:29 which simply read, "This kind cometh out by nothing save by prayer," give no reason to suppose that Jesus laid any stress upon fasting, though apparently He did not positively discountenance it, but regarded it as legitimate so long as it was the spontaneous and unostentatious expression of the religious mood (Matt. 6:16). Prayers and alms are coordinated in the case of Cornelius (Acts 10:4).

As an expression of the speaker's earnestness a prayer is sometimes supported by a vow; for example, Jacob's prayer for guidance (Gen. 28:20–22), Hannah's for a child (1 Sam. 1:11), and Absalom's for a safe return to Jerusalem (2 Sam. 15:8). Even in New Testament times, the lot is once used in connection with prayer (Acts 1:26).

The healthy spirit of the Bible is indicated by the fact that prayer is usually accompanied by work. The biblical men of prayer are not hermits. Like Moses, Jeremiah, Nehemiah, Paul, they are also mighty in word or deed or both. Under God, Moses created, and Jeremiah may be almost said to have recreated Hebrew religion:

Nehemiah reorganized the nation, and Paul, by his practical genius, laid the foundations of the Christianity that was to be. Faith does not supersede effort. The foreign sailors in the Book of Jonah "cried every man unto his god, and then they cast forth the tackling to lighten the ship" (Jon. 1:5). They prayed their gods to help them, and then they helped themselves. The union of work and prayer is splendidly illustrated by the career of the pious and practical Nehemiah. *We made our prayer unto God and set a watch against the enemy day and night* (Neh. 4:9). Instinctively this statement recalls the injunction of Jesus to "watch and pray" (Mark 13:33; Matt. 26:41). This insistence upon the use of means and the exertion of effort is just as characteristic of the Bible as its insistence upon faith. The prayer of faith that was to save the sick was to be accompanied by an anointing with oil (James 5:14, 15). Those who continued steadfastly in prayer were no less to communicate to the necessities of the saints (Rom. 12:12, 13): and "praying in the spirit" did not exempt those whom Jude (1:20) addressed from building themselves up on their most holy faith.

The intense earnestness of biblical prayer is often suggested by the emotion which accompanied it. There is frequent reference, for example, to tears. Hezekiah wept sore as he prayed for recovery from his illness (2 Kgs. 20:3), Nehemiah weeps as he prays for Jerusalem (Neh. 1:4), and Ezra, as he makes his confession for the people (Ezra 10:1); and the priests in Joel 2:17 are called upon to weep while they intercede for the people. Other signs of mourning occasionally accompany prayer. The elders throw dust upon their heads after the defeat at Ai (Josh. 7:6), and Job utters his noble words of resignation, prostrate upon the ground, after rending his robe and shaving his head (Job 1:20, 21). After Paul's farewell prayer with his friends at Miletus, they wept and kissed him (Acts 20:36, 37).

The prayer scenes of the Bible are occasionally dramatic and exciting. The most exciting of all occurs in connection with a heathen prayer, where the Baal priests, as they frantically shout for hours,

"O Baal, hear us," cut themselves with knives and lances till the blood gushed out upon them (1 Kgs. 18:26, 28). Equally terrible and more tragic must have been the scene in which the king of Moab upon the battlefield offered up his eldest son—undoubtedly with a prayer to his god—to secure the victory over Israel (2 Kgs. 3:27).

It is no accident that nothing so terrible as the lacerations on Carmel ever occurs in connection with the prayers of the true worshipers of Jehovah. Israel's conception of God was incomparably more serious and worthy than that of her neighbors, but the Israelites too were Semites, and shared, in their measure, the violence of the Semitic temper. The degenerate worshipers of Hosea's time, in imitation of their heathen neighbors, "cut themselves* for the grain and the new wine" (Hos. 7:14). But even on truly noble levels, prayer takes a dramatic turn. Most conspicuous in this respect is Ezra—all the more that he is a priest. Before the prayer of confession which he made weeping and casting himself down before the house of God (Ezra 10:1), he tells us that he rent his garment and robe, and plucked off the hair of his head and beard, and sat down confounded. "And at the evening oblation I arose up from my humiliation, even with my garment and my robe rent, and I fell upon my knees and spread out my hands unto Jehovah my God; and I said, 'O my God, I am ashamed and blush to lift up my face to Thee, my God' " (Ezra 9:3, 5, 6).

It must not, of course, be forgotten that these scenes were not normal. This was not the formal worship of the sanctuary, but a very exceptional occasion. But after making every allowance, it is very probable that, Oriental nature being what it was, prayer was more violent than it normally is with us. The language of Paul suggests that Christian prayer is, in one aspect, a struggle (Rom. 15:30; Col. 2:1); and while this intensity is in part created by the deadly earnestness of Christianity, it is also in part an inheritance from older Hebrew custom. The publican beat upon his breast (Luke 18:13), and the early Christians groaned in the excess of their emotion

---

* So reads the Greek text, rightly.

(Rom. 8:26). But by far the greatest illustration of intensity in prayer is that of our Savior as He prayed in Gethsemane. Whether or not the statement, omitted by many of the manuscripts, is literally true, as it well may be, that "His sweat became as it were great drops of blood falling down upon the ground" (Luke 22:44), it is certainly true to the spirit of the situation, and is practically corroborated by the other statement that "He offered up prayer and supplications with strong crying and tears" (Heb. 5:7).

The posture most frequently mentioned in connection with prayer is prostration (cf. Gen. 24:26). The worshiper approached his God with the same deference that he showed when presenting a petition to an earthly superior. Unfortunately the Hebrew equivalent for "he prostrated himself" is usually rendered in the English Bible by "he worshiped." The prostration, with the face to the ground (Neh. 8:6), was commonly preceded by the bowing of the head (1 Chr. 29:20; Neh. 8:6), and it is sometimes described as a falling to the earth upon the face (Josh. 7:6); as Ezekiel fell on his face (Ezek. 3:23) when he saw the glory of Jehovah in the plain, and in this attitude he offered his brief intercessory prayers (Ezek. 9:8; 11:13). Jesus, too, falls on His face in Gethsemane (Matt. 26:39), and it is thus that the angels in Revelation 7:11 offer their praise to God. It is adopted in prayers of gratitude (Gen. 24:26; Rev. 7:11) as well as of supplication. A very peculiar posture is that of Elijah, who, on Mount Carmel, put his head between his knees (1 Kgs. 18:42). The context suggests that this may have been the attitude of one who prayed for rain.

Prayer could also be offered kneeling (1 Kgs. 8:54). In point of fact most references to kneeling appear to belong to the later books (cf. Ps. 95:6). Daniel (Dan. 6:10), Stephen (Acts 7:60), Peter (Acts 9:40), Paul (Acts 20:36; Eph. 3:14) knelt: these prayers are all petitions or intercessions.

Sometimes, however, the worshiper stood. It was standing that Hannah prayed for a son (1 Sam. 1:26), that Solomon blessed the people (1 Kgs. 8:54; cf. 14, 22), and that Jeremiah interceded for them (Jer. 18:20). The "hypocrites" in Jesus' time stood at prayer

(Matt. 6:5), but He presupposes the same attitude for His own disciples (Mark 11:25). The Pharisee offered his prayer of gratitude standing (Luke 18:11), so also did the publican his for mercy (Luke 18:13); and in Revelation 7:10 a great multitude in heaven stands to praise God. Thus this attitude could be adopted alike in prayers of petition, intercession, and thanksgiving. It has been suggested, with some probability, that ordinarily prayer was offered kneeling or standing, with prostration at the beginning and the end.

Sitting does not seem to be a particularly natural attitude in prayer, but it occurs at least once, in David's prayer of gratitude (2 Sam. 7:18; 1 Chr. 17:16), and possibly another time (cf. Judg. 20:26), in a context of sorrow.

Whether kneeling (2 Chr. 6:13; Ezra 9:5) or standing, the hands were usually stretched out (Ex. 9:29; 17:11; 1 Kgs 8:22), either towards the Temple (1 Kgs. 8:38; Ps. 5:7; 134:2)—in particular towards the shrine (Ps. 28:2), where Jehovah was supposed preeminently to be—or towards heaven (1 Kgs. 8:22, 54), though when the worshiper was not in the holy land, he could also turn to Jerusalem (1 Kgs. 8:38; 2 Chr. 6:34; Dan. 6:10). Jehovah Himself is even represented as spreading forth His hands (Is. 65:2); and in public worship, not only the leaders pray thus (1 Kgs. 8:22), but also the people, when they respond with the Amen (Neh. 8:6). So characteristic was this attitude that the lifting up of the hands is synonymous with prayer (Is. 1:15; Lam. 2:19; 3:41; Ps. 141:2), and it was a feature also of Christian prayer (1 Tim. 2:8).

In prayer the eyes are open, but they are usually turned upwards, as we may infer from the statement that the publican "would not lift up so much as his eyes unto heaven" (Luke 18:13). Jesus looked up to heaven when saying grace before meat (Mark 6:41; Luke 9:16), and before He healed the deaf and dumb man (Mark 7:34). These are all open-air scenes, where the upturned face of the Master would be strangely impressive. It is not said that He lifted up His eyes in His prayer of gratitude at the institution of the supper, or in the grace which He said before supper at Emmaus (Luke 24:30), but the fact that the high priestly prayer was so delivered (John 17:1) shows that this attitude was not impossible within closed doors.

Women, at least in public, prayed with the head veiled, men with the head bare, though in the Corinthian Church there appears to have been a movement among the women for emancipation from this custom (1 Cor. 11:5, 13). Job shaved his head (Job 1:20) before prostrating himself in prayer, but that, like the rending of his robe, was a symbolical expression of grief.

The prayers of the Bible are nearly all spoken in a loud voice. Nehemiah offers a silent prayer on an occasion when a spoken prayer was impossible (Neh. 2:4), and in Hannah's prayer for a child "only her lips moved, but her voice was not heard" (1 Sam. 1:13). As a rule, however, the worshiper "cries with a loud voice." Often this is explained by the nature of the situation. It is thoroughly in keeping that the Baal priests, who gashed themselves till the blood spurted, should cry aloud (1 Kgs. 18:28). Oaths made (2 Chr. 15:14) or praises offered (Rev. 5:12; 7:10) by a crowd are naturally spoken in a loud voice, and a speaker who is praying before a large assembly also has to exert his voice (1 Kgs. 8:54). But even private prayers seem, as a rule, to have been spoken loudly. This would be no surprise in the case of so rugged a figure as Elijah (1 Kgs. 17:20, 21), or in the first fresh enthusiasm of conscious sonship (Rom. 8:15), but even Ezekiel prays thus, as he lies upon his face, and briefly pleads for "the remnant of Israel" (Ezek. 11:13). The leper whom Jesus healed glorified God with a loud voice (Luke 17:15); and with a loud voice Jesus (Luke 23:46) and Stephen (Acts 7:60) utter their dying prayer.

Most of the biblical prayers are short. The original prayers may, of course, well have been longer than the records would lead us to suppose. The parables of Jesus were no doubt texts rather than sermons, and the extant prophecies are summaries rather than addresses. Many of the minor prophets could be read through in half an hour, and one or two in a few minutes. But, as we cannot suppose that these books exhaust the activity of the prophets, so we need not suppose that the prayers were as brief as the records.

On the whole, however, there can be no doubt that earlier prayers were brief. "O Baal, hear us"—two Hebrew words—that is the whole prayer of the Baal priests, though it rends the air with weird iteration from morning till noon (1 Kgs. 18:26). The prayers of their great opponent Elijah are somewhat longer, but still very brief. "Let this child's soul come into him again" (1 Kgs. 17:21; 18:36, 37). In the earlier times, at least, the speakers said simply and briefly what they had to say, and then stopped. We have already seen how, in the older dialogues, God speaks much and men comparatively little. Few things can be more impressive than the reticence of Isaiah in his inaugural vision. All he says after his first expression of guilt and confusion, is, "Behold me, send me," and "Lord, how long?" (Is. 6:8, 11). A man whose eyes have seen the King will not be very garrulous. Ezekiel had also seen the Divine glory, and his prayers are very brief. After his vision of God, Job laid his hand upon his mouth. In the presence of Jehovah silence is wisdom.

> Jehovah is in His holy temple,
> Let all the earth keep silence before Him
> (Hab. 2:20, cf.; Zech. 2:13).

If words must be spoken, the fewer the better. "God is in heaven, and thou upon earth; therefore let thy words be few" (Eccl. 5:2)–whether they be spoken to God or man.

Reverence is hardly compatible with loquacity, but probably the exceptional brevity of Hebrew prayer is connected with the Hebrew view of the perils and responsibilities of all speech.

> Death and life are in the power of the tongue
> (Prov. 18:20).
> Whoso keepeth his mouth and his tongue,
> Keepeth his soul from troubles (Prov. 21:23).
> In all labor there is profit,
> But the talk of the lips tendeth only to penury
> (Prov. 14:23).

Their wise men were acutely sensitive to the dangers of superfluous speech; and James, a Hebrew prophetsage in the Christian Church, felt that the taming (James 1:26) of the untamable tongue (James 3:8) is no small part of a man's religion. Naturally, if care had to be exercised in the daily speech of man to man, how much more in his solemn speech to God!

It is characteristic of the growing emphasis placed upon prayer, as we have seen, in the post-exilic period, not only that formal prayers are more numerous, but that they are longer. The national confession, led by Ezra, lasted three hours (Neh. 9:3), and this spirit developed till, in the time of Jesus, long prayers are a passion with the officials of the Jewish Church. He, both by precept and example, taught the duty of brevity in prayer, and grounded it upon God's knowledge of our needs: "In prayer, do not babble like the heathen, for your Father knows" (Matt. 6:7, 8).

No doubt private prayer could be offered at any time; the time would depend upon the mood or the need of the man who offered it. Anyone who was sick or suffering or cheerful (James 4:13, 14) could pray then and there. But the needs of an organized religious community would tend to impose a certain regularity upon the hours of prayer, consequently the references to fixed hours practically all belong to the post-exilic period. One Psalmist speaks of praising God seven times a day (Ps. 119:64), but in general prayer was offered three times a day (Dan. 6:10)–evening, morning and noonday (Ps. 55:17)–the evening being mentioned first as the Hebrew day began then (Gen. 1:5); and in the Book of Acts, the three hours of prayer–the third hour (Acts 2:15), the sixth (Acts 10:9), and the ninth (Acts 3:1; 10:30)–are expressly attested, and observed, not only by the Jews (Acts 2:15), and by Cornelius (Acts 10:30), but also by Christians (Acts 3:1; 10:9). Prayer of course would be offered on the Sabbath day (Acts 16:13). Ezra offers his confessional prayer at the hour of the evening oblation (Ezra 9:5; cf. 1 Kings 18:36; Luke 1:9). Prayer was also offered at mealtime (Rom. 14:6). Morning prayers are mentioned in connection with the Temple (Ps. 5:3). Specially earnest private prayer is naturally enough often associated with the night (Lam. 2:19; cf. Ps. 119:62). That was the time when it was specially easy to commune with one's own heart (Ps. 63:6; 77:6; 119:55), and for more reasons than one it was the favorite time of Jesus (Mark 1:35; Luke 6:12). Nehemiah in one age

(Neh. 1:6), and Anna in another (Luke 2:37), are represented as praying night and day for the redemption of Jerusalem: they illustrate what Paul means by prayer without ceasing (1 Thess. 5:17). With that refusal to legislate which characterized all the ministry of Jesus, He laid down no law concerning the time of prayer. Ye, *when ye pray, shut the door* (Matt. 6:5, 6).

With regard to the place of prayer: the local country sanctuaries in early times, and the temple in later, were felt to be places of prayer in a very peculiar sense. Hannah offers a private petition of her own at Shiloh (1 Sam. 1:11), and Hezekiah at the Jerusalem temple (2 Kgs. 19:14). But prayer could be offered *in every place* (1 Tim. 2:8)—in the land of exile (1 Kgs. 8:47; Jer. 29:13) as well as in the holy land; in a house (Acts 10:30, 12:12), on a house-top (Acts 10:9), in bed (Ps. 63:6), in prison (Acts 16:25), in the fields by a well of water (Gen. 24:11, 12), on the hillside (Gen. 28:18–20; Matt. 14:23), on the battlefield, by a riverside (Acts 16:13), on the seashore (Acts 21:5). The hypocrites loved to pray at the street corners (Matt. 6:5), but Jesus taught and practiced secrecy in prayer. If in the house, let the door be shut (Matt. 6:6; cf. 2 Kings 4:33), but He Himself loved the deserts (Luke 5:16), and the mountains, and the great spacious silence of the night, for there and then He could be alone. *He went up into the mountain apart to pray; and when even was come, He was there alone* (Matt. 14:23). The mountain, the evening, the loneliness—these things are the earthly background of the strength of Christ.

A suggestively large place in the gospels is occupied by the word *apart.* Jesus prays apart (Luke 9:18). "Sit ye here while I go *yonder,* and pray" (Matt. 26:36). He calls His disciples apart. " 'Come ye apart into a desert place.' And they went away in the boat to a desert place apart" (Mark 6:31, 32; cf. Gal. 1:17). He took His three favorite disciples up *into a high mountain apart* (Matt. 17:1; Luke 9:28). Public prayer is a religious necessity, but it must have its roots in private prayer. To this, loneliness is essential; and that must be secured in the inner chamber, with the door shut, or, best of all, on the mountains or some desert place apart.

But to the Jew, the temple was, in an altogether unique sense, the house of prayer (Is. 56:7). Prayer was offered before it,[*] for Jehovah's name was in it (2 Chr. 20:9). It is "the beautiful house where our fathers praised Thee" (Is. 64:11). To it the publican and the Pharisee go up to pray (Luke 18:10), but also Peter and John (Acts 3:1), for the early Christians regarded it equally with the Jews as the house of prayer (Luke 24:53; Acts 3:1, 22:17).

But the great word of Jesus "neither in this mountain nor yet in Jerusalem shall ye worship the Father" (John 4:21) was the inevitable corollary of His view of God. For "God is spirit," and the consequences of this for religion are innumerable and inestimable. If God be spirit, and His worshipers must worship Him in spirit, then questions of posture and gesture, time and place, can never be of supreme consequence. The exigencies of practical and ecclesiastical life will compel us to select certain places and times for religious observances, but the soul must not be bound by them or attach to them a fictitious importance. Where the spirit of the Lord is, there is liberty. The only thing of real consequence is that the finite man come face to face with his infinite Friend; and this he may do, as well at midnight as at the third hour or the ninth of the day, as well in the desert place apart as in the holy and beautiful house where our brethren praise Him.

---

[*] Ezra 10:1; in Joel 2:17, "between the porch and the altar."

The Teaching and Practice
of Jesus

No prayers and no teaching about prayer can be so important as the prayers and the teaching of Jesus. Here, as everywhere in religion, He is the Master—with his incomparable union of simplicity and depth, serenity and earnestness; and nothing is more natural than that, "as he was praying in a certain place, when He ceased, one of His disciples said unto Him, 'Lord, teach us to pray' " (Luke 11:1).

It is of more than ordinary interest to ascertain precisely the words He used, as well as the manner and spirit of His prayer. Most of His recorded prayers are brief and striking, and we have every reason to believe that they faithfully represent not only His spirit, but His language. But the facts providentially forbid an idolatrous worship of the letter. The two versions of the Lord's prayer (Matt. 6:9–13; Luke 11:2–4) and the three versions of the prayer in Gethsemane differ—very slightly indeed, but they do differ—from one another. Sometimes, as in the word rendered by *daily* in the English version of the fourth petition of the Lord's prayer, the difference rests upon the difficulty of translating the Aramaic original into adequate Greek, but all the differences cannot be so explained. The question, too, might with some justice be raised whether the idea of prayer being rewarded (Matt. 6:6) does not come from an age or circle in which the pure message of Jesus was somewhat colored by an externalism inherited from the ancient Jewish Church; or whether the story of the unjust judge, in which God is represented as "avenging His elect that cry unto Him day and night" (Luke 18:7) does not, like Revelation 6:10, bear traces of a later day than that of Jesus, when the church was exposed to persecution.

The greatest difficulties naturally lie in the gospel of John. The general characterization of Jesus in that gospel is wonderful: in one sense, it is the truest of all the gospels, because it penetrates most profoundly into the inner nature of Jesus. But just because it has, with such sensitiveness, yet with such power and originality, assimilated His spirit, its language, though we can often feel sure that it breathes the very breath of Jesus, is often very obviously rather that of the writer himself than that of Jesus.

To this statement, the prayers are no exception. Take, for example, the great intercessory prayer in John 17. It is altogether probable that this prayer is, in every essential respect, the prayer then offered by Jesus. It has all the atmosphere of the last days, it contains the characteristic ideas of Jesus, it enables us to look deeper into His heart than perhaps any other of His recorded words do. Yet the writer's hand is unmistakable. After the words, "Thou (the Father) gavest Him (the Son) authority over all flesh, that to all whom Thou hast given Him He should give eternal life" (John 17:2), follows a definition, "and this is life eternal, that they should know Thee, the only true God, and Him whom Thou didst send, even Jesus Christ." This definition is extremely improbable in the course of a prayer. The improbability is heightened by the fact that Jesus, who is the speaker, would thus be made to refer to Himself by name, and even to add to this his quasi-official title "Christ." There can be little doubt that this is a theological interpolation of the writer, suggested by the words "eternal life." A similar motive seems to explain the reference in verse 12 to the fulfilling of the Scripture. This is the language of apologetic rather than of prayer; least of all is it in the manner of Jesus.

A similar criticism might be made of the prayer at the grave of Lazarus. "Father, I thank Thee, that Thou heardest me; and I know that Thou hearest me always" (John 11:41, 42). This is quite in the manner of Jesus (cf. Matt. 11:25), and it points to an unrecorded and probably silent prayer, such as Jesus seems to have been in the habit of offering before a miracle (Mark 7:34). But what of the words that follow? "But because of the multitude that standeth around I said it, that they might believe that Thou didst send me." In other words, it was hardly a real prayer; it was offered simply to produce a certain impression on the multitude. It is hard to believe that such a motive ever dictated any prayer of Jesus. But, after all, most of these criticisms are unimportant, they do not touch the essence of Jesus' prayer.

The occasions on which Jesus is recorded to have prayed are very suggestive. They are nearly all connected with crises in His mission. But we must not be misled by their relative infrequency. His dying prayer, *Father, into Thy hands I commend my spirit,* was no doubt the prayer of all His life. He said nothing but what He had heard from the Father, He did nothing but what He had seen the Father do. His whole public ministry was rooted and grounded in private prayer. "Every day He was teaching in the temple, and every night He went out"—no doubt to pray (Luke 22:39, 40)—"and lodged in the mount" (Luke 21:37). Could the teaching by day have been so brave and true if He had not lodged by night in the mount? It is striking that He is often recorded to have spent the night in prayer after a day with the multitude. For example, in the morning of the day after He had "healed many that were sick with diverse diseases . . . in the morning, a great while before day, He rose up and went out and departed into a desert place, and there prayed" (Mark 1:34, 35). The motives for prayer at such times may have been very various: the need to renew the strength which had gone out of Him, the need of the eloquent silence after the noisy din of the crowd, the need of gathering His soul together before facing the unknown day. In prayer He won new strength and confidence "to preach the good news of the Kingdom of God to other cities also." He may also have felt the need of fortifying His soul against the false Messianic hopes of the people; for, after sending away the multitudes whom He had fed and who would gladly have made Him King (John 6:15), He went up into the mountain apart to pray.*

After healing in the synagogue on the Sabbath day the man with the withered hand, the church dignitaries "were filled with madness and communed with one another what they might do to Jesus. And it came to pass in those days that He went out into the mountain to pray, and He continued all night in prayer to God. And when it was day, He called His disciples, and chose from them twelve" (Luke 6:11–13). The chronological order of the incidents related in the gospels is notoriously difficult to establish, and a loose phrase like "in those days" may be little more than a general connecting link. The prayer offered here undoubtedly refers primarily to the prayer before the choice of the twelve, but read retrospectively, it is also true, whether it is true chronologically or not. We may be sure that when public or private passion was stirred up against Him, He sought strength and comfort in communion with His Father. But of more importance is it to note that the whole night before His choice of the twelve was spent in prayer to God. Humanly speaking, on this step the whole future history of the Kingdom of God depended. The crisis was one of supreme importance: therefore it is not surprising that He prayed not only earnestly, but all night.

Similarly all the great crises of His ministry are accompanied by prayer—the baptism at the beginning (Luke 3:21), and towards the end the confession of His Messiahship at Caesarea Philippi (Luke 9:18). It was necessary that the right moment should be chosen for this confession, and on this point He must have the clearness and certainty which only His Father could give Him. It is also very probable that all His miraculous acts of healing were accompanied by prayer. This is expressly attested for the story of Lazarus (John 11:41), and suggested by His cure of the deaf and dumb man, to whom, *after looking up to heaven,* he said *Ephphatha* (Mark 7:34). The disciples who had failed to cure the epileptic boy had forgotten that

---

* Matthew 14:23; cf. Luke 5:15, 16, when the report went abroad concerning Him and His marvelous cures.

this kind could come out by nothing save by prayer (Mark 9:29): the Master who cast out the evil spirit was fresh from His prayer upon the mountain top. If ever anyone in this world, assuredly Jesus must have prayed without ceasing, but in particular, He seems to have specially committed all that concerned His life-work into His Father's hands. In prayer, He secured that unity of will with the Father which made Him in the deepest sense one with Him.

One of the most prominent features of the prayer-life of Jesus must have been its spirit of thanksgiving. The thanks He offered before feeding the multitude—possibly the regular grace before meat said by the head of a Jewish household—is specially mentioned in all the gospels (Matt. 15:36; Mark 6:41; Luke 9:16; John 6:11) and must have been peculiarly impressive. So at the grave of Lazarus His prayer begins, "Father, I thank Thee" (John 11:41). He has the glad consciousness that His Father hears Him always. His is a happy prayer. *"He rejoiced* and said, 'I thank Thee, Father' "* (Luke 10:21). In the remarkable prayer—unique in the Synoptic gospels—recorded in Matthew 11:25, 26, and Luke 10:21, 22, He confesses His thanks to the Father, whose might and wisdom were incomparable, who was "Lord of heaven and earth," and who revealed His truth only to the simple and childlike of heart. He knows the perfect oneness of His own will with the Father's, and He is therefore conscious of His own uniqueness among men. Thus Jesus thanks His Father alike for the earthly things and the heavenly, the little things and the great, for the mystery of the Father's will and for the bread that perisheth.

Like the great prophets of old, Jesus also appears in the role of intercessor. He intercedes alike for His disciples and for His tormentors. He prayed for Peter that his faith fail not (Luke 22:32), and as He prayed for him, He prayed for them all, that they should be preserved from the evil one, and sanctified in the truth (John 17:6–19); and not only for them, but also for those who should be persuaded by their word to accept Him (John 17:20–24). In His prayer at the parting of the ways, He looks down the avenue of the future, and prays for the unity of those who will believe in Him.

But most wonderful of all is His prayer, "Father, forgive them," for the men who nailed Him to the cross (Luke 23:34). This is primarily a prayer only for them. They literally did not know what they were doing. The church officials who compassed His death and the people who shouted "Away with Him," knew much better what they were doing. At least they knew that they were devoting to death one who had healed their sick, and who had gone about doing good. But it is not to be wondered at if His challenge of official religion and of popular hopes created a deadly hostility among men of deep but natural prejudices and conventional religious attainments. Of them, too, it might be said, that they did not fully know what they were doing, and the prayer for pardon is indirectly, if not directly, also for them.

So far as the words of Jesus go, He never directly exhorts that "intercessions be made for all men" (1 Tim. 2:1). But He does what is more striking: He exhorts His disciples to pray for those who abuse and persecute them (Matt. 5:44; Luke 6:28). This prayer is the highest and the hardest: it includes all the lesser intercessions. Jesus Himself, who urged this duty, performed it upon His cross, at a time when such a prayer must have seemed nothing less than a miracle. One who intercedes for his enemies will not be likely to forget his friends, and the world beyond the circle of his friendships. Jesus prayed for those who nailed Him to the tree, but He also prayed for Peter, for the disciples, and for those who through them should believe on Him. Thus explicitly by teaching and implicitly by practice He taught the duty of intercession.

Jesus had nothing to confess, therefore He confesses nothing. Even in the terrible hour of Gethsemane, when the darkness is such as might be felt; even on the cross, when, for the moment, He feels as if His God had forsaken Him, there is no whisper of such a thing. This would not be wonderful in Jeremiah, but in Jesus, who was sensitive, as none had ever been before, to the stain of sin, it would be wonderful, if it did not rest upon His conscious sinlessness. Confession is the one element which was necessarily absent from His prayers and necessarily present in ours. We have sins to confess and we must pray for their forgiveness, and the prayer must proceed from a heart that is itself ready to forgive the trespasses committed against it. The importance of forgiveness and the condition upon which it depends seem, judging by the peculiar nature and earnestness of the allusions, to have been a favorite theme of Jesus (Matt. 6:14, 15, 18:35; Mark 11:25, 26). The man who prays must love his fellows: the unforgiving remain unforgiven.

The petitions which Jesus Himself offered and exhorted others to offer are, as we might expect, predominantly spiritual. The first thing to be sought was the Kingdom of God. One of the chief prayers of those who love the Lord of the harvest is that laborers be sent into His harvest (Matt. 9:38; Luke 10:2). The prayers of the early Church for boldness in preaching the gospel (Acts 4:29) show that she had learned the lesson of Jesus well.

But while prayer must be predominantly, it will not be exclusively for things spiritual. There is no strained or unnatural idealism in the teaching of Jesus. It is not as if to Him the Kingdom of God stood first and other things nowhere, but His conception of the Kingdom of God is so comprehensive that all these other things find their place and legitimation within it. He taught His disciples to pray, "Give us bread," and this is the eternal justification of prayer for things temporal. Man does not live by bread alone, but neither can he live without it. The heavenly Father knows that we have need of this and similar things, and therefore we may pray for them—briefly indeed and simply, but sincerely, and with no feeling that such a prayer is unworthy of one who aspires to the full stature of spiritual manhood.

The tendency of a later age to give a spiritual turn to the words of Jesus is illustrated by the change of the word *good things* (Matt. 7:11) into *the Holy Spirit* (Luke 11:13) in the sentence "How much more shall your Father who is in heaven give good things to them that ask Him!" The things to be asked must of course be good, but good in the widest and not in any exclusive sense. "Pray that your flight be not in the winter" (Mark 13:18; Matt. 24:20; cf. Luke 21:36), says Jesus to the people, as He foresees the "great tribulation" that is soon to fall upon them. Prayer would thus seem to be justified not only for growth in grace but for deliverance from distress, and the alleviation of misery. Jesus Himself prayed in the hour of His agony that the cup might pass from Him, and the disciple may not count Himself more spiritual than his Master.

But this simple prayer of Jesus in Gethsemane is a model in more respects than one. While it justifies a petition for deliverance from distress, it also shows that the deepest desire of the man who prays must be not for his own deliverance, but for the glory of God and the triumph of the Divine will in him. "Father, save me from this hour, but, Father, glorify Thy name" (John 12:27, 28) "Not my will, but Thine be done." The struggle in Gethsemane was a very real one. Jesus prayed, according to a late but very credible tradition, till His sweat became as it were great drops of blood falling down upon the ground (Luke 22:44). He offered supplications with strong crying and tears unto Him that was able to save Him from death (Heb. 5:7). He prayed that the cup might be removed, that the way might not be so terrible, but through, and above, and crowning all, that the will of God be done. He might have prayed for twelve legions of angels, but He refused to offer such a prayer; for that, at any rate, was not His Father's will. The Father is glorified when His will is done. "I glorified Thee on the earth, having accomplished the work which Thou hast given Me to do" (John 17:4). The glory of God, in this sense, is the goal of history–the establishment of a kingdom in which His will is done as the angels do it in heaven. Considering Christ's consciousness of His own unique relation to the Father and to men (Matt. 11:25–27), it is fitting that His great intercessory prayer should begin with a petition for the glory of the Father and the Son, each through the other (John 17:1).

For once it would seem as if Jesus' sustaining consciousness of fellowship with the Father was momentarily clouded. In indescribable torture of body and spirit upon the cross He meekly asks His God why He had thus forsaken Him (Mark 15:34; Matt. 27:46). It is a cry out of the deepest depths that sorrow has ever sounded. Yet He knows Himself not utterly forsaken: He can still appeal to Him and say *"My* God." It is of peculiar interest that He does not call God here, as everywhere else, Father. The reason can hardly be that the appeal is a literal quotation from Psalm 22:1, because the words, "Father, into Thy hands I commend My spirit," are also a quotation, but here Jesus has substituted *Father* for the *Lord* (or, in the Hebrew, *Jehovah)* in the second half of the verse of the original Psalm (Ps. 31:5). He is free to amplify or adapt the original words; consequently, if He retains them, it must be because they perfectly express the mood of the moment. In that awful crisis God is felt to be God rather than Father, but He is still *"My* God." Afterwards, the feeling of abandonment vanishes. God passes as God, and returns as Father, and into the Father's hands Jesus commends His spirit, with the quietness, the clearness, the simplicity, the triumphant confidence which had marked all His earthly ministry.

The most complete and connected expression of Jesus' conception of prayer is to be found in the Lord's prayer (Matt. 6:9–13; Luke 11:2–4). It is not in the least probable that He intended to bind this prayer upon His disciples. He imparted a spirit, He did not impose a law—as little in prayer as in any other exercise of religion; and we cannot suppose that He prescribed a prayer. That was not His way. The prayer is a model, incomparable and inimitable; and because inimitable, nothing is more natural than that it should very early have fallen into regular use. The *Didaché* already prescribes it repetition three times a day. But it is essentially a model: its object was to present the ideal of prayer.

One cannot but wonder whether the disciples were not disappointed when they heard it for the first time. According to one account (Luke 11:1), it was given in response to one of the disciples who had apparently been struck by Jesus' prayer, and was eager to learn its secret. And what is its secret? Most of the petitions had in some form or other been offered before. In its individual expressions it was not and could not be something absolutely new and original. It but expressed a longing for the deepest things; and that longing had, by devout men, been felt and expressed before.

But assuredly never so expressed: never with such brevity, sureness, clearness, comprehensiveness, depth, power, simplicity. Other men had said more, or less—had often said little when they seemed to be saying much. He said enough, because He said everything. These seven[*] petitions sweep the whole range of religious aspiration, leaving nothing untouched or unilluminated. Like the twenty-third Psalm, the Lord's prayer is appropriate to every stage of religious development. A child can understand it, but the wisest cannot exhaust its depths. As we grow, it grows: we never leave it behind. Like the parables of Christ it has an inexhaustible power of suggestion. Every new experience of life sheds new light upon its meaning, while in its turn it sheds light on every new experience. It "may be committed to memory quickly," as F. D. Maurice says, "but it is slowly learned by heart."

The brevity of the prayer is its first surprise, and this is without doubt one of the lessons Jesus meant to teach. According to its setting in the Sermon on the Mount, it is given as a contrast to the wordiness which characterized heathen and even much Jewish prayer. "When you pray, do not babble, like the heathen; for they think that they shall be heard for their multitude of words. Do not be like them. This is the way to pray." Then follows a prayer of barely more than half a minute's length, if so much. And the prayer is brief, partly because it deals with the fundamental things, which are few—the kingdom and the will of God, the need of bread, of forgiveness and deliverance—and partly because it leaves everything to God. There is no dictation. How the kingdom is to come, how we are to be delivered from temptation, it does not say: these things are left to the omnipotent wisdom of God.

The simplicity of the prayer is as striking as its brevity. Jesus meant to teach that the simplest prayer is also the highest and the truest. It is the natural speech of a child to the holy Father, and an everlasting rebuke to all unnaturalness and exaggeration, whether in expression, thought, or feeling.

Our Father. This, then, was how to address God in prayer; not by calling Him God, and then by heaping high epithet upon epithet—"the great, the mighty, and the terrible God, who keepest covenant

---

[*] Six, according to some, who count the last two as one.

and loving-kindness" (cf. Neh. 9:32)–but simply by calling Him Father, *our* Father, for we are all brethren. The first words usher us into the presence of a great company of brethren whom no man can number. Our Father *who art in heaven*. So Jesus Himself prayed: "I thank Thee, Father, Lord of heaven and earth." As heaven is high above the earth–infinitely more high and mysterious to us than it could have been to the Jews of Jesus' time–so the Father is higher than the children who cry to Him. The trust and familiarity awakened by the thought of the Fatherhood are touched to the deepest humility and reverence, as the worshiper faces the God whose home is the infinite universe, and the heart is expanded by the contemplation of such a Father and such a home. How anyone who thus addresses God can remain narrow in mind or heart is a mystery; for in this address the finite man faces the universe, he acknowledges his kinship with humanity and with the infinite Father.

Hallowed be Thy name. To a Semitic ear the name meant far more than to us. The name of God represented all that was covered by the term God–His being and character, including of course His name. All this must be held in holiest reverence. His name must not be used in a spirit of frivolity or thoughtlessness, profanity or superstition. Even in prayer this reverence has to be carefully guarded. It is forgotten by the garrulous, who make long prayers, use vain repetitions, and seem to suppose that they will be heard for their much speaking. This prayer is a petition for a worthy attitude to God, to religion, to worship. It implies a rebuke of the indifference to religion which characterizes many who profess it, and of the noisy and unseemly familiarity which characterizes the worship of many who really believe in it.

Thy kingdom come. There is a growing belief that much of the New Testament in general, and such phrases as this in particular, are to be interpreted in an eschatological sense. Whether or not, the kingdom of God would, in any case, be in its essence a moral and spiritual kingdom. The time and the nature of its coming might be differently conceived, but in its essence it was righteousness, peace and joy (Rom. 14:17), and, as such, was already in the midst of them (Luke 17:20, 21). Apart from all historical and theological questions, the prayer is essentially a petition for the triumph of the cause of God in the world–of truth, and goodness, and love. It suggests visions of a day when all the world will be united as one, under the kingship of God, and when all the interests and ambitions of men will be controlled by the necessities of the kingdom.

His subjects must be willing, for in the kingdom of God there is no constraint: therefore *Thy will be done,* as in heaven, so on earth. The angels, "mighty in strength, hearken unto the voice of His word" (Ps. 103:20), and like those obedient messengers of Hebrew narrative and poetry, so are we to do His will, swiftly, gladly and without constraint; for the will must be willingly done: it is the will of the Father whose children we are. It would hardly be just to the spirit of the prayer to trace any rigid logical connection between its petitions–indeed, in one aspect, they are practically synonymous–and yet it is perhaps not altogether fanciful to see in them a certain simple progress. The will of God can only be done by men who honor the name and live for the kingdom. Where and when the name is hallowed, the kingdom comes and the will is done.

In the fourth petition we turn–but without any sense of break–from the contemplation of God's majestic universe, kingdom and will, to the more specific needs and frailties of men. *Give us our bread for the day,* whether today or tomorrow: the phrase is hard and need not be here discussed, but the meaning is plain. We cannot be too grateful for this simple recognition on the part of our Lord of the material basis of human life. True, only one petition of the seven is for material things, but, in One whose outlook on life was so sane and true, that one could not fail. "Ye have need of these things." That is His will, and His will be done. The petition is at once modest and comprehensive; it is not a prayer for prosperity, far less for luxury, but simply for that which makes life possible, and even that simply for the day–not for that abundance which will deliver us from anxiety for the morrow. But, on the other hand, it is implicitly a prayer for *all* that is needed to make life possible. How much more than bread that may mean each man has to determine for himself. To all it will include clothing and shelter, to some it may mean more. It suggests and includes, in its grandly simple way, all that is necessary to sustain the life—in the largest sense—of men. No healthy recognition in prayer of the natural basis of life can be unworthy. The whole earth is the Lord's, and the fullness thereof. Every creature of God is good, and may be sanctified through prayer (1 Tim. 4:4).

But more pathetic than man's need of bread is his need of forgiveness. The petition *forgive us our debts* excludes all possibility of self-righteousness: the worshiper implicitly confesses his guilt and acknowledges its seriousness, for he also confesses his need of forgiveness. His petition implies a longing to be at one again with the Father, and his confession of guilt is useless unless it be sincere, for he must be prepared to show the same mercy to others that he craves for himself. If he will not forgive others, then it is the simple fact that God cannot forgive him (Matt. 6:15).

As the past is full of sin that needs to be forgiven, so the future is full of peril, in which the old sins may be repeated, and new ones committed; therefore *lead us not into temptation, but deliver us from evil.* The latter petition, though, in a sense, independent, in another sense explains and deepens the former. The former is essentially a prayer that we may not be led into situations that will tempt us. But the power of temptation lies in our susceptibility to evil; if we are delivered from that, the temptations into which the casual circumstances of our life may bring us will have no more power over us.

And thus the Lord's prayer ends; for the doxology, though altogether worthy, is no part of the original prayer. It ends with the thought of the great antagonist, whether we call that evil or the evil One, and thus forms a somber contrast to the great Father in heaven at the beginning of the prayer. It makes us feel the terribleness of life to all who take it seriously; life is threatened and, apart from God, is overpowered by the strong man who can spoil it of all its goods. But the great antagonist meets his match in the great Redeemer of human life, and the prayer ends, not with the thought of the antagonist, but with that of redemption—*deliver us*—and thus carries us back from the pain and struggle and temptations of earth to the serene atmosphere of the opening petitions, with its outlook upon the glorious kingdom and the will of the Father in heaven.

Like all the words of Christ, this prayer searches. What do we care for the name and the kingdom and the will of God? And how do we show that we care? These questions must rise to the heart of one who is praying sincerely. And the prayer is also a confession. In our prayer for bread, we confess our impotence over the mysterious forces of nature, and our absolute dependence upon God. In our prayer for forgiveness and deliverance, we confess our utter and infinite weakness.

It is often said that this prayer indirectly teaches that in prayer the things of God must come first: after a petition for the triumph of His cause, we may then petition for our own affairs. This is to ignore, however, the very intimate connection between its two parts, and can hardly be in the spirit of Jesus. The kingdom comes through the practice of loving forgiveness between man and man, the will of God is done by men who fear and shun temptation. The last three petitions are but the translation, in terms of human life, of conditions which the first three regard from the standpoint of God. Man is implicated in the first half of the prayer, as surely as God is in the second. The kingdom of God is not in the air, it is "among you." The will of God is to be done *upon the earth*. The divine interests are not to be separated from human interests, they are the same. The hallowing of His name, the coming of His kingdom, the doing of His will are as truly our affair as daily bread and forgiveness of sins and redemption from evil.

The Lord's prayer illustrates what men ought to pray for: it goes without saying that such prayer, if sincere, would be earnest. It could only be offered by a man to whom the kingdom of God and the forgiveness of sins were dear. The more earnestly it was offered, the more surely it would be answered; for the interest betokened by the petitions would be, in a sense, their fulfillment. It is not surprising therefore that Jesus should teach the duty of persistency in prayer. He Himself prayed with strong crying and tears; and when His request was not granted the first time, or the second, "He prayed a third time, saying again the same words" (Matt. 26:44). Prayer He compared to knocking, as if the door remained closed till the knock was heard. But how long has the suppliant to knock till the door is opened? There are two parables which seem to suggest not only the duty of persistence, but of importunity—the parables of the friend who came at midnight (Luke 11:5-8), and the unjust judge (Luke 18:1-8).

In the sense that one cannot pray such a prayer as the Lord's Prayer too earnestly, importunity is intelligible and unobjectionable. But the first impression made by the parables seems to carry us beyond this. The friend within is surly. "Don't worry me. I can't get up and give you." But "I tell you," says Jesus, "though he won't rise and give him because he is his friend, yet because of his importunity he will rise and give him as many as he needs." This is a very bold illustration, altogether in the manner of Jesus, but we must not draw from the parable more than it was intended to yield. It is surely obvious that the friend within does not adequately represent God. He has no sympathy for the needs of the man at his door, but he finally gets up for the sake of peace and gives him all he needs, perhaps to make sure that he will not soon be back again. Anything more unlike what is elsewhere called "the philanthropy of our Savior God" (Titus 3:4) it would be almost impossible to conceive. The one thing the parable is intended to teach is the need of persistence; and the reasonableness of that—considering the things we ought to pray for, *as suggested by the Lord's Prayer*[*]—we have already seen. Persistence, importunity if you like, is the test of sincerity, but it is not for a moment to be supposed that importunity could extort from God gifts which He is initially unwilling to grant.

An almost more daring illustration of the need of persistency is furnished by the parable of the unjust judge. The judge is determined to refuse the widow's request, but he finally grants it. "Though I have no fear of God, and no regard for man, yet because she worries me, I will give her satisfaction, to keep her from wearing me out by her everlasting visits." Surely it is as plain as day that this man cannot represent God. He is unjust and irreligious,

---

[*] It is of great importance to note that this parable immediately follows the Lord's prayer.

but he, like the friend in bed, finally grants the request simply to secure his own comfort. If the figure of the judge is so totally inadequate to represent God, why should we suppose that his conduct
can typify that of God—that God, like him, can, as it were, be co-
erced, by the persistence of the petitioner, into granting a request
which He is at first disposed to refuse? Here we must say, as before, that the lesson is simply one of the duty of persistency; and
the reasonableness of this persistency must be obvious to one who
has learned his conception of prayer from the example of Jesus.

If there is any analogy at all, it is rather this: If an unwilling
friend and an unjust judge will yield to a persistent petition for
earthly things, how much more will the heavenly Father to a petition for the heavenly things! It is altogether alien to the spirit of
Jesus and of healthy religion to speak of assaulting the walls of
heaven and of wresting a blessing from God Almighty. The ultimate prayer is, "Thy will be done"; and the more earnestly we
offer that prayer, the better it will be for ourselves and the world.
But earnestness is one thing, and violent importunity another. If it
is the will of God we desire to see accomplished, and not our own
will, we shall be content to be earnest without being violent.
Against an importunity which may sometimes only be a disguised
selfishness, we have to remember that we shall not be heard for
our much speaking, and that our Father in heaven knows what
things we have need of.

It may even fairly be questioned whether the moral of the parable of the unjust judge really originates, at any rate in its present
form, with Jesus. The prayer of the elect, which can count on being
answered, is a prayer for vengeance—such a prayer as was natural
enough to Jeremiah and Nehemiah, and apparently even to Jewish
Christians (Rev. 6:10), but hardly such a prayer as could have been
offered or prescribed by Him who said, "Pray for them that persecute you" (Matt. 5:44), and who almost with His last breath prayed
for His own tormentors. It is much more like a cry from a later
time of persecution: there is a vehemence about it which suggests
dark days. "Shall not God avenge His elect? I tell you, He will
avenge them speedily."

The manner of Christ's prayers must have been as striking as their contents. Into the mystery of His private prayers we are seldom permitted to look. He loved the loneliness—the mountains and the desert places. Even from His disciples "He was parted about a stone's throw" when He knelt down and prayed (Luke 22:41). He believed in the closed door, and He left the street corners to the hypocrites.

But He also knew the joy and help of fellowship, and more than once He took Peter and James and John with Him to pray. Special influences were in the air when "two or three were gathered together." It is to this that we owe our knowledge of the scene in Gethsemane and on the mount of transfiguration, which was the mount of prayer. *As He was praying, the fashion of His countenance was altered* (Luke 9:29). We can well suppose that not only then, but every time He prayed, His face was transfigured. The effect of prayer upon the face—its permanent expression of quiet and the temporary light that kindles it in the moment of devotion—this may be witnessed today; and what must have been its effect upon that face? When He spoke, everyone was astonished, for He spoke with authority; when He prayed, everyone was equally astonished, for He prayed with transfigured face. It is the old phenomenon we witnessed in the prophets: they had power with men, because they had prevailed with God.

The extraordinary impressiveness—shall we say fascination?—of Jesus' prayer is suggested over and over again. It was this, according to one version, that led one of the disciples to put to Him the question which led to the Lord's prayer. In prayer, especially in the open air, He is often recorded as having looked up. This He did before His healing miracles (Mark 7:34; John 11:41), and this trait is mentioned in one group of the narratives of His feeding of the multitude (Matt. 14:19; Mark 6:41; Luke 9:16). Nothing could have been more impressive than to see that shining face upturned in prayer before a great expectant multitude sitting on the grass.

The prayer which Jesus offered before the feeding of the multitude is not recorded; it is simply said that He blessed (or gave thanks [Matt. 15:36; Mark 8:6]) and brake and gave. It so happens that all the illustrations of prayer before a meal in the New Testament are important for other reasons: the feeding of the multitude, the institution of the supper (Matt. 26:26, 27; Mark 14:22, 23), the evening meal at Emmaus (Luke 24:30), the meal after Paul's shipwreck (Acts 27:35)—these are all occasions which may well have called forth special prayer. Yet it is quite possible that the prayers then offered were simply the ordinary thanksgiving or grace before meat, offered by the head of a Jewish family. What this was in the time of Jesus, we cannot be sure, but it was probably not unlike the later prayer, "Blessed be the Creator of the fruits of the earth." The prayer was brief, but as Jesus would offer it, with His eyes lifted up to heaven, those who heard it would carry the impression of it with them to their graves.

That there was a peculiar solemnity about the way in which Jesus gave thanks and broke bread is made very plain by the Emmaus story. "When He had sat down with them to meat, He took the bread and blessed, and He broke it and gave it to them. And their eyes were opened, and they knew Him" (Luke 24:30, 31). Nobody had ever broken bread or given thanks like Him. A curious confirmation of this view of the special solemnity of Jesus' thanksgiving before meat occurs in an altogether incidental remark in John 6:23: "there came boats from Tiberias nigh unto the place where they ate the bread *after the Lord had given thanks."* Surely, in the simple description of a place, this is a very remarkable addition, but it points to the extraordinary and indelible impression produced by the prayers of Jesus.

Thrice happy those who were privileged to hear Jesus pray! His manner can never be recalled or repeated, because He stands alone among the sons of men, but the prayers themselves are for us and for all men. Among all the dissensions that have dishonored the name of Jesus, and stained the history of the Christian Church, the prayer He taught His disciples has been an ideal bond throughout the centuries, binding together all that believe in Him; and, whatever the future may have in store, that prayer will continue to hold His Church together, while the world stands.

The Prayers of Paul

Beyond all comparison Paul is the greatest figure in the history of the early Church. He was the Master's aptest pupil; and the truth he learned from Him he applied with a courage, a penetration, a versatility, and an originality which are beyond all praise. The tremendous force that was brought into history by Jesus is well seen in the restless creative energy of Paul. Jesus lives in Him; and because he possesses the spirit of Jesus, he breathes new life into all that he touches—the men he meets, the theology he inherits, the prayers he offers.

The contrast between Jesus and Paul is, in one respect, as striking as it could be. There are few, if any, verbal parallels between them. The direct reminiscences of the Master's teaching are not many; the intricate and impetuous prayers of Paul (cf. Eph. 1:16–19; Col. 1:9–12) are unlike the simple serenity of Jesus. But the contrast is so great just because Paul is so completely overmastered and controlled by Jesus. He is at once His slave and His freeman. He does not so much possess the spirit of Jesus, rather He is possessed by it, and that spirit scorns imitation. It seeks out—as it always must, wherever its freshness and freedom are felt—new methods of expression and attack. It shows its true kinship with the Master by the originality with which it works.

The contrast between the prayers of Jesus and Paul is great, nevertheless the similarity is very real. In particular, he had caught the Master's note of *thanksgiving*. In everything, prayer and supplication have to be blended with thanksgiving (Phil. 4:6). He begins almost all his epistles with thanksgiving and often ends his arguments with doxology (Rom. 11:33). "Thanks be unto God" is the motto of his life. It makes a very interesting study to compare the petitions and the prayers of thanksgiving offered by Paul: the latter far outweigh the former. The joy which had welled up in the heart of the Old Testament worshiper as he entered the courts of Jehovah was intensified in Paul a thousand times by his gratitude to God for His unspeakable gift (2 Cor. 9:15). In Jesus Christ salvation had been brought nigh. All who enjoyed it and all who witnessed its triumph in the hearts of other men could not but "rejoice in the Lord always; and again I will say, 'Rejoice' " (Phil. 4:4). It was a duty "in everything to give thanks, for this is the will of God" (1 Thess. 5:18)—a duty to which all who loved God and men were invincibly constrained. *"We are bound* to give thanks to God always for you, because God chose you unto salvation" (2 Thess. 2:13). *"We are bound* to give thanks to God always for you, brethren"—for your faith and love to one another (2 Thess. 1:3): bound to give thanks for the salvation and spiritual progress of men.

The number of allusions to thanksgiving is more than surprising upon an area so relatively small as the epistles of Paul. His many exhortations to gratitude show how much his own mind was controlled by this thought, and suggest, on the other hand, the tendency of average men to "forget His benefits." "Be ye thankful," "abound in thanksgiving," "do all in the name of the Lord Jesus, giving thanks unto God," "continue steadfastly in prayer, watching therein with thanksgiving" (Col. 3:15, 2:7, 3:17, 4:2)—all these admonitions come from one short epistle. He himself had taken to heart the advice he gave the Ephesians (Eph. 5:20) to "give thanks always for all things to God."

Though thanks must be given for all things, in point of fact the thanksgivings of Paul are nearly always connected with the salvation that came to men through Jesus. That was the fact that dwarfed all others in importance, and its effect upon the heart of himself and other men causes him to rejoice evermore. It is the depth of the riches of the wisdom of God (Rom. 11:33) in sending one who had delivered men out of the power of darkness and translated them into the kingdom of the Son of His love (Col. 1:13), one who had given them the victory over sin and death (1 Cor. 15:55–57), one in whom they had been blessed with every spiritual blessing (Eph. 1:3)—it is this that kindles the heart of Paul to rapture.

The amazing unselfishness of the life of Paul is seen as clearly in his thanksgiving as in his petitions. His thanks are nearly always connected with the welfare of his converts or the progress of the gospel. Once he expresses gratitude for a specific gift of his own—that "I speak with tongues more than you all" (1 Cor. 14:18), but he at once proceeds to speak somewhat depreciatingly of this power, at least insofar as it does not tend to the welfare of the Church. The thing to be grateful for is the progress of the truth, and any personal gift that contributes to that progress. In keeping with this altruistic view of life, Paul blesses God for the power he possesses of comforting others (2 Cor. 1:4), he thanks Him for the fidelity of Titus (2 Cor. 8:16), and he cannot find words to express his rapture at the thought of his Thessalonian converts (1 Thess. 3:9).

The acceptance of Jesus by men and their fidelity to Him whom they had accepted—these are the things that chiefly inspire Paul to thanksgiving. He thanks God at the sight of men who had been the servants of sin becoming the servants of righteousness (Rom. 6:17, 18), or when they received his message not as the word of man but as the word of God (1 Thess. 2:13), or—in more theological language—that God had chosen them unto salvation (2 Thess. 2:13). But especially did Paul rejoice over the fruits of conversion, over the visible signs that his converts were really possessed of the spirit of Jesus. He gives thanks for the universally acknowledged fidelity of the Roman Church (Rom. 1:8), for the faith in Jesus and the love towards each other which characterized the Thessalonians (1 Thess. 1:2, 3; 2 Thess. 1:3), the Colossians (Col. 1:3, 4), and the Ephesians (Eph. 1:15, 16), for the faith and love of Philemon (Phile. 1:4, 5), for the gifts of the Corinthians (1 Cor. 1:4–6), for the fellowship of the Philippians in furtherance of the gospel (Phil. 1:3–5).

Surely there were never more remarkable prayers of thanksgiving than these. Self is forgotten: Christ, the converts, the progress of truth, faith, and love–these are everything. And the thanksgiving becomes all the more astonishing when we remember the fierce, hard life that Paul was compelled to lead: in affliction, in distresses, strifes, imprisonments, tumults, labors, vigils, fasting (2 Cor. 6:4, 5). "Five times I received forty stripes save one. Three times I was beaten with rods, once I was stoned, three times I suffered shipwreck, I have been a day and a night in the deep, in journeyings often, in perils of rivers and robbers, of countrymen and heathen, of city, desert and sea, of hunger, thirst, cold, and nakedness" (2 Cor. 11:24–27). But Paul remained more than conqueror. In all these things he rejoiced evermore, because of the unspeakable gift.

It was inevitable that one who so rejoiced over the salvation and progress of his converts should pray for them. *Intercessory prayer* plays a great part in the life of St. Paul. It is the old story: the true prophet, the preacher who means what he says, will be an intercessor. The man who loves the truth and who also loves the men to whom he preaches it, will plead for them. So not only Paul's heart's desire, but also his supplication to God for the Jews (Rom. 10:1) was that they should be saved. And once men have been won for Jesus, he prays that they may be sustained in the good life (1 Thess. 3:13), and enabled to bring forth much fruit, and this to the ultimate end "that the name of our Lord Jesus may be glorified" (2 Thess. 1:12; Rom. 15:5, 6; cf. Phil. 1:11). He prays not only that they may do no evil (2 Cor. 13:7), but that they may, in a spirit of blameless sincerity (Phil. 1:10), do much good, especially that they may put into practice the Master's royal lesson of love to one another and to all men (1 Thess. 3:12; Phil. 1:9).

But as the quality of the outward life depends entirely upon the inward spirit, it is usually towards this that the supplications of Paul are directed. If men are "to walk worthily of the Lord, bearing fruit in every good work," then they must be "filled with the knowledge of His will" (Col. 1:9, 10). He therefore prays that God may give them a spirit of wisdom that they may realize all that is theirs in

Christ—the hope of the Divine calling, and the greatness of the Divine power as attested by the resurrection of Christ (Eph. 1:17–20). What is needed is an inward strength and this can only come through the indwelling of Christ in the heart; it is therefore for this that he prays (Eph. 3:16, 17). These requests are summed up in the prayer, "The Lord direct your hearts into the love of God, and into the patience of Christ" (2 Thess. 3:5), and "give you peace at all times in all ways" (2 Thess. 3:16).

Paul's unbounded interest in his converts is attested by the almost extravagant language in which he describes his prayer for them. He struggles for them, he prays night and day exceedingly that he may see their face (1 Thess. 3:10). Like most great leaders of men, he probably knew personally those who were devoted to him and never forgot any with whom he had had individual personal relations. He speaks of "making my supplication with joy on behalf of you all" (Phil. 1:4). The names of long-forgotten men and women are scattered over his letters—unknown to us, but dear to him. He gave his life not for an abstraction, nor even for a gospel, but for Jesus and for men. In words of moving sincerity, he discloses the secret of his earnestness in intercessory prayer. He prayed for men because he loved them. "God is my witness," he says, "how I long after you all in the tender mercies of Christ Jesus" (Phil. 1:8); and still more touchingly and simply, "I have you in my heart" (Phil. 1:7).

So thoroughly is Paul in earnest about the duty and power of intercessory prayer that not only does he himself pray for his converts, but he asks them to pray for him. He knows that their supplications can help him (Phil. 1:13; 2 Cor. 1:11; cf. Phile. 1:22). The very last injunction before his parting salutations to the Thessalonians is "Brethren, pray for us" (1 Thess. 5:25). As we might expect, the prayers he requests them to offer on his behalf are never selfish prayers: they are always intimately related to the progress of the gospel. Once indeed he beseeches his brethren (Rom. 15:30, 31) to strive with himself in their prayers to God for him that he might be "delivered from them that are disobedient in Judea"—in another case, "from unreasonable and evil men" (2 Thess. 3:1), but the context shows that this is really a prayer that his work, and the work of the Lord—which was the same—should move on unhindered. That the prayers he requested his converts to offer were really for the gospel's sake rather than his own is usually made very explicit. They are to pray that he be enabled boldly to declare the mystery of the gospel (Eph. 6:19; Col. 4:3). That is the supreme ambition of Paul, for which he enlists the prayers of others—that the gospel may triumph, and that he may be equipped to proclaim it.

Considering the power and fidelity with which Paul apprehended the teaching of Jesus, to say nothing of his own unselfish and enthusiastic devotion to the cause of evangelization, it can hardly be regarded as other than striking that he never directly recommends prayer for the heathen.[*] Jesus prayed for His enemies, Paul prayed for his friends. He even pronounces anathema upon anyone who preaches other than the unadulterated gospel (Gal. 1:8, 9), and upon any man who does not love the Lord (1 Cor. 16:22). This anathema is nothing but the corollary—natural to a man of his impetuous temperament—of his flaming devotion to Christ. The absence of allusions to prayer for the heathen, though it cannot be accidental,[†] must not be unduly strained. The love recommended to the hungry and thirsty enemy (Rom. 12:20), and extolled in one of the noblest prose-poems ever written (1 Cor. 13), must surely also have expressed itself in prayer for the heathen. Such prayers are really involved in his prayers for the success of the gospel and in his requests for the similar prayers of others. First and last, he was a missionary; and what was all his crowded life but an unremitting prayer for the men for whom Christ died and rose again?

The absolute selflessness of the life of Paul is very plainly seen in his *petitions*. He recommends indeed that in everything requests be made known unto God (Phil. 4:6), but his own recorded requests are nearly all for others. Very characteristically he assures

---

[*] In Romans 10:1 Paul prays for the salvation of the Jews.
[†] Cf. John 17:9, where Jesus is made to say, "I pray not for the world."

the Philippians (Phil. 4:19), "My God shall supply every need of *yours.*" His own needs were practically summed up in the desire for the new creation and preservation of men through Christ. For himself he prayed only that he might become a fitter instrument and win a wider opportunity (cf. 1 Thess. 3:11). He prays night and day that he may see the faces of the Thessalonians, but it is that he may make perfect that which is lacking in their faith (1 Thess. 3:10). He prays that he may be permitted to visit Rome, but it is that he may impart to them some spiritual gift (Rom. 1:11).

Only once does he offer a prayer for his own welfare, and even that is of a very modest and negative kind (2 Cor. 12:8, 9). It was for the removal of a physical disability, which he doubtless considered was an impediment to his life-work; so that even in this desire his passion for the gospel may have been implicated. But it is significant that this, his only recorded prayer for his own welfare, was not granted. Like the Master in Gethsemane, he prayed earnestly, three times, so that it must have been a matter lying heavily upon his heart. But when his petition is not granted, he knows what to do. He not only submits, but rejoices, because, through his weakness, he reaches a deeper experience of the power of the grace of Christ.

The very numerous incidental allusions to prayer in the life of Paul show what an enormous place it must have had in his life. Often he speaks of "making mention of you in my prayers" (Rom. 1:9; Eph. 1:16; 1 Thess. 1:2). This phrase does not necessarily imply that Paul had regular hours of prayer, though this may well have been the case. He urges the Ephesian (Eph. 6:18) and the Thessalonian (1 Thess. 5:17) Christians to pray at all seasons, and this he does himself, praying ceaselessly (Rom. 1:9; Eph. 1:16; 1 Thess. 2:13; 2 Thess. 1:11), night and day exceedingly (1 Thess. 3:10). This last phrase, together with Paul's advice to the married (1 Cor. 7:5), and a few allusions to "watchings" (cf. 2 Cor. 6:5; 11:27; Eph. 6:18), have created the impression that he believed in regular nightly vigils for prayer. But this seems to strain the words unduly. Paul was a practical genius; and knowing the spiritual value of order and regularity, it is highly probable that he carried over into his Christian life his Jewish habit of praying three times a day. But he was no legalist. He, of all men, was a man of the spirit; and though, in his days of travel, it may not always have been possible for him, more than three times a day, to "bow the knee to the Father, from whom every family in heaven and on earth is named" (Eph. 3:14), we may be sure that, like Nehemiah at the court of Artaxerxes (Neh. 2:4), he sent up many a swift and silent prayer to God, so that, apart from the conscious God-ward attitude of all his life, it may have been almost literally true that he prayed without ceasing.

We have now to raise the very important question of the attitude of Paul to Jesus in prayer. Did he pray to God only or to Jesus also? Before dealing with this question, it will be well to consider whether, apart from his epistles, there are other illustrations of prayer to Jesus, and whether Jesus ever directly prescribed or indirectly suggested this.

During the lifetime of Jesus, appeals, usually brief, were occasionally directed to Him, which sound like prayers. "Jesus, Thou son of David, have mercy upon me" (Mark 10:47, 48). Thus He is addressed by the blind Bartimaeus (cf. Matt. 9:27; 20:30, 31; Luke 18:38). The request is nearly always one for mercy or help, and was made to Him as the Messiah, but as the Messiah, though divinely equipped, was not necessarily regarded as Himself divine, this proves nothing for the possibility of prayer to Jesus. In a similar situation, He is addressed simply as "Jesus, Master" (Luke 17:13).

Addresses to Him as Lord look, at first sight a little more in the direction of worship. "Lord, have mercy on my son" (Matt. 17:15), says the father of the epileptic boy. "Lord, save me" (Matt. 14:30), is the cry of Peter, and "Lord, save us, we perish" (Matt. 8:25), of the disciples on the sea. The word Lord, however, while it was a common designation of God in the time of Jesus, could be equally well applied to man. It was a polite or deferential address: it is thus that the servants in the parable of the unfaithful steward address their master (Matt. 25:20, 22, 24). It was not unlike our "Sir," and is the regular word in modern Greek for "mister." Considering, however, the religious use of the word, it was very natural that, soon after the resurrection of Jesus, His followers should apply the term to Him in the profounder religious sense: He was Lord, as God was Lord. But no inference can be drawn from the use of the word as addressed to Him during His lifetime. The dying thief, according to the true text in Luke 23:42, says, *"Jesus, remember me,"* but *Jesus* is transformed into *Lord* by the reverent instincts of a somewhat later age. We can here see the process at work (cf. Luke 18:38, 41; John 6:34).

Nor can any inference be drawn from the use of the word *worship,* which occurs in the story of the visit of the Magi (Matt. 2:2, 11), and of the meeting of Jesus with the eleven disciples after His resurrection.[*] The Greek word really implies no more than the prostration with which an inferior honored a superior: it is the word used to describe the attitude of the servant in the parable who could not pay his dept. "He fell down and prostrated himself and said, 'Have patience with me and I will pay thee all' " (Matt. 18:26). It cannot be denied that in the two stories alluded to, especially as they are late, the idea of worship may have been more than remotely suggested, but that is not the essential meaning of the word. The fate of mistranslation has befallen alike the Greek word and the corresponding Hebrew word of the Old Testament.

It is altogether improbable that Jesus directly counseled or even countenanced the worship of Himself during His lifetime (cf. Mark 10:18). He disclaimed omniscience: "Of that day or that hour knoweth no one, not even the angels in heaven, nor yet the Son" (Mark 13:32). He refused to accede to the request of James and John in the words: "To sit on my right hand or on my left is not mine to give" (Mark 10:40). There may have been moments when the disciples felt towards their Master something more than reverence—moments when, under the influence of His manifest power and His strangely searching words, there arose instinctively in their

---

[*] Matthew 28:17; in Luke 24:52 the word is omitted in some manuscripts.

hearts the consciousness that here was a being unlike any other. But it is another question whether they worshiped Him.

Many influences would contribute to render that, during His lifetime, practically impossible. First, there was the intense monotheism of Jewish religion. Jehovah was one, He was spirit; He was like man, but He was not man. He could speak through men and in them, but He could not be identified with man. Anything like the worship of a living man, however possible it may have been in other parts of the Roman empire, must have been inconceivable upon the soil of Judaism. Besides this, there was Jesus' own express injunction to worship the Father. The manner of His own prayers and His own teaching on prayer must have gone to confirm, if it needed confirmation, the Jewish view of the exclusive right of God to worship.

On the other hand, it cannot be denied that prayers are addressed to Jesus in the New Testament. Sometimes, indeed, the question is complicated by the ambiguous use of the word Lord, to which we have already alluded. For example, the prayer of the disciples for a successor to Judas is addressed to the Lord (Acts 1:24). Is this God or Jesus? The epithet "who knowest the heart" suggests that the address is to God, and this is confirmed by Acts 15:8, where this epithet is directly applied to God. But, on the other hand, three verses before the prayer, we meet the phrase *the Lord Jesus;* so that the prayer may, after all, be addressed to Jesus.* Against this, however, we may set the prayer of the Church for Peter in prison, which is expressly said to have been made *to God* (Acts 12:5), though a prayer to Jesus, for whose sake Peter was suffering, would not have been unnatural, had prayers to Jesus been common.

The truth is that, leaving out the Pauline epistles, prayers to Jesus are exceedingly rare in the New Testament. An undoubted case is the dying prayer of Stephen—*Lord Jesus, receive my spirit* (Acts 7:59)— which can at least be no later than the composition of the Book of Acts. There is further the brief prayer in Revelation 22:20, *Come, Lord Jesus.* These simple appeals are probably the earliest form of

---

* Acts 9:17, the Lord, (even) Jesus, etc.

prayer to Jesus. A prayer to the risen Jesus, in a crisis into which one had been brought through fidelity to Him, would be very natural; and at a time when both the Jewish and the Christian atmosphere was filled with eschatological hopes, *Come, Lord Jesus,* would no doubt be a very common prayer on the lips of Christians.

Thomas's address to Jesus (John 20:28), "My Lord and my God"—the only passage[*] which suggests the worship of Him in the gospel which, more than any other, emphasizes His divinity—is an address rather than a prayer. There is a doxology to Jesus in 2 Peter 3:18, and in Revelation 5:6–13 the Lamb is praised by a multitude of angels round about the throne in heaven. Though the Lamb, with the seven horns and seven eyes, is symbolical, and the scene is in heaven, not on earth, it seems not unfair to conclude from this, supported as it is by the other doxology and two prayers, that divine honors were early paid to Jesus. Christian, Jew and heathen could all alike appeal to God; Christian and Jew could alike address God as Lord; the Christian could distinguish himself from both by praying to Jesus.

Such warrant for prayer to Jesus as may be supposed to be derived from His own words comes from the Gospel of John, where occasional reference is made to prayer in His name (John 14:13, 14; 15:16; 16:23). It is not without significance that this phrase, in this connection, is not found in the Synoptic Gospels, and it may reflect the later practice of the Church. But it is quite possible that Jesus did actually use the expression in the promises of those farewell days.

What does it exactly mean? The phrase "in the name of" has its roots deep in the past: it had once carried with it ideas of magic and superstition. To Semitic peoples the name meant far more than to us. It covered all that we mean by character, personality; it was mystically connected with the person named. But it also seemed sometimes to be regarded almost as an entity separable from the person with whom it was associated, and enjoying, in a sense, an

---

[*] In John 14:14, "If ye shall ask *me* anything in my name," *me* is omitted in the best texts.

independent existence alongside of him. The higher the being, the more powerful the name. There was hardly anything that could not be effected by the help of the Divine name. It could control the demons. The good spirits obeyed willingly, the evil could be compelled by the name to service. In the prayer of Manasseh, God is addressed as the one who has "shut up the deep and sealed it by Thy terrible and glorious name."

Belief in the power of the Divine name existed long before the New Testament, and colors much of the language of both Old and New. When we read that certain strolling Jews, exorcists, took upon them to name the name of Jesus over those that had evil spirits (Acts 19:13), we cannot but suppose that a certain magical power was ascribed to the name. The nature and quality of the apostles' faith in the name of Jesus must have been very different from that of these exorcists, and yet there were points of contact between the two. Their miracles were wrought in the name of Jesus (Acts 3:6, 4:30; cf. James 5:14). Very singular are Peter's words with reference to the healing of the lame man: "By faith in His name hath *His name* made this man strong" (Acts 3:16). It is hardly possible to deny that the name here is more than simply an equivalent for Jesus. Its curious prominence and its repetition in this verse, together with the fact that the name is actually pronounced when the cure is about to be effected, all seem to suggest, in accordance with ancient Semitic belief, that the manifestation of the power of the person addressed is connected with the naming of his name. Similarly, in the late appendix to Mark those who believe in Jesus are to cast out devils in His name (Mark 16:17), and even those whom He rejects in the final judgment claim to have enjoyed the same power (Matt. 7:22).

Does not this indisputable use of the word throw light upon the passages in which Jesus speaks of His disciples as "asking in His name"? To ask in the name of Jesus would mean to pray, and, in praying, to utter His name.* A prayer so offered would be answered

---

* From this point of view, the statement, "Hitherto ye have asked nothing in my name," is striking.

either by Himself or His Father (John 14:13, 14, 15:6). It is not impossible that the ordinary Christian of those early times—heir as he was to the Semitic past—would, in a somewhat mechanical and superstitious way, associate the power of Jesus, whether to act or to mediate, with the mere naming of His name. That, of course, cannot have been, in the remotest degree, the intention of Jesus. Here, as everywhere else, He takes familiar words, and transforms them. Only those could count on being heard who believed on Him as they uttered His name. In other words, the thing of essential importance was their faith in Him (Acts 3:16), indicated by their appeal to Him, and not the mechanical utterance of His name. The person who offered a prayer in His name would be one whose will was in unison with His; so that prayer in the name of Jesus comes to mean practically prayer in His spirit, and carries also with it an implicit confession, on the part of the worshiper, of his supreme debt to Jesus for his new relation to God.

Let us now return to the consideration of the prayers of Paul: did he pray to God only, or to Jesus also? It is remarkable that, in spite of Jesus' injunction to pray to the Father, the address to God the Father—with the exception of the simple exclamation "Abba, Father," which occurs twice (Rom. 8:15; Gal. 4:6)—is found only four times (Col. 1:2, 12; Phil. 4:20; Eph. 3:14). Everywhere else Christ is in some way implicated in Paul's address to God, for whom the usual designation is "the Father of our Lord Jesus Christ."* This is certainly no accident. It is an eloquent testimony to the difference that Jesus made in Paul's relations to God. What God now is to Paul, He is through Jesus.

But does the phrase imply more? The answer to this question is somewhat facilitated by noting other expressions—chiefly two—in which Paul describes his approach to God; namely, "in the name of Christ," and "through Christ." As an illustration of the former, take Ephesians 5:20, "giving thanks always for all things *in the name*

---

* Colossians 1:3. It is interesting to note that here this fuller address *immediately* follows the simpler address to "God our Father" (v. 2).

of our Lord Jesus Christ to God, even the Father," and of the latter, Romans 1:8, "I thank my God *through Jesus Christ* for you all." It does not, of course, go without saying that these expressions are identical in meaning, but, as they occur in very similar contexts, they cannot lie far apart.

The meaning of "the name" we have already discussed. Strictly speaking, to thank God in the name of Jesus would naturally mean to thank Him, uttering aloud—for whatever purpose—the name of Jesus. The purpose for which Jesus is appealed to is supposed by some to be indicated in the other phrase, where the thanks are offered to God *through* Jesus. In other words, it is contended that Jesus is summoned to convey the thanks to God.

But there are serious objections to this view. While a certain magical force may well have been attributed to the name by average Christians of that time, we can hardly suppose this to have been the case with Paul. Any such mechanical conception can hardly be ascribed to one who saw so clearly into the essence of religion, any more than it can be ascribed to Jesus Himself. There would be something peculiarly wooden about this explanation as applied to so spontaneous an utterance as "I thank God through Jesus Christ our Lord" in Romans 8:25. Besides, it would be very remarkable if this explanation were correct, that Paul always thanks, and never entreats, through Jesus: it would be at least as natural, if not more so, to suppose that Jesus would also be summoned to convey petitions.

Through Jesus suggests mediation indeed, but probably mediation of the salvation rather than of the prayer. A presumption in favor of this view is created by the triumphant words of 1 Corinthians 15:57, "Thanks be to God, who giveth us the victory through our Lord Jesus Christ." If this be the meaning of thanking God through Christ, some light is thus thrown on the other phrase—thanking Him "in the name of Christ." The name of Christ is all that rises to the mind of the worshiper when He utters His name—notably the salvation which He mediated. Thus there would be in the expression a reminiscence of the older associations that clung to the name, but into it there would also be poured the grateful memory of the work wrought by Christ.

Thanks in the name of Christ does not therefore necessarily imply that Paul prayed to Christ; and even more direct phrases, such as the description of Christians as "those who call upon the name of our Lord Jesus Christ" (1 Cor. 1:2; cf. Phil. 2:9–11), do not necessarily lead to this conclusion. This, while it might indeed involve prayer to Christ, may mean no more than that Christians implicated the name of Christ in their prayers to God, as Paul himself did. Immediately after the phrase just quoted, Paul simply says, "I thank my God" (1 Cor. 1:4), and his prayers must certainly have been, in the main, directed to God (Rom. 10:1).

But are there no exceptions? Paul's view of Christ is so exalted that the worship of Him is certainly anything but inconceivable. He is far above all rule and authority, not only in this world, but in that which is to come (Eph. 1:20–23). He had existed in the form of God, before He emptied Himself and took upon Him the form of a servant (Phil. 2:6–11). He is the image of the invisible God, the first-born of all creation (Col. 1:15–18), and in Him dwelleth all the fullness of the Godhead bodily (Col. 2:9). The conception of Christ being so exalted, the surprise rather is that there should be so few passages which can, with any plausibility, be regarded either as direct prayers to Him, or as implying the possibility of such prayers, especially as in the introductory greetings to the letters, the Lord Jesus Christ is so frequently coordinated with "God our Father" as the giver of grace and peace (1 Cor. 1:3; 2 Cor. 1:2).

This may be explained by the relativity or subordination of Christ to the Father which comes clearly to light in many other passages. God sent Him (Gal. 4:4), delivered Him up (Rom. 8:32), raised Him from the dead (Rom. 4:24). "When all things have been subjected unto Him, then shall the Son also Himself be subjected"–or shall subject Himself–unto God the Father (1 Cor. 15:28). Even in the lofty passages just quoted, this sense of subordination is not absent. The Father of glory raised Christ from the dead, and set Him at His right hand (Eph. 1:20). He gave Him the name which is above every name (Phil. 2:9); and He is the first-born of all creation (Col. 1:15). Sometimes there is a sharp distinction drawn between God and Christ. "There is one God the Father, of whom are all things and we unto Him; and one Lord Jesus Christ, through whom are all things and we through Him" (1 Cor. 8:6; cf. Eph. 4:5, 6). When Paul became a Christian, he did not forget the strict monotheism he had learned as a Jew. "There is no God but one" (1 Cor. 8:4, 6; cf. Rom. 3:30; Eph. 4:6), and "of Him and through Him and unto Him are all things" (Rom. 11:36).

Yet there are phenomena which leave room for the possibility that Paul did address Christ in prayer. The revelation of God in Him was so complete that, in spite of the historical and theoretical distinction between them, there is, for the devotional life, where logical categories are forgotten, a practical identity. Sometimes, immediately after both have been named, the verb that follows is in the singular, and of course the function expressed by the verb is equally ascribed to both. For example: "May our Lord Jesus Christ Himself, and God our Father . . . comfort your hearts and establish them in every good work" (2 Thess. 2:16). It is not impossible that the double address at the beginning of the verse has been forgotten under the influence of the parenthetic clause of twelve Greek words which follows it. But this explanation of the singular verbs will not hold in 1 Thessalonians 3:11, where the verb immediately follows its two subjects: "May our God and Father Himself and our Lord Jesus Christ direct our way unto you." In these passages, Jesus equally with God is the comforter, the strengthener, and the guide of life, and the possibility of prayer to Him must be conceded.

The passage which is supposed to raise this possibility into an actuality is 2 Corinthians 12:8. "Concerning this thing"–his thorn in the flesh–"I besought *the Lord* thrice, that it might depart from me." But who is the Lord? We have already seen how naturally the early Church applied this term to Jesus; it is also Paul's favorite designation of Jesus. But though there are many cases where the term may equally refer to God or Christ, and few, if any where it necessarily refers to God,* it is altogether probable that Paul could also have applied the word quite naturally to God, especially as it was so familiar a designation of Him in the Greek version of the Old Testament. Indeed, from this he quotes passages containing the word Lord (Rom. 4:8 [=Ps. 32:2]; 1 Cor. 3:20 [=Ps. 94:11]), which he must have felt referred primarily to God, though it would be begging the question to say that, in the mind of Paul, the reference to Christ was absolutely excluded.

The prayer then, for the removal of the thorn in the flesh may, after all, be a prayer to God. But in candor it must be confessed that the context seems to point the other way. "He"–that is, the Lord–"said unto me, 'My grace is sufficient for thee; for (the) *power* is made perfect in weakness.' " That is the answer to the prayer. Paul goes on: "Most gladly therefore will I rather glory in my weaknesses, that the *power of Christ* may rest upon me" (2 Cor. 12:9). It is impossible not to hear in these words an echo of the answer; in that case, the answer must have come from Christ, and the prayer been directed to Christ.

This would seem to be the only indubitable instance of prayer to Christ in the epistles of Paul. Such prayer could be justified by the completeness with which God was revealed in Jesus, and would be facilitated by the use of the term Lord for each alike. Nevertheless it is significant that such prayers should be so very few–elsewhere in the New Testament only the prayer of Stephen, and the brief cry "Come, Lord Jesus." There is no direct word of Jesus enjoining prayer to Himself. Even in the gospel of John, though Jesus urges His disciples to "ask in His name," He seems deliberately to avoid urging them to ask Himself,† and explicitly urges them to ask the Father (John 15:16, 16:23).

At first the impulse to pray to Jesus would be hindered by the deep-seated monotheistic instincts of His contemporaries, by His own command to pray to the Father, and not least, by their recollection of

---

* Perhaps Romans 14:6 is such a passage; he who eateth eateth to *the Lord,* for he giveth *God* thanks.

† John 14:13, 14. Note the dogmatic addition of *me* in certain texts; of v. 14.

Him as a man. But the farther men receded from the times of the historical Jesus, the more easy and natural would prayer to Him become. If the question of the legitimacy of prayer to Him has to be settled on the basis of His own demands alone, then it would have to be settled in the negative. He did not claim this honor for Himself. But the greatness of His personality is not to be measured by His formulated claims, great as these sometimes were. The stupendous impression He made upon the world issued naturally in the offering to Him not only of praise, but of prayer. History was so moved by Him that, without any express warrant from Himself, she thrust this homage upon Him.

The Difference That Jesus Made

🔳

Jesus was at once conservative and revolutionary. In fulfilling, He destroyed; in destroying, He fulfilled. The prayers that follow His appearance in history have something, even much, in common with those that precede Him; yet, in the main, they are different. It will therefore be worthwhile to gather up here the scattered impressions that the argument has made, and to look briefly at the difference that Jesus made.

That difference must have been more or less obvious to all who heard Jesus pray. "As He was praying, when He ceased, one of His disciples said to Him, 'Lord, teach us to pray, *even as John also taught his disciples*' " (Luke 11:1). Here is a recognition of the felt importance of prayer, and also of knowing its true method or secret, but it is also an acknowledgment of the difference that was felt to exist between John and Jesus in prayer as well as in preaching. The prayer that follows the answer to this question, while it is primarily intended to serve His disciples as a model, is also an implicit criticism of existing practice, from which it differed partly in form, and partly in content.

After this manner pray ye: briefly. That was not the existing manner—the scribes made long prayers (Mark 12:40)—nor is it the manner of the later prayers of the Old Testament. It is as if Jesus said: A true prayer must be brief; ye shall not be heard for your much speaking. The publican's prayer, which is approved, is little more than a cry; the Pharisee's, which is condemned, is relatively much longer (Luke 18:11, 13). The former prayer forms, in particular, a very striking contrast to the elaborate confessional prayer of Manasseh.

Again, "when ye pray, say, 'Father.' " This is the correct text in Luke 11:2, and is in itself very probable. That it was the favorite word of Jesus is made practically certain by the cry *Abba, Father* (Rom. 8:15; Gal. 4:6; Mark 14:36; cf. Matt. 11:25; John 17:1), uttered by those who possess the spirit of sonship. The Aramaic word of Jesus—Abba—appears to have been so integral a part of His prayer that it was perpetuated even among the Greek-speaking Christians. He no doubt also said, *"My* Father" (cf. Matt. 26:39, 42). The word Father had been used centuries before in prayer (Is. 63:16, 64:8), though God had usually been regarded as the Father of the nation. Before the time of Jesus, however, the word Father appears also to have been addressed to God by the individual, but, even so, we have the incontrovertible testimony of Paul that, after the revelation of Jesus, the Fatherhood seemed to be a different thing. Since Jesus, sonship was realized in another way, or another degree; the thought of it stirred an emotion which had never been so stirred before, with the result that the sons *cry* Abba, Father (Rom. 8:15).

Jesus had, for the first time, placed the fatherhood of God in the center of religious thought. It is characteristic that neither the Pharisee nor the publican, though the one offers a prayer of gratitude, and the other for mercy, uses the term Father; they both address God simply as God (Luke 18:11, 13). The difference that Jesus made in this connection is very strikingly seen in the use He made of the words "Into Thy hands I commend My spirit," on the cross (Luke 23:46). These words come from Psalm 31:5a; and that they are addressed to the Lord, or Jehovah, is clear from 5b. But by the simple change of Lord to Father, the words are transfigured. In this little word lies the real difference between the Old Testament and the New, and that word we owe to Jesus.

With it, of course, goes a whole wealth of new associations, and a totally different attitude to God. In the Old Testament, the attitude is rather that of a servant to his master. Especially in the later period God is felt to be far away (cf. Eccl. 5:2). There is an importunity about some of the Psalms, for example, which suggests that God may be ultimately worn into granting His grace by the worshiper's vehemence and persistency (cf. Luke 18:5). Though New Testament prayer is not less earnest, it is more restful and confident. It is sure of the divine love, for it has seen Jesus. God is not now distant, but nigh. His worshipers therefore speak of approaching Him not only with confidence, but with boldness, for the spirit of bondage has been cast out and replaced by the spirit of sonship. The reverence due to God is not forgotten. He is still the invisible (Col. 1:15), the incorruptible (Rom. 1:23), the only wise God (Rom. 16:27), the Father of glory (Eph. 1:17), but He is also now the God of peace (Rom. 15:33, 16:20; Phil. 4:9; 1 Thess. 5:23), of love (2 Cor. 13:11), of hope (Rom. 15:13), of consolation (Rom. 15:5).

When ye pray, say Father—simply Father. It had been the custom for three or four centuries before Jesus' time to enrich the divine name with epithets. The tendency is already quite marked in the prayers of Ezra.

A prayer probably contemporary with Jesus and certainly in the contemporary manner, begins thus:

> Blessed art Thou, O Jehovah, our God and the God of our fathers, God of Abraham, God of Isaac, God of Jacob, the great and mighty and terrible God, God most High, maker of heaven and earth, our shield and the shield of our fathers.

How profound, simple, original and welcome, would be the simple "Father." This word did not indeed imply an absolute condemnation of all titles in prayer—Jesus Himself also prayed to the "Father, Lord of heaven and earth"; also, according to John, to the "holy" and "righteous Father"—but they must be chosen with regard to their relevance and propriety. They will in any case be few, and will be often, if not usually, absent altogether. Again, in addressing God simply as Father, Jesus obliterates all the old national*

---

* For the value and relative justification of the national element in prayer, cf. "The Nature and Content of Prayer," pp. 139–150.

associations of prayer. *"All* flesh shall come to Thee." God is not now the God of Israel, or of Abraham, Isaac and Jacob, but the Father of all. Whereas ancient Jewish prayer was fond of enumerating what God had done for Israel (cf. Neh. 9), Paul dwells rather on what He had done for men in Christ: He is the God "who reconciled us to Himself through Christ" (2 Cor. 5:18).

The difference which Jesus made is very conspicuous if we contrast His prayers with those of Jeremiah. The similarity between their careers is more than remarkable. No Old Testament figure is so prophetic of Jesus as Jeremiah. Each was rejected by his own townsmen (Jer. 11:21; Mark 6:1–3), the life of each was sought by the priests of Jerusalem (Jer. 26:8), each was led as a lamb to the slaughter (Jer. 11:19), each was a man of sorrows and acquainted with grief, each sought and found strength in prayer. But how different was the temper of the prayer! Jeremiah's passionate readiness to reason the cause with God, his challenges of the divine ways (Jer. 12:1), which are repeated in the still bolder challenges of Job, and find an echo in Psalms as late as the second century B.C. (Ps. 44:23), have nothing to match them in the prayers of Jesus, except the single heart-broken cry, wrung from the depths of an agony incomparably deeper than Jeremiah's, "Why hast Thou forsaken me?" (cf. Jer. 15:18).

Again, we have already seen how frequent and terrible are Jeremiah's prayers for vengeance. "Bring upon them the day of evil, and destroy them with double destruction" (Jer. 17:18). "Deliver up their children to the famine, and give them over to the power of the sword, and let their wives become childless and widows, and let their men be slain of death, and their young men smitten of the sword in battle. Forgive not their iniquity, neither blot out their sin from Thy sight, but let them be overthrown before Thee; deal Thou with them in the time of Thine anger" (Jer. 18:21, 23). Such prayers are common in all periods of Hebrew history. Joshua (Josh. 10:13) and Samson (Judg. 16:28), at the beginning of Hebrew history, pray for vengeance upon their enemies. So Nehemiah (Neh. 4:5)–"Cover not their iniquity, and let not their sin be blotted out"–and these terrible petitions ring throughout the whole history (Ps. 69:22–28, 109). What a contrast they form to Jesus' command, "Pray for them that persecute you," and to His dying prayer, "Father, forgive them." The Jewish passion for vengeance was hard to slay, and it was not at once destroyed by the spirit of Jesus; its voice is still heard plainly enough in early Jewish Christianity (Rev. 6:10, 16:5, 6). But, in the main, such prayers are offered no more. The dying prayer of Samson ran: "O Lord Jehovah, remember me, I pray Thee, and strengthen me, I pray Thee, only this once, O God, that I may be avenged of the Philistines for my two eyes" (Judg. 16:28). The dying words of Stephen were: "Lord, lay not this sin to their charge" (Acts 7:60). That was the difference that Jesus made.

Another difference lay in the predominant emphasis which He placed on prayer in spiritual things. Even the Old Testament occasionally touches this height. "Though the fig-tree flourish not, and there be no herd in the stalls, yet will I joy in the God of my salvation" (Hab. 3:17, 18). If I have but Thee, I ask for nothing in heaven or earth (Ps. 73:25). But, as a rule, these heights were reached only after a struggle, and they were held by very few. Jesus Himself recognized both in practice and in prayer the place of things material. Much of His ministry was given to caring for the bodies of men, and He taught His disciples to pray for bread. Nevertheless, with Him the kingdom of God is first and everywhere; and in the epistles of Paul, as we have already seen abundantly, the supreme and almost the exclusive place is occupied by the things of the spirit. That was another difference that Jesus made.

But perhaps the most remarkable difference of all was the shifting of the emphasis from petition to thanksgiving. The Old Testament is indeed a glad book. Worshiping a God of Salvation, a God who had saved and who could save in real and tangible ways, the people could not but be happy in their worship. This at least was the mood of pre-exilic times. From the exile on, the religion became much more somber, but joy was far from being obliterated. The call to "give thanks to Jehovah, for He is good; for His mercy endureth forever," is peculiarly frequent in post-exilic times. The one hundred and seventh Psalm is an eloquent and grateful testimony to the goodness of Jehovah. Many of the later Psalms form one continuous shout of jubilation (Ps. 145–150), and some of the later prayers acknowledge very fully the goodness of God to Israel in history (Neh. 9).

Nevertheless, petition vastly outweighed thanksgiving. With a deepening recognition of the majesty of God, petition becomes more reverent. The old complaints, in which man spoke to God as to a friend with whom he was angry, become fewer and fewer. They are common still in Jeremiah, but, except for the book of Job, which is practically a dramatic poem, and some stray utterances in the Psalms, complaints practically disappear. But, with the coming of Jesus, the absence of complaint merges into positive thanksgiving. "Father, I thank Thee"–that was the motto of Jesus. The change is very obvious in the prayers of His greatest disciple. We have already seen how the epistles of Paul are crowded with prayers of thanksgiving, and this proportion between thanksgiving and petition is an altogether new thing in prayer.

Further, the thanks is more personal than was customary in Jewish prayer. A common introductory formula was, "Blessed be God," etc.; and this more distant and impersonal form is occasionally retained by Paul himself, who would naturally carry into Christianity many of the usages of the Judaism in which he had been trained (Eph. 1:3). But the characteristically Christian prayer is, "I thank Thee" (Phil. 1:3; Rev. 11:17). It is warm with the gratitude of a human heart. It implies a definite personal relationship of reverent affection. With full heart, the finite man kneels before his infinite Benefactor and says–not merely "Blessed be God," but–"*I thank Thee.*"

And that personal note is made more intensely personal by the thought which, even when unexpressed, must ever be present to Christian prayer, of the worshiper's infinite debt to Christ. The frequency of Paul's references to Christ in prayer to God is very significant. It was He who taught men their new relation to the Father, and He who brought them into it. The Christian cannot even call God Father without acknowledging his debt to Christ. And the Christ who taught him that dear name is also the Christ who loved him and gave Himself for him (Gal. 2:20). He knows what he has to be grateful for. He thanks his Father for rain and sunshine, food and raiment, seedtime and harvest, day and night, sorrow and joy, defeat and victory, friendship and love, the inspiration of the past and the opportunities of the present, but, most of all, for His unspeakable gift.

The form and spirit that characterize true Christian prayer ultimately rest upon a clear recognition of all that is involved in the fatherhood of God. This is what makes prayer brief—for the Father knows; and it is this that makes it grateful and glad—for the Father cares.

Part 2

Modern Prayer

The Nature and Content
of Prayer

It is the simple truth to say that the Hebrews have taught the world how to pray. Prayer is an instinct of the unsophisticated soul. Whether to gods or saints or demons or the dead, all nations have prayed. But the prayers differ as the religions differ; and as the Hebrews are the world's acknowledged masters in religion, it is from their prayers that we have by far the most to learn. *Ye shall not pray as the Gentiles do.* Hebrew prayer itself, as we have seen, underwent development, and the difference that Jesus made was very great, but it is still to the Bible, to the Old Testament and New alike, that we must go when we would learn to speak with God. Old Testament aspirations were fulfilled rather than abolished by Christ. The piety of the millennium which preceded Him has a value of its own, and a value even for us. For more than twenty centuries men have lifted up their hearts to God on the words of the Hebrew Psalter, because there they have found their deepest thoughts most finely interpreted and expressed; and the older the world grows, the more profound and wonderful seems that prayer which Christ taught His disciples. These things can never be outgrown or superseded; they are eternal, because they are simple and true. *We know not how to pray as we ought,* but the Bible may be our teacher and guide. For prayer, though in its nature spontaneous, may be directed; though an instinct, it may, like any other instinct, be trained. "One of His disciples said unto Him, 'Lord, *teach* us to pray.'" So prayer can be taught, and the modern Church has much to gain by recalling her prayers to the biblical standard. We shall therefore call attention to a few considerations, suggested by a study of biblical prayer, which may help to guide the devotional usage—whether public or private—of today.

One of the most remarkable phenomena—confined, however, in the nature of the case, practically to the Old Testament—is the prominence of history in prayer, alike in prayers of petition, thanksgiving and confession. The worshipers beseech the Divine help, because it has already been in the past so signally manifested; or they offer their thanks for the Divine guidance of the nation in ages long gone by; or they look at the sins which they confess in the light of the ancient goodness of God of which they have proved themselves so miserably unworthy. But the striking thing is this: they do not content themselves with vague assertions of that goodness; they relate it definitely—sometimes briefly, and sometimes very elaborately—to their national history.

It is done briefly, but characteristically, by Jehoshaphat when, in his prayer for help in battle, he says, "Didst not Thou, O our God, drive out the inhabitants of this land before Thy people Israel, and give it to the seed of Abraham Thy friend forever?" etc. (2 Chr. 20:7, 8). David, in a prayer of thanksgiving, is also represented as recalling the goodness of God in the time of the Exodus: "What one nation in the earth is like Thy people, even like Israel, whom God went to redeem unto Himself for a people, and to make Him a name, and to do terrible things for Thy land, before Thy people, whom Thou didst redeem to Thee out of Egypt, from the nations and their gods?" (2 Sam. 7:23).

A very beautiful and striking illustration of this phenomenon occurs in the prayer of thanksgiving which is offered for the first-fruits (Deut. 26:5-9). The prayer at first seems curiously out of place in this connection: it is a tolerably minute summary of the facts of Israel's early history. "A wandering Aramean was my father, and he went down into Egypt and sojourned there, few in number, and he became there a nation, great, mighty and populous. And the Egyptians dealt ill with us and afflicted us, and laid upon us hard bondage, and we cried unto Jehovah, the God of our fathers, and Jehovah heard our voice and saw our affliction, and our toil and our oppression; and Jehovah brought us forth out of Egypt with a mighty hand, and with an outstretched arm, and with great terribleness, and with signs, and with wonders; and He hath brought us into this place, and hath given us this land, a land flowing with milk and honey." Then at the end come the simple words: "And now, behold, I have brought the first of the fruit of the ground, which Thou, O Jehovah, hast given me."

In many ways, this prayer is most characteristic and instructive. Behind it lies the thought: We love Him, because He first loved us. It further suggests that gratitude must be expressed, not in word only, but also in deed. It links the ages each to each: God did that *then,* therefore we do this *now.* It keeps alive the memory of the gracious past. But the point with which we are immediately concerned is that the goodness of God is vividly brought before the mind of the worshiper by a historical recital. The great words "goodness and loving-kindness" were not allowed to degenerate into empty phrases, but they were filled with radiant and indisputable historical fact. So much is this the case that some of the longer Psalms (Ps. 78, 105, 106) practically form a brief history of early Israel. The past was ever with them: it was kept alive not only in history, but in prayer.

Similarly, in the great prayer, half petition, half confession, of Isaiah 63:7–64:12, history holds a prominent place. The speaker begins by saying, "I will make mention of the loving-kindnesses of Jehovah, and the praises of Jehovah, according to all that Jehovah hath bestowed on us, and the great goodness toward the house of Israel, which He hath bestowed on them according to His mercies, and according to the multitude of His loving-kindnesses." But he does not leave the matter there. He at once proceeds, through seven verses, to amplify the Divine mercies and loving-kindnesses by recalling the days of Moses and the divided sea.

One would hardly expect a strongly historical element in prayers of confession. It would be natural to suppose that the sinner would be occupied chiefly with the thought of his own sin. Not so in the Hebrew confession. In it the sinner thinks also of that goodness against which he has sinned, and that goodness is writ

large in history. Three-fourths of the very elaborate confession of
Ezra in Nehemiah 9 are occupied with a historical summary which
passes in review the call of Abraham, the affliction of the fathers
in Egypt and their deliverance, the giving of the law on Sinai, the
ordinance of the Sabbath, the Divine guidance through the wilderness, the manna and the water from the rock, the obstinacy, disobedience and idolatry of the people, their victories over foreign
kings, their conquest of Canaan.

These prayers hold vividly before the people the goodness of
God as manifested in the national history, and they keep alive the
names of national heroes, like Abraham and Moses. It must not be
forgotten, of course, that these are all special prayers, and we cannot from them infer with certainty the contents of average Hebrew
prayer. Indeed, more or less is this true of all the biblical prayers:
the only prayers preserved are those which, for some reason or
other, were considered to be significant or important. Nevertheless,
a feature so conspicuous among prayers so different was probably
a general feature of the longer prayers, at least of public prayers.
This becomes all the more probable, when we consider the universal emphasis of the Old Testament on history. Wherever else
God is, He is there. A very large proportion of the book is taken up
with historical narrative, which lovingly follows the sternly gracious purpose of God throughout the centuries. His mercy was not
only in the heavens; it was the most palpable of the realities that
walked the earth. And the people were never weary reminding
themselves of it: it was a spur alike to gratitude and penitence.

> We have heard with our ears,
>   Our fathers have told us
> What work Thou didst in their days,
>   In the days of old (Ps. 44:1).

Has the Old Testament not something here to teach the modern
Church? Might not that emphasis on history, which so largely inspired Hebrew prayer, find a more adequate recognition in modern prayer? It goes without saying that any influence which would
tend to encourage a narrow nationalism would be altogether alien

to the religion of Christ, in which there can be neither Jew nor Greek, French nor German, British nor American, but man as spirit stands before his God, who is also spirit. But the religious value of history is no less than ever. God is the same today as yesterday, and His kingdom is achieved among the kingdoms of this world. Its subjects are men who do His will, and its history is the story of the march of His will through time.

A prayer must indeed never degenerate into a sermon or historical narrative; it must always remain an address to God. But why may not men, out of a full heart, thank God for those of the fathers who, like Abraham and Moses, nobly did his will, or who were called to conspicuous service in the older time? Why, when they are met in the sanctuary to meditate on His goodness, may they not gratefully, and more frequently than they do, recall what they have read, and their fathers have told them, the work that He did in their days, in the days of old? This would not be to encourage a nationalistic or materialistic religion: it would be to recognize the inevitable contact of religion with history.

Again, it may be questioned whether—especially in the light of the New Testament—much of the customary language regarding the power of prayer does not need to be revised. Prayer is said to move the hand that rules the world, and the implication frequently is that, if it only be persistent enough, the petition cannot be withheld. But what of Jesus and Paul? Surely never did more earnest or persistent prayers rise to God than that the cup might pass and the thorn be removed. For these things each prayed three times; yet in the literal sense the prayers were not answered. The cup did not pass, it was drunk to the dregs; and the flesh was still tormented by the thorn.

Prayer is therefore not omnipotent in the sense that, whatever it earnestly asks, it can secure. It must sincerely subordinate itself to the will of God; and then, whatever be the issue, it must remain content, believing that the will is done. The Divine will is the thing that triumphs, and is the only thing that is sure of its triumph. To that all aspirations and petitions must be related, and the value of prayer lies partly in this, that it compels a deliberate reference of earthly life, with its activities and ambitions, to the heavenly will. In prayer the suppliant is compelled to look at himself, not as others see him, but as God sees him. And further, from out the innumerable uncertainties of his own life he looks at God the certain, the eternal, the unchangeable.

Its value is therefore inestimable. It humbles him by revealing to him the truth about himself. It clears his mind of false ambitions, by letting him feel the emptiness of all that is not eternal. It cultivates in him a temper of quietness and confidence; for, in true prayer, his will is in glad and solemn harmony with the omnipotent will of God: the peace and strength of God come back upon him. Whatever else prayer may do, these things at least it does; and surely this is much. It might be better then to speak of the influence of prayer than of its power. Power, properly understood, would not be an inappropriate term, but it too easily deflects attention to external and material effects and loses sight of that more mysterious transformation of the soul within.

As He was praying, the fashion of His countenance was altered. There, in a figure, is the true effect of prayer. For the transfigured countenance is but the outward expression of the inward transfiguration of the spirit, which is effected by prayer; and then any kind of work may be quietly attempted and triumphantly done. The soul is sure of itself and its God; and, with immovable confidence it can go down from the mount to face the devils on the plain. It is literally true that certain kinds can come out by nothing but by prayer. They yield to the touch only of the man with the transfigured face, the man who has won his soul by patient prayer. It is the transfigured man who transfigures the world. It is he whom no shouts of demons can appall, he who rids the world of its devils, he who does the work which the prayerless cannot do. So prayer has its power as well as its influence. Its effects are visible not only in the man within but in the world without.

This is one of the most indubitable effects of prayer—to possess the soul with a habitual peace and confidence, which are especially conspicuous in the midst of danger and difficult duty. *Let your re-*

quests be made known unto God; and the peace of God which passeth all understanding, shall stand sentry over your hearts and your thoughts (Phil. 4:6, 7). This effect of prayer is repeatedly illustrated in the Bible. It is quite clear that Nehemiah's brief silent prayer heartened him to proffer his bold request to Artaxerxes (Neh. 2:4), just as Jeremiah was heartened when the thought of his youth and inexperience tempted him to recoil from the mission to which he felt himself divinely impelled. The heavenly voice whispered, *Be not afraid, for I am with thee* (Jer. 1:8); and with that confidence in his heart he quietly faced the surging crowd in the temple and the fanatical priests and prophets who thirsted for his blood (Jer. 26:15).

So, throughout those dreary days and nights upon the sea and amid the impending terrors of shipwreck, Paul remains clear and calm. It was the man who had stayed his soul on God that was able to issue practical orders to his confused companions, and who succeeded in inspiring them with a calmness like his own. *He gave thanks to God in the presence of all, and then they were all of good cheer* (Acts 27:35, 36). And through that other notable prayer, which was not answered, for the removal of the thorn, he won a deeper peace and a richer experience of the grace of Christ (2 Cor. 12:9). Prayer can never be in vain: it calms, strengthens and purifies the soul of the man who offers it.

Most of all is this power of prayer illustrated by Gethsemane. At first the prayer of Jesus is: "If it be possible, let this cup pass away from Me; nevertheless not as I will, but as Thou wilt" (Matt. 26:39). The desire that the cup should pass is terrible in its reality: the prayer is offered with strong crying and tears. But, as the awful struggle proceeds, this prayer merges in the other, "If this cup cannot pass away except I drink it, Thy will be done" (Matt. 26:42). The first cry is, "Save me from this hour" (John 12:27), but the last is, "Father, glorify Thy name" (John 12:28). From the beginning, the deepest desire of Jesus was that the will of God be done, but the human will prayed vehemently that the cup should pass. But through the deadly earnestness of His prayer, He reached the absolute harmony of His will with God's; and He came forth from the garden, calm and triumphant, to face the treachery of a disciple, the fanaticism of the mob, and the jealous cruelty of the priests.

And what may be said of petition may also be said of intercession. It is twice blessed: it blesses the man who prays, not less than the man for whom he prays. It is touching to read how often Paul, in spite of his unique experience in the spiritual life, requests his converts to pray for him. Probably here most modern congregations grievously fail. Unquestionably a preacher would be enormously helped if he had reason to believe that he was being sustained by the prayers of his people. In such an atmosphere he could be his best. He would feel that his people had met, in a devout spirit, to worship God and to be helped to the better life, and that criticism was therefore disarmed; and, other things being equal, he would have a freedom, joy and power, such as is seldom possible where the people are apathetic, or at best, bring to the service little more than curiosity.

It is hard to conceive of an influence more likely to preserve in temptation and to strengthen for duty than the knowledge that prayers are offered in our behalf, or even the memory of prayers once offered. The voices, some hushed, that once pled with God for us—voices of father or mother or some faithful friend—plead with us still, and it is hard to resist such a plea. It can wake old and blessed memories, stir a long-slumbering conscience, stifle the incipient passion, quicken the better nature, brace, strengthen and purify. Jesus interceded for Peter that his faith should not fail, and, in a crucial moment, it failed: he denied and cursed and swore. Nevertheless the prayer bore fruit; for afterwards he wept bitterly, and became one of the Master's mightiest servants. Verily great is the power of intercession.

But its power over the man who prays is perhaps even greater and more certain. Intercession is love at prayer. Every true exercise of it deepens our interest in others, and develops in us a sympathy which must have its ultimate effect upon the happiness and well-being of the world. As William Law has said, "Intercession is the best arbitrator of all differences, the best promoter of true friendship, the best cure and preservative against all unkind tempers, all angry and haughty passions." Besides, the interest in men which lies behind intercessory prayer will, if it be genuine, also be likely to express itself practically. "He who prays to God to make men happy will do what he can to make them happy himself." He will hope, bear, believe and do all for the man whom he prays; and so its influence upon himself in restraining impatient and uncharitable tempers, and its influence, through him, upon the world, will be very great.

Not only intercession, but all prayer is fitted to expand the heart; for we pray to *our* Father, as well as *my* Father, to our God and my God. The need which a man brings to God in prayer is his own: but in the deepest sense, it is also every other man's; for, in a word, it is the need of God. In prayer all flesh can come, because between the deepest needs of men there can be no conflict. The house of prayer is for all nations, because in the things that they crave in prayer, national distinctions do not count. *Moreover, concerning the foreigner . . .* (1 Kgs. 8:41); every prayer must be offered in this large-hearted spirit. There is a Jewish story of a mother who had two sons, one a potter and one a gardener. The gardener asked her to pray for rain to water his plants, the potter asked her to pray for dry weather to dry his vessels. She loved them both: whom was she to pray for? The moral is that prayer must lie within the realm of common interests. Where two or three are gathered together, that which is individual falls away: one could not deliberately pray for that which he knew would injure some other.

Hence public prayer is less liable to abuse in this direction than private prayer, but even private prayer cannot go far astray, when it is directed to *our* Father. This is only a warning, reached along another line, that prayer should be predominantly for things spiritual. There can be no conflict of interests so long as men pray that God's name be hallowed, His kingdom come, and His will be done, that their trespasses be forgiven, that they may be delivered from evil and not led into temptation. The more these prayers of the individual are answered, the better it will be for everyone else. Prayers for things temporal must also have their relation to the Kingdom and the Will; and even they will be modest. "Give us this day our daily bread." That is not much to ask. The range of the prayer is wide, but the needs that it covers are simple; and my neighbor will not be injured if God answers so unambitious a prayer of mine.

Further, prayer is one of the best avenues to self-knowledge. We do not know how to pray as we ought, but we begin to learn, when we begin to interest ourselves in our spiritual welfare, and to understand our needs. It is as if we heard a divine voice say, *What wilt Thou that I should do unto thee?* And we were under the obligation to answer as sincerely, explicitly, and intelligently, as we can. We pray for the things which we miss, the defects which we deplore. *Lord, that I may receive my sight.* Vague words like "Bless us," which are not common in biblical prayer, and which, in any case, had for the Hebrew a more definite signification than for us, often only help to hide from us our real needs. Definite prayer has therefore the effect of bringing a man face to face with himself as well as with God.

But also with God as well as with himself. It is a fearful thing to fall into the hands of the living God, but it is a more fearful thing not to fall into His hands; for those are gracious arms that will uplift the soul that casts itself upon them. The life that in prayer habitually lets itself be searched by the divine gaze cannot continue in conscious, deliberate sin. As someone has said, either the sin will kill the prayer or the prayer the sin. The purifying influence of sincere prayer is undeniable. One cannot court temptation who has earnestly prayed that he be not led into it: he cannot pamper his baser nature if he has prayed for deliverance from evil. In the world into which his prayer introduces him, these desires stand rebuked and abashed; and, when the prayer is over, and he faces the world again, and meets there and in his own heart a thousand unsought solicitations to evil, there will lie upon him the holy obligation to become a co-worker with God in the answering of his own prayer.

The other side of petition is confession. In it, if it be definite enough, we get to know ourselves best of all. But the necessarily general language of public prayer is not sufficiently searching. "Forgive us our debts." This may mean everything or nothing. It cannot mean much unless we are at the trouble to recall our debts, as we should recall our blessings, one by one. We must call upon our soul and all that is within us to forget not any of His benefits nor any of our own shortcomings. True, the real enemy is not our sins, but our sin: it is out of the heart that these things proceed, and therefore the heart that must be renewed. But we learn our sin through its manifestations; and it is by confessing and fighting these that we come to know ourselves, and, by the grace of God which touches the life at its springs, that we overcome ourselves. "If the sins of the present day require a new confession, it must be such a new confession as is proper to itself." Character has everything to gain by the self-examination which must accompany petition and confession.

We have already seen how peculiarly characteristic of Christianity is thanksgiving. This is one of the last lessons which the individual learns. It is more or less amply recognized in the formal prayers of the Church, but the ordinary individual, if we may judge by the proportion of thanksgiving to petition in his prayers, still stands practically on the level of the Old Testament. Robert Louis Stevenson's wife says of him: "When he was happy, he felt impelled to offer thanks for that undeserved joy; when in sorrow or pain, to call for strength to bear what must be borne." It is to be feared that, with most men, the latter art is very much better understood than the former. The impulse to pray is usually a sense of need rather than of grateful and abounding joy. "We beseech Thee to give us that due sense of all Thy mercies that our hearts may be unfeignedly thankful." That such a prayer should be necessary shows our habitual and deep-grained inattention to the goodness of God, so unlike the spontaneous, open-eyed gratitude of the Bible.

If prayers of thanksgiving were commoner, the whole life would be indefinitely enriched. The eye would ever be kept awake and clear for the hundred tokens of a Father's love that fall unnoticed about our path every day, and the heart would be more sensitive and responsive to the great salvation. We are far enough yet from the enthusiasm of the New Testament. Perhaps indeed that can never be quite recalled. The men who had looked upon the face of Jesus or stood very near Him in history, and who had literally seen the world turned upside down by His gospel, must have been moved, as it is hardly possible for us to be moved, who have been born into an atmosphere more than nominally Christian—a world whose type of civilization has, generally speaking, been created by Christianity; a world which is, indeed, far enough from being in all its departments controlled by the Christian spirit, but which nevertheless can show much genuinely Christian thought, activity and aspiration. It may be that in a world so different, that ancient enthusiasm can never be altogether repeated. Nevertheless, the thanksgiving of the New Testament remains an eloquent rebuke to our more sluggish Christianity, and a standard to which it must be continually recalled.

The Form of Prayer

Many questions affecting the form of prayer receive a suggestive answer in the prayers of the Bible. In their noble combination of simplicity and solemnity they stand unsurpassed and almost unapproached. The language is so simple and unstudied that, but for the context, one could often suppose it was the petition of a man to his earthly friend. This at least can be said of the Old Testament prayers, and of the prayers of Jesus, though hardly of the prayers of Paul. It must not be forgotten, however, that no direct prayers of Paul have been preserved in their spoken form; they are woven into the course of his epistles, and are characterized by the same rapidity and disregard of the literary proprieties as characterize his writings generally.

But biblical prayer, as a whole, is simple. "Heal me, and I shall be healed; save me, and I shall be saved; for Thou art my praise" (Jer. 17:14). The vivid and passionate simplicity of such prayers could not be surpassed. They are the outcome of the Hebrew mind which saw clearly, and, whether in narrative or prayer, said what it had to say without circumlocution or affectation. Indeed, one test of a good prayer, from the literary point of view—if we may speak of such a thing—would be whether it easily lends itself to translation into Hebrew; in other words, whether it has the directness and simplicity of the Old Testament or the Lord's prayer. The *Te Deum* could stand this test. Assuredly the Lord looketh upon the heart more than upon the form of a prayer. Yet the form is not altogether unimportant, and least of all in public prayer, which, like every other part of public worship, ought to be inspired by a sense of "comeliness and order." Nor is the form so very separable from the content after all. A clumsy, confused, or complicated prayer hardly tends to the edifying of the Church (1 Cor. 14:12). Doubtless God can take these weak things, and let His Spirit shine through them. The heavenly treasure may be enclosed in a very earthen vessel, but the vessel should be as worthy of the treasure as possible. The precious ointment deserves the alabaster box.

"The best prayers," says Dr. John Hunter, "are those which express in the simplest language the simplest needs, trusts and fidelities of the Christian soul." The language must be such that "the other is edified" (1 Cor. 14:17); and, in considering the differences of age and of education in every Christian congregation, that means, in other words, that it must be simple and readily intelligible. It hardly needs to be said that prayer must not be, as the Latin Mass of the Roman Catholic Church, in a foreign language, but there are other kinds of unintelligibility besides that of a foreign tongue. The use of soaring polysyllables, of exaggerated expressions, of poetical quotations, of lengthy sentences, of complicated syntax, of antiquated forms of language or thought—all this goes to defeat the end for which prayer is offered. Instead of edifying, they mystify; and "how is he that fills the place of the unlearned to say the Amen to your thanksgiving, if he does not know what you are saying?" (1 Cor. 14:16).

How the heart warms to the simple words of the Bible!

Thy loving-kindness, O Lord, is in the heavens:
Thy faithfulness reacheth unto the skies.
They righteousness is like the mountains of God:
Thy judgments are a great deep.
O Lord, Thou preservest man and beast.
How precious is Thy loving-kindness, O God.
And the children of men take refuge under the shadow of Thy wings.
They shall be abundantly satisfied with the fatness of Thy house,
And Thou wilt make them drink of the river of Thy pleasures.
For with Thee is the fountain of life:
In Thy light shall we see light (Ps. 36:5–9).

The language is simple, but its power of suggestion is inexhaustible. "It is high as heaven; the measure thereof is longer than the earth, and broader than the sea." True prayer must be simple, not only in the sense that it is plain and intelligible, but also in that it is free from exaggeration. The publican expresses his penitence in half a dozen words; he calls himself a sinner, but not a miserable sinner. It is the simplicities, alike in form and thought, that touch the heart.

Perhaps the exquisite simplicity of the Bible can never, on the same scale, be repeated; and yet the Christian era has also been blessed with prayers which express the needs of men with fidelity, simplicity and beauty. There is a certain noble austerity, as well as simple comprehensiveness, about the sixth century prayer:

> O Lord, we beseech Thee mercifully to receive our
> prayers; and grant that we may both perceive and
> know what things we ought to do, and also may
> have grace and power faithfully to fulfill the same,
> through Jesus Christ our Lord.

More poetic and almost equally simple is the following prayer from the Mozarabic sacramentary:

> Grant us, O Lord, to pass this day in gladness and
> peace, without stumbling and without stain; that,
> reaching the eventide victorious over all tempta-
> tion, we may praise Thee, the eternal God, who
> art blessed, and dost govern all things, world with-
> out end.

Perhaps the simplicity and beauty of the Bible have never been so completely and continuously sustained in subsequent prayer as in the *Imitation of Christ*. Take, for example, the following prayer, addressed to the "most merciful Jesus":

> Grant to me Thy grace that it may be with me,
> and work with me, and continue with me even to
> the end. Grant that I may always desire and will

> that which is to Thee most acceptable and most
> dear. Let Thy will be mine and let my will ever fol-
> low Thine, and be in most excellent accord there-
> with. Let my will be all one with Thy will, and let
> me not be able to will or forego anything but what
> Thou willest or dost not will. Grant to me above
> all things the desire to rest in Thee and to quiet my
> heart in Thee. Thou art the true peace of the heart,
> Thou its only rest: out of Thee all things are full of
> trouble. In this peace, that is, in Thee, the one
> supreme eternal good, I will lay me down and rest.

Such prayers as these exercise an unconscious influence, apart
from their content, by the singular beauty and musical cadence of
the language. The ear is satisfied as well as the heart. And when, in
addition to this, the thought is fresh and unhackneyed, the prayer
is like a breath from the hills of God. Such a prayer, for example, is
that of Robert Louis Stevenson:

> The day returns and brings us the petty round of
> irritating concerns and duties. Help us to play the
> man, help us to perform them with laughter and
> kind faces, let cheerfulness abound with industry.
> Give us to go blithely on our business all this day.
> Bring us to our resting beds, weary and content
> and undishonored, and grant us in the end the gift
> of sleep.

Or still more this:

> We are here upon this isle, a few handfuls of men,
> and how many myriads upon myriads of stalwart
> trees. Teach us the lesson of the trees. . . . Let us
> see ourselves for what we are, one out of the
> countless number of the clans of Thy handiwork.
> When we would despair, let us remember that
> these also please and serve Thee.

No doubt original prayers of this kind may easily degenerate into
the fantastic, but that tendency may be held in check by an ac-

quaintance with the less daring language of the Bible and the more formal prayers of the Christian Church.

Prayer is the outpouring of the heart to God (Ps. 62:8; Lam. 2:19), and, if the heart be that of a poet, the language, which normally tends to be severe and chaste, may well blossom forth into figure. Such figures are found in some of the most passionate prayers of the Bible. Compare, for example, the prayer in Isaiah 63:7–64:12: "As the cattle that go down into the valley, the Spirit of Jehovah caused them to rest" (Is. 63:14). Almost more striking is the reference, a little later on, to the "fire that kindleth the brushwood and causeth the waters to boil" (Is. 64:2). So Jesus prayed that the *cup* might pass from Him. Metaphorical language is quite compatible with the most intense sincerity: it is the natural expression of a poetical mind.

But it does not follow that such language should be imitated. When a prosaic mind expresses itself thus, there is always the suspicion of artificiality; and better a thousand times that prayer be unadorned, even clumsy, than artificial. The garnishing of prayer with quotations from the poets and the hymn-writers is, as a rule, a breach of literary taste, as well as of religious propriety. It is certainly not incompatible with sincerity, but it lacks that simplicity which one has a right to expect in the speech of a child to his father. *When ye pray, say Father.* A child does not quote poetry when he talks confidentially to his father.

On the other hand, where there is a real poetic gift, this may well come to light in the emotional speech of prayer; and this speech will be as natural to one soul as bolder and more prosaic speech to another. No one could fail to be moved by the following beautiful prayer of Christina Rossetti:

> O Lord, with whom is the fountain of life, give us all, we entreat Thee, grace and goodwill to follow the leadings of Thy Holy Spirit. Let the dew of Thy grace descend and abide upon us, refreshing that which droops, and reviving that which is ready to perish, until the day when all Thy faithful people shall drink of the river of Thy pleasures.

The propriety of quoting Scripture extensively in prayer may also be doubted. Sometimes the quotations are ludicrously unnatural on western lips; as when in public prayer a preacher says, "Thou art our Father, though Abraham be ignorant of us, and Israel acknowledge us not" (Is. 63:16); or when, on behalf of his people, he assures God that Assyria shall not save them, and they will not ride upon horses (Hos. 14:3). These touches are completely unnatural to any but members of the ancient people of Israel; and quotations of this kind will tend to disappear the more the historical relations of the Bible are understood.

But there are countless passages in the Psalms and prophets, the gospels and the epistles, which lend themselves very readily to citation in prayer, and a question may be fairly raised as to the propriety of this practice. Unquestionably the temptation is very great. Assuming that the prayer is a real prayer, it is often those very words that have awakened in the mind of the speaker the thought he desires to express. He may find other words, but he is not likely to find better. The thing he would say is there to his hand; why should he not avail himself of it?

Obviously such a question cannot be fully settled by an appeal to the Bible itself, as, in the nature of the case, such citations could only appear in the later books. Time had to elapse and many circumstances had to conspire together before the earlier books could rise to the rank of "Scripture." In the post-exilic literature such allusions begin to be found. Nehemiah, for example, calls upon Jehovah to remember the word which He commanded His servant Moses saying, "If ye trespass, I will scatter you abroad among the peoples, but, if ye return unto me," etc. (Neh. 1:8). This is not an exact quotation, but it is a close reminiscence of Leviticus 26:33 and Deuteronomy 30:2, 3. In a prayer of Ezra (Ezra 9:11) there is a still more elaborate reminiscence of a law—"which Thou hast commanded by Thy servants the prophets"—against intermarriage with the Canaanites, which recalls Deuteronomy 7:3. Similarly the confessional prayer of Daniel acknowledges that the disasters that have befallen the Jewish people are in accordance with that which is written in the law of Moses (Dan. 9:11, 13).

By the time the New Testament was written, practically the whole of the Old Testament was what we may call, for want of a better word, canonical, but, so far as this question is concerned, the early Christians were drawn in opposite directions. On the one hand, there was the exuberant sense of the possession of a new life, which, like all true life, had the desire and the power to create its own forms of expression. This is very conspicuous in the prayers of Paul, which do not reproduce even the prayers of Jesus, though there are naturally a few faint reminiscences (cf. 1 Cor. 10:13; 2 Thess. 3:3; Gal. 1:4). But, on the other hand, there was a very powerful Messianic influence at work in the early Church, impelling the Christians to "show by the Scriptures that Jesus was the Christ" (Acts 18:28). This would naturally affect the prayers, which would often take the form of thanksgiving that the Messiah had come, as had been predicted in ancient Hebrew Scripture. Therefore the tendency to spontaneous prayer would be balanced by a tendency to quote.

An excellent illustration of this is furnished by the prayer offered by the friends of Peter and John after their acquittal: "O Lord, Thou that didst make the heaven and the earth and the sea, and all that in them is; who by the Holy Spirit, by the mouth of our father David, Thy servant, didst say, *Why did the Gentiles rage, and the peoples imagine vain things? The kings of the earth set themselves in array, and the rulers were gathered together, against the Lord and against His Anointed,* etc."* Such a prayer does not make upon us one tithe of the impression made by the simple appeals of Jesus, nor would it be natural to us, but—unless we regard it, with some, simply as a later literary prayer—it is the spontaneous utterance of men filled with the idea that at last had come the Messiah "by prophet-bards foretold."

Jesus does not refer to Scripture in this way,† but He uses it in prayer. On the cross, He prays in the language of Psalm 22:1, "Why hast Thou forsaken Me?" and in a sentence of Psalm 31 He

---

* Acts 4:24–26: the quotation is from Psalm 2:1, 2.
† But cf. John 17:12, which probably comes in part from the author.

commits His spirit into His Father's hand. These quotations are not sufficient, however, to justify the extravagant use of Scripture which is frequently made in modern prayer. The situation must be borne in mind. Jesus was on the cross, in agony: at such a time, what was more natural than that the mind should fall back upon old familiar words? The creative impulse is not at its highest when the body is racked with pain. Then the apt words of others are doubly welcome, and they seem to be our own. But it has to be further noted that, in the case of the second prayer, Jesus gave the familiar words a touch distinctively His own by the addition of the word *Father*. In borrowing from the Psalmist, He did not so much adopt as adapt. There is a sovereign freedom even in His use of the quotation; for the Psalmist commits His spirit to Jehovah for life, while in His words Jesus commits His spirit to His Father in death.

In biblical prayer, reminiscences of Scripture are relatively frequent–consider, for example, the *Magnificat*–but direct quotations are few; and even these are always justified by special circumstances. Perhaps this principle might be applied with advantage to modern prayer. Where there is life, there should be liberty and power: we have perhaps not only the right, but the duty, to express our own thoughts in our own way. But as the Bible is at once the inspiration and the finest expression of those thoughts, its language cannot fail to be a constant stimulus, and it may even be directly appropriated, but, as we have said, if it be used at all, it should, as a rule, be adapted in the spirit of free and living men rather than indolently adopted.

Prayer is an address to God, not to man; therefore it must have a very different ring from the sermon, which is addressed to man, not to God. Yet this very obvious distinction is occasionally forgotten. Some prayers are so didactic and rhetorical that a somnolent person is inclined to suspect that he has slept through the prayer and into the sermon. That ought not to be; nor could it be, if the prayer were a prayer. Prayer is speech, but it ought not to be *a* speech. It is the speech of the heart to God, but it must not be a speech to men in the form of a prayer. This is one of the dangers of public prayer, where the presence of other men can hardly be altogether forgotten—a special danger for one whose profession is preaching.

It is from the prayers that we pray when "the door is shut," and especially in hours of trial, danger, or temptation, that we learn the real nature and meaning of prayer—such a prayer as was offered, for example, by Principal Harper, of Chicago, shortly before his death: "May there be for me a life beyond this life; and in that life may there be work to do, tasks to accomplish. . . . If in any way a soul has been injured or a friend hurt, may the harm be overcome, if it is possible." That is how men pray, when they are face to face with death and reality; and that is the spirit also which should control public prayer. No rhetoric, pyrotechnics, or argument, but reverence, humility, awe, and filial confidence. A child does not preach to his father; no more should the preacher when he speaks to the Father in heaven.

In some of the later prayers of the Old Testament there can be detected a slight tendency to preach. The reminiscence of Deuteronomy 7:3 in Ezra's confession (Ezra 9:11, 12), to which we have already alluded, gives a certain hortatory turn to the prayer: "Now, therefore, give not your daughters unto their sons, neither take their daughters unto your sons, nor seek their peace or their prosperity forever; that ye may be strong, and eat the good of the land, and leave it for an inheritance to your children forever." Of course this may be explained away on the ground that it is a quotation, but it shows how real and obvious the danger is. The same homiletic tendency comes out in another prayer of Ezra, which, though a real prayer, both in form and spirit, might yet also be not unfairly characterized as half-narrative, half-sermon. "They dealt proudly, and hearkened not unto Thy commandments, but sinned against Thine ordinances, *which, if a man do, he shall live in them,* and withdrew the shoulder, and hardened their neck, and would not hear" (Neh. 9:29).

It is obvious that this can only be a feature of long prayers: the danger becomes less as the prayer grows shorter, and therefore, for this reason among many others, short prayers are to be recommended. Biblical prayers are usually short—very much shorter than the average modern prayer. The very earnest prayer of Hezekiah (2 Kgs. 19:15–19) for deliverance from Sennacherib could easily be spoken in less than a minute and a half; and the beautiful thanksgiving of David in 1 Chronicles 29:10–19 in between three and four minutes.

But most of the prayers are much shorter than this; and the teaching and practice of Jesus, as we have seen, go to confirm the impression that the ideal prayer is short. Many public prayers are undoubtedly much too long. The so-called "long prayer" in Scotland has little biblical sanction. In essence the long prayer is a heathen prayer: *your Father knoweth what things ye have need of.* It is refreshing to turn from the elaborate prayers of Ezra to the simple ejaculations of Nehemiah. It is the difference between the practical man of affairs and the professional clergyman. Allowance of course must also be made for the difference in the situation. Nehemiah's prayers are private, Ezra's are public; and the unusual length of Ezra's confession in Nehemiah 9—about nine minutes, and it appears to be unfinished—is explained by the exceptional gravity of the situation. All the long prayers of the Bible—and they are very few—are similarly connected with situations of critical importance. The prayer put into the lips of Solomon in 1 Kings 8 occupies about eight minutes, and that of Daniel in Daniel 9 about five, but the one is connected with the dedication of the temple, an event of epoch-making importance, and the other with its desolation (Dan. 9:17). But the ordinary biblical prayer is short, often astonishingly short; and modern prayer, public and private alike, would do well to recover this essentially biblical quality.

A brief prayer will be more likely than a long one to concentrate itself upon the matter in hand. In the prayer of Hezekiah just alluded to, after a simple ascription of praise to Jehovah as the only God and the Creator, the king at once makes his request: "Hear the words of Sennacherib, wherewith he hath sent him to defy the living God . . . Now save us, I beseech Thee, out of his hand." Besides securing concentration, brevity has the further advantage of keeping the speaker in mind of the elementary fact, which some speakers appear to forget, that prayer is an address to God. There are some who habitually speak of God in the third person. The motive might conceivably be one of reverence, though this was certainly not how Jesus taught His disciples to pray. In other cases, the habit may be unconsciously produced by the influence of preaching, in which God is spoken of, not to. Prayer addressed to God in the third person is, in reality, devout meditation—an excellent thing in its way, and not far removed from prayer, but not to be confused with it.

The long prayer of Ezra to which we have already referred (p. 159), in spite of its narrative and homiletic drift, is a real prayer. *Thou* and *Thee* and *Thine* are everywhere: we are never allowed to forget that we are in the presence of God. Occasionally, indeed, the third person appears in Hebrew prayer, but, except in the Psalms, it is seldom sustained for any length of time; its place is usually at once taken by a second person. Take the prayer of Jacob for example: "If *God* will be with me and keep me . . . of all that *Thou* shalt give me, I will give the tenth unto Thee" (Gen. 28:20–22). Or of Solomon: "Will *God* in very deed dwell on the earth? Behold, heaven and the heaven of heavens cannot contain *Thee*" (1 Kgs. 8:27). Or of Daniel: "Jehovah our God is righteous in all *His* works which He doeth, and we have not obeyed His voice. And now, O Lord our God, that hast brought *Thy* people out of the land of Egypt" (Dan. 9:14, 15). Similarly, a man may refer to himself in the same sentence in the third person and in the first: "*Thy servant* doth know that *I* have sinned" (2 Sam. 19:20).

Especially interesting are the rapid transitions of the Psalms from the second person to the third and *vice versa*.[*] It is this that makes it so difficult to use the Psalms in their entirety as prayers, but it very powerfully suggests the reality and naturalness of the communion of these writers with God. God was the background of

---

[*] Cf. Psalm 23:3, 4. So the third person in Isaiah 63:7–14a glides into the second in 14b–19.

the Hebrew mind. He was never far from any one of them; and whether they speak to Him or of Him, they are with Him. He besets them behind and before, and in a real sense, all their religious speech is speech to Him. Meditation is on the borderland of prayer: Hebrew meditation has crossed the border.

Apart from the Psalms, allusions to God in the third person are rare in Hebrew prayer. As we have seen, they are usually displaced at once by the more direct address; and where the transitions are frequent, as in the Psalms, it is because the devout Hebrew had an unusually powerful consciousness of God. *Nevertheless I am continually with Thee.* But in modern prayer, the use of the third person in addressing God is usually a sign of inattention. The suppliant is forgetting that he is appealing to God, as a man to his heavenly Friend.

God should therefore be directly, not allusively addressed: but how, and how often? When we pray, say *Father.* That ought to settle the first question. This is not of course an absolute condemnation of all other names and epithets whatever. Jesus Himself also said "My God," and to Father He added "Lord of heaven and earth." But it indicates the name by which He should be predominantly addressed, and any epithets which may be added should express His nature not only truly but simply. "O God, Light of the hearts that know Thee, and Life of the souls that love Thee, and Strength of the thoughts that seek Thee; from whom to turn away is to fall, to whom to turn is to rise, and in whom to abide is to stand fast forever." This introduction is very noble, but perhaps a little artificial; it is a literary prayer, and lacks the naïve simplicity of the Bible.

In the light of the teaching and practice of Jesus, and of the Bible generally, which never really overloads its titles, even when, as in the later prayers, it makes liberal use of them, it is interesting to find that Law sets a high devotional value on these epithets, and deliberately recommends their use. We may begin our prayers, he tells us, in words like these: "O Being of all beings, Fountain of all light and glory, gracious Father of men and Angels, whose universal Spirit is everywhere present, giving life, and light, and joy, to all Angels in Heaven, and all creatures upon earth," etc. And again, when we direct petitions to our blessed Lord, let it be in some expression of this kind: "O Savior of the world, God of God, Light of Light: Thou art the brightness of Thy Father's glory, and the express Image of His Person: Thou art the Alpha and Omega, the Beginning and End of all things; Thou that hast destroyed the power of the devil; that hast overcome death; Thou that hast entered into the Holy of Holies, that sittest at the right hand of the Father, that art high above all thrones and principalities, that makest intercession for all the world; Thou that art the Judge of the quick and the dead; Thou that wilt speedily come down in Thy Father's glory, to reward all men according to their works: be Thou my Light and my Peace."

Law justifies the use of epithets by insisting on their power to raise our hearts to lively acts of adoration. We are to begin by using such expressions as may make us most sensible of the greatness and power of the Divine Nature; and he observes rightly enough that, as words have a certain power of raising thoughts in the soul, so those words which speak of God in the highest manner are the most useful and edifying in our prayers. But there is something artificial, or at least unbiblical, about this attempt to create an atmosphere in which the nature of God can be more readily apprehended. When a Hebrew sought to kindle in his audience a sense of the divine goodness, he pointed them to history (Hos. 11:1–4; Amos 2:9, 10, etc.); or he revived his own wavering faith by meditating on the mysteries of the moral world, and on the ultimate destinies of the good and the bad (Ps. 73:16–20). The exercise prescribed by Law may have its uses, but it is not in the spirit of biblical prayer. The men of the Bible did not have to whip themselves into a devout mood: they spoke to God as a man speaks to his father or his friend.

Nor is it necessary to repeat the name of God often in prayer. A man does not name in every sentence the friend to whom he speaks. There is even a certain unreality about the too frequent use of the divine name in prayer; if the speaker really felt that God were as near him as the men about him, he would probably not

name Him so often. It is striking that, in some of the most passionate prayers of the Old Testament, God is named very seldom, and
even then very simply. There can, of course, be no law on such a
point. Elijah, at a critical moment on Carmel, addresses Jehovah
three times within two verses (1 Kgs. 18:36, 37).

But in the great prayers the direct addresses are few. For twenty-
five verses in the prayer at the dedication of the temple (1 Kgs.
8:28–53), there is no direct address at all. In Ezra 9 the addresses
are few, chiefly at the beginning and the end. When Jeremiah
pleads in 12:1–3 with all the energy of perplexity and disappointment, he only says, "O Jehovah," and that only twice. Similarly,
this is the only address (Is. 63:16, 17; 64:8) in the very powerful
appeal of Isaiah 43:7–64:12. Job, in 10:2–22, a prayer delivered at
white heat, never mentions the name of God at all. This very curious circumstance, that the most passionate prayers have the very
simplest addresses, and sometimes none at all, should perhaps be
more generally borne in mind in modern prayer. The custom of
multiplying epithets grew up very early in the Christian Church,
and it has more or less influenced all subsequent prayer. On this,
too, the word of Jesus has a bearing, that men will not be heard
for their much speaking.

There is a certain solemn stateliness about biblical prayer. The
threefold invocation of Jacob:

> The God before whom my fathers Abraham and Isaac did walk,
> The God who hath shepherded me all my life long unto this day,
> The Angel who hath redeemed me from all evil
> (Gen. 48:15, 16; cf. Dan. 9:19).

reminds me of the threefold priestly blessing:

> Jehovah bless thee, and keep thee:
> Jehovah make His face to shine upon thee, and be
>   gracious unto thee:
> Jehovah lift up His countenance upon thee, and give thee peace
> (Num. 6:24–26).

What is perhaps less often noticed is the orderliness of prayer in the Bible. In discussing tragedy, Aristotle (*Poetics,* 7:3) defines a whole as that which has beginning, middle, and end. A good prayer, like a good poem, should be, in this sense, a whole; it should have a beginning, a middle, and an end. Its parts may not be strung together anyhow: it must move on from point to point, controlled by a sense of decency and order. It must not be obtrusively logical, for prayer is not argument, but it ought to have a natural consecution. Nothing could be more orderly, for example, than the Lord's prayer. It is not a series of disconnected petitions; it is the development of a single thought, presented, with an almost Greek regard for symmetry, from two complementary sides.

The same sense of order characterizes all the longer prayers of the Old Testament. The prayer of Solomon, for example, begins with an ascription of praise. Its first real petition (1 Kgs. 8:31, 32) is for the visible establishment of the moral order; and then, with much variety, beneath which is a real unity, the prayer beseeches the mercy of God upon sinners who turn in penitence to Him. So the prayer in Isaiah 63:7–64:12 begins by "making mention of the loving-kindnesses of Jehovah," and then continues with entreaty and confession. In Nehemiah 1:5–11 an introduction emphasizing the might and the faithfulness of Jehovah is followed by an elaborate confession and a short petition. Similarly the prayer of Ezra in Nehemiah 9:6–37 begins with an ascription of praise to Jehovah for His might manifested in creation and His love in history, and this is followed by confession and petition.

Generally speaking, the order of the longer prayers is: ascription of praise or thanksgiving, confession, petition. Especially secure is the place of praise or thanksgiving at the beginning of the prayer. Besides the cases mentioned, Hezekiah's prayer for deliverance from Sennacherib so begins (2 Kgs. 19:15), David's prayer of thanks for the free-will offering (1 Chr. 29:11–13), Jehoshaphat's prayer before the battle (2 Chr. 20:6), and the probably post-exilic prayer in Jeremiah 32:17–23 (cf. Jer. 10:6, 7). One lesson to be learned from this is a lesson that the New Testament, as we have seen, teaches with exceptional power—that praise and thanksgiving are the first duty in prayer. But another is that prayer should be orderly. God is a God of order, not of confusion.

Again, prayer must be intelligent, as well as orderly: indeed it cannot be orderly without being intelligent. The speaker must know what he is praying for, and what he is thanking God for. *For this cause,* says Paul more than once: "for this cause I bow my knees unto the Father," (Eph. 3:14) and "thank God without ceasing" (1 Thess. 2:13). This is the attitude of the man who said, "I will pray with the spirit and *with the understanding also"* (1 Cor. 14:15).

But while intelligent, it will not be obtrusively theological. Doubtless every thinking man will endeavor to concatenate his religious thought; and he will not be intellectually satisfied till he sees it in its relations. But prayer is not the place for theological opinion or doctrine, as such. "Though I walk through the valley of the deep shadow, I will fear no evil, for Thou art with me." How He will be with me I cannot tell, and on that I may speculate, but that He will be with me I know, and with these and similar words I may gratefully approach Him in prayer. I have heard a man pray, "We thank Thee, O God, for the doctrine of the Trinity." There is no biblical warrant for a prayer like that. We thank God for facts, not for doctrines. Doctrines have their day and cease to be, but the facts abide forever.

Occasionally, though seldom, in the longer prayers, simple statements occur, which, strictly speaking, do not belong to the essence of prayer, and which have perhaps a remotely theological flavor. For example: "Thou knowest the hearts of all the children of men" (1 Kgs. 8:39); "there is no man that sinneth not" (1 Kgs. 8:46). Here again we may say, "Your heavenly Father knows," and such statements should not be frequent. But they are not in themselves objectionable; for they are statements, not of doctrine, but of fact. Everyone who believes in God and who knows the human heart must admit their truth. Prayer gathers about the fundamental needs, confessions, and gratitudes, and expresses these in language that is simple and free from the technicalities of theology. We pray as children, not as scholars. When ye pray, say Father, and let the thought of this simple human relationship control all our speech to God.

The religion of Jesus Christ is a religion of freedom; and the New Testament is true to itself in making no prescriptions as to the time and place of prayer. It does not even prescribe family worship any more than it enjoins the abolition of slavery. But it is supremely practical, just because it prescribes so little. It creates a spirit, and the spirit must express itself: how and when and where will depend upon circumstances. But where the circumstances are normal and regular, the expression is likely also to be regular. Regularity, however, so easily degenerates into routine that, by the very regularity, the real object of prayer may be defeated, and its seriousness forgotten. In every possible way, therefore, it is necessary for those who lead the devotions of others, whether in church or home, to preserve the vitality of prayer, without which it is of no more value than the sounding of brass or the tinkling of cymbals.

Every day we must allow ourselves to be impressed anew, and as if for the first time, by the wonder of God's goodness, and by the mystery, the pathos and the frailty of our little lives. "Morning by morning He brings His justice to the light: He faileth not" (Zeph. 3:5). That prayer will be hearty and spontaneous which rises from the lips of one who, with ever new delight and wonder, meets that goodness which unfailingly greets him in the morning, and un-slumberingly watches over him in the night. Every day is a fresh reminder of the need of God—for bread to eat and for deliverance from evil. If *He* fails not, but comes to us more bright and sure than the shining of tomorrow's sun, why should we fail? Why should we not gladly come with regular, fresh, unwearied gratitude to Him who renews His loving-kindness in the morning, and His faithfulness every night?

Among these regular prayers may be included grace before meat. This is not prescribed any more than they are, though, as we have seen, it must have been practiced (cf. Rom. 14:6). A question might fairly be raised, however, whether it is reasonable to connect so deliberately the taking of food with religion, while few would so readily think of formally beseeching the blessing of God upon a lecture or a concert they were about to attend. The nurture of the spirit should surely stand as high in the estimation of a Christian man as the sustenance of the body; and we should be at least as grateful for the one as the other. *Give thanks,* says Paul, *always for all things* (Eph. 5:20); and in consistency it might be said that one was bound either to give thanks aloud for these things as well, or to allow his gratitude for food to remain unspoken, or to express itself practically in a deeper sense of brotherly fellowship with his companions at table, who are all sons of a common Father.

Charles Lamb says, "I own that I am disposed to say grace upon twenty other occasions in the course of the day besides my dinner." Though "theoretically no enemy to graces, practically they seem to me to involve something awkward and unreasonable"—at any rate "at the heaped-up tables of the pampered and luxurious," though he admits that they are proper enough at a poor man's table or at the "simple and unprovocative repast of children." There is a good deal of truth in this distinction; and many another besides Lamb has "felt in his mind the incompatibility of the scene of the viands before him with the exercise of a calm and rational gratitude." Such were certainly not the dinners contemplated by Jesus, when He encouraged His disciples to pray for their daily bread.

But for the simple meal, a prayer which raises a natural act into a sacrament, though it cannot be said to be necessary, is peculiarly appropriate. There is no reason why we should not also express our gratitude to God for the anticipated blessings of music or literature. Better level up than down. Better thank Him *for all things at all times,* than never formally thank Him at all. But grace before meat, as Law says, is a proof that religion is to be the rule and measure of all the actions of ordinary life.

With regard to the length of such prayers, it is interesting to see how he characterizes the custom of his times. "To such a pass are we now come that, though the custom is yet preserved, yet we can hardly bear with him that seems to perform it with any degree of seriousness, and look upon it as a sign of a fanatical temper, if a man has not done, as soon as he begins." Certainly, if prayer is to be offered at such times, it must be offered reverently, but even a very brief prayer may be reverent. The prayer Jesus offered may have simply been, "Blessed be the Creator of the fruits of the earth," but the effect was indescribable.

Free and Liturgical Prayer

One question which can never lose its interest or importance, is that of the legitimacy and use of fixed forms of prayer; and we shall now consider what contribution the teaching and the practice of the Bible make towards its solution. There can be no doubt that free prayer is, on the whole, more consonant with the idea of prayer than fixed. If prayer be a real intercourse of the human heart with God, prescribed or studied words would seem to be no more natural than in intercourse with men; and, as Dr. Rainsford has said, "If all men prayed always as some men pray sometimes, there would be no need of a liturgy."

In particular, it might be argued that the true Protestant not only feels the impulse, but is under the obligation, to pray in his own words. Just as he claims the right and the duty to think for himself, so it might be said that he has a similar right and duty to express his thoughts, to God no less than to man, in his own way. But the retort would be easy. The Protestant, if he be an educated man, does not, in his thinking, ignore the thoughts of other men. He is not, and could not be if he would, an absolutely independent worker. He builds upon the labors of others, welcomes the help of all who have done or are doing work similar to his own. His independence is not absolute, but relative; it is the independence of a man who stands in human society, a debtor to the present, and a very heavy debtor to the past. Even his independence, though in a sense his birthright, was historically won for him. He can never rid himself of the obligation to learn from others, and his life would be infinitely the poorer if he could. This indeed would not be an argument for the use of fixed forms, but it would be an argument for the study of the best devotional literature that the world has produced; and even those who insist most vehemently on the duty of free prayer confess, by their frequent use of the Lord's prayer, sometimes also by the abundance of Scripture quotations with which they embellish their own prayers, their enormous debt to the Bible.

Naturally the question we are discussing is not directly raised in the Bible. The only prescribed prayer in the Old Testament is that to be offered at the presentation of the firstfruits (Deut. 26); and, with the exception of the Lord's prayer, the New Testament prescribes no prayer at all. Nor is it possible to believe that Jesus, who was the uncompromising foe of the mechanical in religion, *prescribed* that prayer. It is simply given that men may learn how to pray: in the spirit of sons and free men they are to pray that prayer or any other like it they please. But it must be borne in mind that even the Lord's prayer is a consecration of the past. It is original in the noblest sense of the word, but most of its individual petitions can be paralleled more or less closely from the Old Testament and other Jewish prayers. It is fresh and spontaneous—nothing could be more so—but it does not sweep haughtily aside the prayers of the past. It recognizes their abiding value by the way in which it uses them. It at once legitimates and transforms them.

We have further seen that, on the cross, Jesus made use of the ancient prayers of His people, when His own need was very sore, and thus established the principle, in itself so natural, that our thoughts may be sent to God upon words composed by others. This meets the objection so commonly made to liturgical prayer, that, as it is not the immediate and spontaneous expression of the speaker's own feeling, it is very apt to be thoughtless or even insincere. But there is no reason why another, who has been in a situation essentially like my own, should not completely succeed in expressing my feeling within that situation; and there is no reason why I should not adopt that expression and utter it with the same sincerity, as if it were my own. In the deepest sense it is my own.

Like lyric poetry, it belongs to all whose mood it adequately expresses. No one who, in public worship, sings psalms or hymns which partake of the nature of prayer, can consistently object to the use of fixed forms of prayer. If he can lift his thoughts to God on the words of another in song, why should it be less possible in a spoken prayer?

In private and family devotions, the help of others will be, in certain cases, almost indispensable. Native timidity, lack of experience or initiative, and many other reasons may practically compel those who are anxious to maintain such prayers, to resort to devotional helps. Just as Jesus laid the religious literature of His own people under contribution, so may we. Besides finding expression for those who cannot express their thoughts and feelings for themselves, such helps, if wisely chosen, may do much to enlarge the range of their religious interests. But the helps must be used in the spirit of free men. Here again, the words of Law, whether we agree with them entirely or not, are apposite: "Though I think a form of prayer very necessary and expedient for public worship, yet if anyone can find a better way of raising his heart unto God in private than by prepared forms of prayer, I have nothing to object against it. It seems right for everyone to begin with a form of prayer; and if, in the midst of his devotions, he finds his heart ready to break forth into new and higher strains of devotion, he should leave his form for a while, and follow those fervors of his heart, till it again wants the assistance of his usual petitions."

The advantages of fixed prayer at public worship are obvious. Most of all perhaps is the sense which it brings—if the prayers be ancient—of continuity with the past, and with the present Church of Christ throughout the world. We pray to *our* Father; and the feeling of continuity and solidarity would undoubtedly be strengthened, if, at least in certain parts of public worship, the same prayers persisted throughout the ages and across the world. Religion has a past as well as a present, and no reverent man would wish to cut himself from that. Rather would he wish to do everything that was not inimical to his spiritual welfare, to encourage his sense of fellowship with his ancient and distant brethren in Christ. The Holy

Catholic Church would be even more impressive to the imagination, if she raised her prayer petitions to God, not only with united heart, but with united voice. Besides, religion, though it is creative, is also, in the deepest sense conservative. It has to do with the things that abide, the needs and the hopes of men, which are ever the same; and if a worthy expression has been found for these things—simple, true and beautiful—why may it, too, not be suffered to abide, especially as it comes to us fragrant with the memory of myriads of faithful souls?

But the prayer must be a real prayer, not a recitation. The conduct of public worship must, it is to be feared, often create the impression that the liturgy is a performance rather than a prayer. Where a speaker is not under the obligation to create expressions for his own thoughts, but finds them ready made in the book before him, he is apt to go too fast. His own devotional mood is very seriously imperiled, while that of the people may be completely destroyed. When to this it is added that the Lord's prayer may be repeated twice and even three times in the course of a single service, one is compelled in candor to ask whether it is ever really prayed at all. *Do not use vain repetitions, as the heathen do.* Saying a prayer is not praying; and a prayer which is galloped instead of being uttered with reverent and befitting solemnity, is not likely to do much for the edifying of the Church.

It must, of course, be presupposed that, if liturgical forms are used, the worshipers must pray *with* the speaker. Public prayer is necessarily expressed in general terms; it cannot deal, like private prayer, with specific situations. It is offered for the forgiveness of sins, for the consolation of the suffering, etc., but such a prayer can leave the worshiper completely untouched unless he pours into it his own experience, asking forgiveness for the sins which he has committed, and consolation for the sick whom he personally knows. Free prayer easily introduces the personal element which, in the more guarded language of liturgical prayer, the worshiper has to supply by an effort of his own imagination; and, if the prayer is not eccentric or too specific, the worshiper may be touched and helped. The atmosphere of personal experience lies about spontaneous prayer. This is its advantage over liturgical prayer, but it constitutes also a weakness and a danger.

For behind liturgical prayer lies the wisdom, the piety, the dignity of the whole Church: the congregation can depend upon "comeliness and order." This is by no means so certain where prayer is free. It is interesting to note that Paul was led to lay down this great principle, *Let all things be done with seemliness and order*, by observing the dangers of an unbridled individualism (1 Cor. 14:40). The ecstasy created by the spirit of the new religion had thrown the Corinthian Church into disorder. Sometimes two even seem to have spoken at once; and under such conditions, especially where some of the members were so powerfully moved as to express themselves in ways completely unintelligible to others, edification was an impossibility.

Similar dangers will always be possible where individualism is not under some more or less official control. In a church in which free prayer holds, the congregation is absolutely at the mercy of the leader. If he be a man of piety and culture, he can speak and pray to the edifying of the church (1 Cor. 14:3–5); and in his prayer there may be a warmth of personal feeling and a ring of personal conviction which are apt to be lacking in the more impersonal prayers of a liturgy. But what if he be a man of bad taste or little culture, a man with no sense of the serious dignity which ought to mark the worship of the Most High God? Far be it from us to over-estimate the value of culture and taste; nor must we forget that those who are in a position to know have assured us that, during the recent marvelous movement in Wales, simple uneducated people, who had never before opened their lips in public, could pour out their hearts to God in language of astonishing beauty. But the fact remains that many a service has been spoiled by the slovenliness, vulgarity, and even irreverence of the public prayer. In a liturgical service this is all but impossible. The preacher has the Church behind him; and, if he does her justice, she will do him justice. If he brings to the liturgy feeling and conviction, she will give him words which will move by their beauty and edify by their truth.

In free prayer, not only the speaker's education, but even his temperament and the condition of his health will affect the nature of the prayers he offers. He will not always be able to say the thing he would. He may be dull or depressed, and this mood may be reflected in his prayers; or—especially in his earlier efforts—he may suffer from nervousness or temporary loss of memory, and this may easily disturb the devotional temper of the congregation. Public prayer is attended by all the difficulties that beset public speech generally. Only men of great natural gift, wide reading, and much experience, can address their fellows extempore in language that is really noble and graceful; and though, in the moment of prayer, feeling may be more exalted, and a man may express a better and deeper self than he can in the more critical atmosphere of a public meeting, it does not follow that his exaltation will exempt him from idiosyncrasies and errors due to inexperience, temperament or the state of his health.

A liturgy affords an absolute safeguard in cases of this kind. The speaker may be depressed, but the prayer will not suffer; for it is not so much he that prays as the Church that prays in him, and her noble words may cheer and strengthen not only the congregation, but himself. He may be nervous when he faces the people, and his thoughts may swim away from him, but the prayer is not impoverished, for he says the thing that needs to be said. As a protection against the eccentricity, the frailty and the inexperience of the individual, the service of the liturgy is inestimable.

But what does the Bible say thereto? At first sight, it cannot be said to give much direct encouragement to, or supply much direct material for, liturgical prayer. The prayers of the Bible are relatively very few; and anyone who has ever taken the trouble to go carefully through them will be surprised to find how comparatively little there is in them that can be used today in its biblical form; and most of that little comes from the Psalms. The reasons for this are many. Ancient Hebrew prayer is often rendered impossible by the spirit of Jesus. Jeremiah and Nehemiah could pray for vengeance upon their enemies, but *with you it shall not be so.* Even the prayers of Jesus cannot all be used by us. We may learn much from the great prayer in John 17, but it can never be our prayer. It is the Lord's prayer, and His only.

The principal reason, however, why only a few fragments of biblical prayer are available for modern use is that those prayers are rooted in history. Prayer, like prophecy, has a historical context. *In that day shall this song be sung in the land of Judah* (Is. 26:1). Only on that day and on days like it would such a song have been appropriate. The biblical prayers are prompted by particular situations; and as history never quite repeats itself, a prayer composed for one situation—if it be at all specific, as Old Testament prayers at least usually are—would not be strictly appropriate to any subsequent situation. It is these specific allusions that help us to feel the reality of biblical prayer and how truly it is the child of the moment. Ezra prays, for example: "O our God, let not all the travail seem little before Thee, that hath come upon us . . . *since the time of the kings of Assyria unto this day*" (Neh. 9:32). And again: "Our God hath not forsaken us in our bondage, but hath extended lovingkindness unto us *in the sight of the kings of Persia*" (Ezra 9:9). The prayer is created by the immediate, specific, historical need, and can therefore, in that particular form, never be offered again.

Yet how does it come that so many of the Psalms which are most, if not all, born in a definite historical situation, can be sung, at least in part, at the public worship of a people so remote in historical experience and mental outlook as we are from the Hebrews? Is it not because their writers instinctively grasped the universal element in the situation? By dropping that which is adventitious and by expressing, with superb simplicity, only that which is essential to the situation, they touch the universal heart and earn an unchallengeable immortality. In other words, where ultimate religious needs and emotions have found perfect expression, that expression may be gratefully acknowledged and conscientiously retained. Where the needs are the same, the words may be the same. In Gethsemane, Jesus "prayed a third time, *saying again the same words*" (Matt. 26:44). Here is an argument for a fixed form in prayer. If the situation is the same, we may pray three times, or a thousand times, "saying again the same words."

Now is not this directly applicable to the situation created by public worship? The ultimate needs of any Christian congregation, formally assembled for worship, are ever the same. There are always the young and the old, the happy and the sad, the earnest and the indifferent, the tempted and the defeated; and it is only their common needs that can form the subject of public petition. Those, for example, for whom intercession is offered will, speaking generally, be always the same: for those in authority over us, for those in danger, doubt and difficulty, for the sick and the suffering, the bereaved and the dying, for all sorts and conditions of men, for ourselves, for the Church of Christ throughout the world. This point need not be further amplified. In every congregation these elements are constant; and if fitting expression has once been found for needs that are ever the same, why should it be abandoned in favor of an expression that is, in most cases, pretty sure to be less noble and beautiful, without necessarily being any more sincere?

Besides, the prayer which we call extempore is seldom really extempore. It is like many a so-called extempore speech—carefully prepared beforehand, and probably in the case of most conscientious ministers the thought to be expressed has at least been considered. In this respect the man who prays is like the true orator who, in the words of a French writer, "knows what he will say, but does not know how he will say it"; and this is perhaps the ideal of free prayer. So that the contrast between what is commonly called free and liturgical prayer is nothing like so absolute as is usually supposed. There would be a real contrast between liturgical prayer and a prayer which the speaker, without the least premeditation, uttered in immediate dependence upon the inspiration of the Spirit.

But it may be very seriously doubted whether such public prayer would be fruitful or edifying. Volubility is one thing; worshipful prayer is another. God is a God of order, and the Church meets to be edified. In point of fact, however, this is not, as a rule, the sort of prayer that is offered in the formal worship of the non-liturgical churches, but a prayer whose contents have at least been considered, if not prepared. Besides, almost everyone, who has to engage regularly in public prayer, falls into ruts of his own, and creates a liturgy for himself—only, as a rule, infinitely less beautiful, dignified, and comprehensive than that of the liturgical churches. So that it is not so much a question whether there shall be a liturgy or not, as whether the liturgy which, in a sense, is inevitable, shall be worthy or unworthy.

It is sometimes argued that a liturgical service is more likely to produce listlessness and inattention among worshipers than free prayer. No one will deny the great dangers associated with the frequent repetition of familiar words. But it is not by any means certain that the average congregation will follow a free prayer much more attentively than a fixed. The feeling of expectancy, with which it may be supposed a new prayer is listened to, is greatly blunted by the congregation's familiarity with the minister's particular turns of thought and expression. The "degraded liturgy"—as it has been called—of the individual, can produce an effect just as narcotic as the noble liturgy of the church. And even when the prayer is unhackneyed, the thoughts of many will wander, especially if the prayer be long. All public prayer, whether free or fixed, demands an effort of appropriation on the part of the congregation. They must *say the Amen* (1 Cor. 14:16): they must pray with the leader, must make his prayer their own by a mental and spiritual effort; and those who do this in any church are perhaps not so numerous as we imagine.

Both free and liturgical prayers are beset by serious dangers. Much more than liturgical prayer does free prayer bring the temptation to make an impression. It is speech before men, and is therefore very apt to become speech *to* men. This is the most hideous caricature of prayer. No disposition is so inimical to the spirit of prayer as ostentation, and one does not wonder at Jesus' scathing rebuke of the prayers at the street corners. The same spirit can too easily animate the public prayer in the congregation. The ancient "hypocrites" prayed, "that they might be seen of men"; and the modern, that they may be heard of them. Of course, the religion of Christ is a social religion, and public prayer is therefore a necessity, but its dangers are many and subtle. It is difficult, almost impossible to secure that detachment of spirit which is essential to prayer. The leader must both remember the people, and forget them. He must remember them, for it is their united needs he has to voice. Yet he must forget them: he must hold direct and unimpeded speech with God, he must speak as if he were alone. And that is difficult: it is not easy to remain entirely uninfluenced by the presence of others.

But if extempore prayer has its difficulties and dangers, no less has liturgical prayer. It was instituted partly in the interests of form; and form very easily becomes formality. Where there is little variety in the service, and the same words are repeated week after week, the spirit may easily grow insensible to their meaning. Here, more than anywhere else, the letter can kill. Custom can make fools of us all. The noble prayers may be babbled instead of being prayed, and their spiritual effect upon leader and people may be no more than would be secured by a Tibetan praying machine, moved by wind or water. This danger may be partly obviated by variety in the liturgy, and by giving the congregation a greater part in the service, but it comes back to this, that a prayer, whether free or fixed, as it is a deliberate appeal to God, must always be regarded as one of the most solemn and responsible acts of the religious life, and has therefore ever to be entered upon with a sincerity which custom must not be allowed to dull. Probably the spiritual effort necessary to interpret feelingly a familiar liturgical prayer is greater than that needed to offer an extempore prayer.

Both kinds of prayer have their advantages. In liturgical prayer there can be no unpleasant surprises. It prevents liberty from degenerating into license: it offers the same safeguard against irresponsible individualism as a creed offers against heresy. *If two of you be agreed* . . . a liturgy secures this agreement. Again, in prayer a man speaks to God as to his friend, that is, not formally, but the conditions of public worship demand form, and liturgy secures this. The "comeliness and order" which ought to characterize public worship may certainly be present when much is left to the initiative of the individual, but in a liturgical service they are guaranteed. On the other hand, if religion is a real and living thing, the individual can hardly help feeling at times the impulse to express his emotion in words of his own, and he ought not to be deprived of this liberty which is his birthright as a son of the Heavenly Father. In the prayers of the Bible, pious men speak as they are moved by circumstance; out of the depths each man cries in his own way. And this great lesson of the Bible must never be forgotten or repudiated. We are often told that Jesus prayed, but seldom what He prayed. He does not bind a yoke upon the neck of His disciples: He wishes us to be ourselves.

The free churches have something to learn from the dignity, beauty, and order of the liturgical churches; while these, in their turn, have to learn from the freedom, the initiative, the versatility of the others. The ideal church would combine the excellences of both, the dignity of the one with the fervor of the other. Some of her prayers would be fixed, and some would be free. The leader of a congregation which believes in free prayer should not be deprived of the right to express his thoughts in a way more beautiful and dignified than any expression of his own is ever likely to be; the leader in a liturgical church should not be deprived of the right to speak to God as a man to his friend. The past may be an inspiration, but it must not be allowed to become an incubus. We shall cherish and perpetuate all that is best in it, but we too will create something which posterity would not willingly let die; and so the religious instinct, as ancient as humanity, and as fresh as the morning, will continue to enrich the world forever.

Part 3

The Prayers of the Bible
Collected

The Prayers of the
Old Testament

10. The prayer of Noah.

Cursed be Canaan;
A servant of servants may he be to his brethren,
Blessed be Jehovah, the God of Shem;
And let Canaan be his servant.
God enlarge Japheth,
And let him dwell in the tents of Shem;
And let Canaan be his servant.
(Gen. 9:25–27)

11. Lot's prayer during his escape from Sodom.*

Behold now, Thy servant hath found favor in Thy sight, and
Thou hast magnified Thy loving-kindness which Thou hast
showed unto me in saving my life; and I cannot escape to the
mountain, lest evil overtake me and I die. Behold now, this city is
near to flee unto, and it is a little one. Oh, let me escape thither,
and my soul shall live.
(Gen. 19:19, 20)

*12. Prayer of Abraham's servant, that he might be guided to the right wife
for Isaac.*

O Jehovah, God of my master Abraham, I pray Thee, send me
good speed this day, and show kindness unto my master Abraham.
Behold, I am standing by the well of water and the daughters of
the men of the city are coming out to draw water; and, let it come
to pass, that the damsel to whom I shall say, "Let down thy pitcher,
I pray thee, that I may drink"; and she shall say, "Drink, and I will
give thy camels drink also": let the same be she that Thou hast appointed for Thy servant Isaac; and thereby shall I know that Thou
hast showed kindness unto my master.
(Gen. 24:12–14, 42–44)

---

* This prayer is addressed, probably not to Jehovah, but to one of the two angels, from whom, in v. 13, Jehovah is expressly distinguished.

13. Jacob's prayer, on his return, for deliverance from Esau.

O God of my father Abraham, and God of my father Isaac, O Jehovah, who didst say unto me, "Return to thy country and to thy kindred, and I will do thee good." I am not worthy of the least of all the mercies and of all the faithfulness which Thou hast showed unto Thy servant; for with my staff I passed over this Jordan, and now I am become two bands. Deliver me, I pray Thee, from the hand of my brother, from the hand of Esau; for I fear him, lest he come and smite me, the mother with the children. And Thou didst say, "I will surely do thee good, and make thy seed as the sand of the sea, which cannot be numbered for multitude."
(Gen. 32:9–12)

14. Jacob's prayer for a blessing.

I will not let Thee go, except Thou bless me.
(Gen. 32:26)

15. Moses' prayer for the presence of God with himself and the people.

If I have found favor in Thy sight, show me now Thy ways, that I may know Thee, so that I may indeed find favor in Thy sight; and consider that this nation is Thy people. . . . If Thy presence go not with us, carry us not up hence. For wherein now shall it be known that I have found favor in Thy sight, I and Thy people? Is it not in that Thou goest with us?
(Ex. 33:13–16)

16. Moses' prayer for a vision of the Divine glory.

I pray Thee, show me Thy glory.
(Ex. 33:18)

17. Moses' prayer regarding the rebels.

Respect not Thou their offering: I have not taken one ass from them, neither have I hurt one of them.
(Num. 16:15)

18. Moses' prayer that he might be permitted to set foot upon the promised land.

O Lord Jehovah, Thou hast begun to show Thy servant Thy greatness, and Thy strong hand; for what God is there in heaven or in earth that can do according to Thy works, and according to Thy mighty acts? I pray Thee, let me go over and see the good land that is beyond the Jordan, that goodly hill-country, and Lebanon.

(Deut. 3:24, 25)

19. Prayer of the Baal priests on Mount Carmel.

O Baal, hear us.

(1 Kgs. 18:26)

20. Elijah's prayer on Mount Carmel.

O Jehovah, the God of Abraham, and of Isaac and of Israel, let it be known this day that thou art God in Israel, and that I am Thy servant, and that I have done all these things at Thy word. Hear me, O Jehovah, hear me, that this people may know that Thou, Jehovah, art God, and that Thou hast turned their heart back again.

(1 Kgs. 18:36, 37)

21. Elijah's prayer for death.

It is enough. Now, O Jehovah, take away my life; for I am not better than my fathers.

(1 Kgs. 19:4)

22. Elisha's prayer regarding the Aramean army which invaded Israel.

Smite this people, I pray Thee, with blindness.

(2 Kgs. 6:18)

23. Solomon's prayer for wisdom.

O Jehovah, my God, Thou hast made Thy servant king instead of David my father; and I am but a little child: I know not how to go out or come in. And Thy servant is in the midst of Thy people

which Thou hast chosen, a great people that cannot be numbered
nor counted for multitude. Give therefore Thy servant an understanding heart to judge Thy people, that I may discern between
good and evil; for who is able to judge this great people of Thine?
(1 Kgs. 3:7–9)

24. Hosea's prayer for the infertility of his sinful people.
Give them, O Jehovah—what wilt Thou give? give them a mis-
carrying womb and dry breasts.
(Hos. 9:14)

*25. Hezekiah's prayer, terrified by the taunts of the Assyrians, and their threat-
ened assault upon Jerusalem.*
O Jehovah, God of Israel, that sittest above the cherubim, Thou
art the God, even Thou alone, of all the kingdoms of the earth:
Thou hast made heaven and earth. Incline Thine ear, O Jehovah,
and hear; open Thine eyes, O Jehovah, and see; and hear the words
of Sennacherib, wherewith he hath sent him to defy the living God.
Of a truth, Jehovah, the kings of Assyria have laid waste the nations
and their lands, and have cast their gods into the fire; for they were
no gods, but the work of men's hands, wood and stone—therefore
they have destroyed them. Now therefore, O Jehovah, our God,
save Thou us, I beseech Thee, out of his hand, that all the kingdoms of the earth may know, that Thou, Jehovah, art God alone.
(2 Kgs. 19:15–19; Is. 37:16–20)

*26. Hezekiah's prayer, when he receives the announcement of his impending
death.*
Remember now, O Jehovah, I beseech Thee, how I have walked
before Thee in truth and with a perfect heart, and have done that
which is good in Thy sight.
(2 Kgs. 20:3; Is. 38:3)

27. Isaiah's response to the Divine call.
Here am I; send me. (Is. 6:8)

28. Prayer for help, perhaps shortly before Sennacherib's invasion.

O Jehovah, be gracious unto us;
We have waited for Thee.
Be Thou our arm every morning,
Our salvation also in the time of trouble.
(Is. 33:2)

29. Prayer of Judah "in the time of their trouble."

Arise, and save us.
(Jer. 2:27)

30. Prayer that Jehovah would punish the heathen, for their treatment of His people.

O Jehovah, I know that the way of man is not in himself; it is not in man that walketh to direct his steps. O Jehovah, correct me, but in measure; not in Thine anger, lest Thou bring me to nothing. Pour out Thy fury upon the nations that know Thee not, and upon the families that call not upon Thy name: for they have devoured Jacob, yea, they have devoured him, and consumed him, and laid waste his habitation.
(Jer. 10:23–25)

31. Jeremiah, persecuted, commits his cause to God.

O Jehovah of hosts, who judgest righteously, who triest the heart and the mind, I shall see Thy vengeance upon them; for unto Thee have I committed by cause.
(Jer. 11:20; 20:12)

32. Jeremiah, in his perplexity, prays for vengeance upon his persecutors.

Righteous art Thou, O Jehovah; how could I contend with Thee? Yet there are questions of justice that I would speak of with Thee. Why doth the way of the wicked prosper? Why are all they at ease that deal very treacherously? Thou hast planted them, yea, they have taken root; they grow, yea, they bring forth fruit; Thou art near in their mouth and far from their heart.

But Thou, O Jehovah, knowest me, Thou seest me and triest my heart toward Thee. Pull them out like sheep for the slaughter, and prepare them for the day of slaughter.

(Jer. 12:1–3)

33. Prayer of Jeremiah for the people, perhaps in time of drought.

Though our iniquities testify against us, act Thou, O Jehovah, for Thy name's sake; for our backslidings are many, we have sinned against Thee.

O Thou hope of Israel, the Savior thereof in the time of trouble, why shouldest Thou be as a sojourner in the land, and as a wayfaring man that turneth aside to tarry for a night? Why shouldest Thou be as a man affrighted, as a mighty man that cannot save?

Yet Thou, O Jehovah, art in the midst of us, and we are called by Thy name; leave us not.

(Jer. 14:7–9)

34. Prayer for forgiveness and mercy upon sinful Judah.

Hast Thou utterly rejected Judah? hath Thy soul loathed Zion? Why hast Thou smitten us, and there is no healing for us? We looked for peace, but no good came; and for a time of healing, and behold! dismay.

We acknowledge, O Jehovah, our wickedness, and the iniquity of our fathers; for we have sinned against Thee. Do not abhor us, for Thy name's sake; do not disgrace the throne of Thy glory: remember, break not Thy covenant with us. Are there any among the vanities of the nations that can cause rain? or can the heavens give showers? Art not Thou He, O Jehovah our God? Therefore we will wait for Thee; for Thou hast made all these things.

(Jer. 14:19–22)

35. Jeremiah's prayer for his own deliverance and for the punishment of his persecutors.

Heal me, O Jehovah, and I shall be healed; save me, and I shall be saved: for Thou art my praise.

Behold! they say unto me, "Where is the word of Jehovah? let it come now." As for me, I have not desired the woeful day—Thou knowest: that which came out of my lips was before Thy face.

Be not a terror unto me: Thou art my refuge in the day of evil. Let them be put to shame that persecute me, but let not me be put to shame: let them be dismayed, but let not me be dismayed. Bring upon them the day of evil, and destroy them with double destruction.

(Jer. 17:14–18)

36. Jeremiah's prayer for the punishment of his persecutors.

Give heed to me, O Jehovah, and hearken to the voice of them that contend with me. Shall evil be recompensed for good? for they have dug a pit for my soul. Remember how I stood before Thee to speak good for them, to turn away Thy wrath from them. Therefore deliver up their children to the famine, and give them over to the power of the sword. Let their wives become childless and widows; let their men be slain of death, and their young men smitten of the sword in battle. Let a cry be heard from their houses, when Thou shalt bring a troop suddenly upon them; for they have dug a pit to take me, and hid snares for my feet. Yet, Jehovah, Thou knowest all their counsel against me to slay me; forgive not their iniquity, neither blot out their sin from Thy sight, but let them be overthrown before Thee. Deal Thou thus with them in the time of Thine anger.

(Jer. 18:19–23)

37. Prayer to be offered, after the triennial tithe has been given to the Levite, the sojourner, the fatherless and the widow.

I have put away the hallowed things out of my house, and also have given them to the Levite, to the sojourner, to the fatherless and to the widow, according to all Thy commandment which Thou hast commanded me. I have not transgressed any of Thy commandments, neither have I forgotten them. I have not eaten thereof in my mourning, neither have I put away thereof, whilst unclean, nor given thereof for the dead. I have hearkened to the voice of Jehovah my God: I have done according to all that Thou hast commanded me.

Look down from Thy holy habitation, from heaven, and bless Thy people Israel, and the ground which Thou hast given us, as Thou swarest unto our fathers—a land flowing with milk and honey. (Deut. 26:13–15)

38. Prayer composed for the dedication of the temple of Solomon.

O Jehovah, God of Israel, there is no God like Thee in heaven above, or on earth beneath; who keepest covenant and loving-kindness with Thy servants that walk before Thee with all their heart; who hast kept with Thy servant David my father that which Thou didst promise him. Yea, Thou speakest with Thy mouth, and hast fulfilled it with Thine hand, as it is this day. Now therefore, O Jehovah, God of Israel, keep with Thy servant David my father that which Thou hast promised him, saying, "There shall not fail thee a man in My sight to sit on the throne of Israel, if only thy children take heed to their way to walk before Me as thou hast walked before Me." Now therefore, O God of Israel, let Thy word, I pray Thee, be verified, which Thou spakest unto Thy servant David my father.

But will God in very deed dwell on the earth? Behold, heaven and the heaven of heavens cannot contain Thee; how much less this house that I have built! Yet have Thou respect unto the prayer of Thy servant, and to his supplication, O Jehovah my God, to hearken unto the cry and to the prayer which Thy servant prayeth before Thee this day, that Thine eyes may be open toward this house night and day, even toward the place of which Thou hast said, "My name shall be there"—to hearken unto the prayer which Thy servant shall pray toward this place. And hearken Thou to the supplication of Thy servant, and of Thy people Israel, when they shall pray toward this place; yea, hear Thou in heaven Thy dwelling-place; and, when Thou hearest, forgive.

If a man sin against his neighbor, and an oath be laid upon him to cause him to swear, and he come and swear before Thine altar in this house; then hear Thou in heaven, and do, and judge Thy servants, condemning the wicked, to bring his way upon his own head, and justifying the righteous, to give him according to his righteousness.

When Thy people Israel are smitten down before the enemy, because they have sinned against Thee; if they turn again to Thee, and confess Thy name and pray, and make supplication unto Thee in this house: then hear Thou in heaven, and forgive the sin of Thy people Israel and bring them again unto the land which Thou gavest unto their fathers.

When heaven is shut up, and there is no rain, because they have sinned against Thee; if they pray toward this place, and confess Thy name, and turn from their sin, when Thou dost afflict them: then hear Thou in heaven, and forgive the sin of Thy servants, and of Thy people Israel, when Thou teachest them the good way wherein they should walk, and send rain upon Thy land which Thou hast given to Thy people for an inheritance.

If there be in the land famine, if there be pestilence, if there be blasting or mildew, locust or caterpillar; if their enemy besiege them in the land of their cities; whatsoever plague, whatsoever sickness there be: what prayer and supplication soever be made by any man, or by all Thy people Israel, who shall know every man the plague of his own heart and spread forth his hands toward this house: then hear Thou in heaven Thy dwelling-place, and forgive, and do, and render unto every man according to all his ways, whose heart Thou knowest—for Thou, even Thou only, knowest the hearts of all the children of men—that they may fear Thee all the days that they live in the land which Thou gavest unto their fathers.

Moreover, concerning the alien that is not of Thy people Israel, but comes from a far country for Thy name's sake—for they shall hear of Thy great name, and of Thy mighty hand, and of Thine outstretched arm—when he shall come and pray toward this house, hear Thou in heaven Thy dwelling-place, and do according to all that the alien calleth to Thee for: that all the peoples of the earth may know Thy name to fear Thee, as doth Thy people Israel, and that they may know that this house which I have built is called by Thy name.

If Thy people go out to battle against their enemy, by whatsoever way Thou shalt send them, and they pray unto Jehovah toward the city which Thou hast chosen, and toward the house which I have built for Thy name: then hear Thou in heaven their prayer and their supplication and maintain their cause.

If they sin against Thee—for there is no man that sinneth not—and Thou be angry with them and deliver them to the enemy, so that they carry them away captive unto the land of the enemy, far or near; yet if they shall bethink themselves in the land whither they are carried captive, and turn again, and make supplication unto Thee in the land of them that carried them captive, saying, "We have sinned, we have done perversely, we have dealt wickedly"; if they return to Thee with all their heart and with all their soul in the land of their enemies, who carried them captive, and pray unto Thee toward their land, which Thou gavest unto their fathers, the city which Thou hast chosen, and the house which I have built for Thy name: then hear Thou their prayer and their supplication in heaven Thy dwelling-place, and maintain their cause, and forgive Thy people who have sinned against Thee, and all their transgressions wherein they have transgressed against Thee, and give them compassion before those who carried them captive, that they may have compassion on them—for they are Thy people and Thine inheritance, which Thou broughtest forth out of Egypt, from the midst of the furnace of iron—that Thine eyes may be open unto the supplication of Thy servant, and unto the supplication of Thy people Israel, to hearken unto them whensoever they cry unto Thee. For Thou didst separate them from among all the peoples of the earth, to be Thine inheritance, as Thou spakest by Moses Thy servant, when Thou broughtest our fathers out of Egypt, O Lord Jehovah.

(1 Kgs. 8:23–53; 2 Chr. 6:14–40)

39. Benediction at the consecration of the temple.

Blessed be Jehovah, that hath given rest unto His people Israel according to all that He promised: there hath not failed one word of all His good promise which He promised by Moses His servant.

Jehovah our God be with us, as He was with our fathers; let Him not leave us, nor forsake us, that He may incline our hearts unto Himself, to walk in all His ways and to keep His commandments, and His statutes and His judgments which He commanded our fathers. And let these my words, wherewith I have made supplication before Jehovah, be nigh unto Jehovah our God day and night, that He maintain the cause of His servant, and the cause of His people Israel, as each day shall require; that all the peoples of the earth may know that Jehovah is God, and none else.

(1 Kgs. 8:56–60)

40. *Prayer from the siege of Jerusalem.*
Behold, O Jehovah; for I am in distress,
My heart is troubled.
My heart is turned within me,
For I have grievously rebelled,
Without, the sword bereaveth,
Within, death.
Hear how I sigh:
There is none to comfort me.
All mine enemies have heard of my trouble,
They are glad at what Thou hast done.
Thou hast brought on the day that Thou didst proclaim,
Because of my sins.
Let all their wickedness come before Thee,
May they be like unto me.
As Thou hast done unto me,
Do also unto them.
For my sighs are many,
And my heart is faint.
(Lam. 1:20–22)

41. *The prayer of Jerusalem, oppressed and enslaved.*
Remember, O Jehovah, what is come upon us;
Behold, and see our reproach.
Thou, O Jehovah, abidest forever,

Thy throne is from generation to generation,
Why dost Thou forget us forever,
And forsake us so long time?
Turn us unto Thee, O Jehovah, and we shall be turned;
Renew our days as of old.
Or hast Thou rejected us utterly?
Is Thine anger against us so very sore?
(Lam. 5:1, 19–22)

42. Another prayer of sorrowful Jerusalem.
O Jehovah, Thou hast seen my wrong;
Judge Thou my cause.
Thou hast seen all their vengeance,
And all their devices against me.
Thou hast heard their reproach, O Jehovah,
And all their devices against me,
The lips of those that rose up against me,
And their devices against me all the day.
Behold Thou their sitting down, and their rising up:
I am their taunt-song.
Thou wilt render unto them a recompense, O Jehovah,
According to the word of their hands.
Thou wilt give them hardness of heart,
Thy curse upon them.
Thou wilt pursue them in anger and destroy them
From under Thy heavens.
(Lam. 3:59–66)

SECOND PERIOD

43. Prayer for the interposition of God in national affairs.
Look down from heaven, and behold,
From Thy holy and glorious habitation.
Where is Thy zeal and Thy strength,
And the yearning of Thy heart?
Restrain not Thy pity,
For Thou art our Father.
Though Abraham knoweth us not,
And Israel acknowledge us not,
Thou, O Jehovah, art our Father;
Our Redeemer is Thy name from of old.
O Jehovah, why dost Thou make us to err from Thy ways,
And hardenest our heart from Thy fear?
Turn again for the sake of Thy servants,
For the sake of the tribes of Thine inheritance.
Our adversaries have trodden down Thy sanctuary.[*]
We are become as they over whom Thou never barest rule,
As they that were not called by Thy name.
Oh that Thou wouldst rend the heavens, and come down,
That the mountains might quake at Thy presence,
As fire kindleth the brushwood,
As water, which fire makes to boil,
To make Thy name known to Thine adversaries,
That the nations might tremble before Thee,
Whilst Thou didst terrible things, which we looked not for,
And which from of old men have not heard.
No ear hath perceived,
Nor eye hath seen,
A God besides Thee,
Who worketh for him that waiteth for Him.
Thou meetest those that work righteousness,
And remember Thy ways.

---

[*] The first clause of v. 18, the meaning of which is very uncertain, has been omitted.

Behold, Thou wast wroth, and we sinned.*

And we are all become as one that is unclean, And all our right-eousnesses are as a polluted garment;

And we all fade as a leaf,

And our iniquities, like the wind, carry us away.

And there is none that calleth upon Thy name,

That stirreth up himself to take hold of Thee;

For Thou hast hid Thy face from us,

And consumed us by means of our iniquities.

But now, O Jehovah, Thou art our Father,

We are the clay, and Thou our potter.

And we all are the work of Thy hand.

Be not wroth very sore, O Jehovah,

Nor remember iniquity forever.

Behold, look, we beseech Thee,

We are all Thy people.

Thy holy cities are become a wilderness,

Jerusalem a desolation.

Our holy and our beautiful house

Where our fathers praised Thee,

Is burned up with fire;

And all our pleasant places are laid waste.

Wilt Thou refrain Thyself for these things, O Jehovah?

Wilt Thou hold Thy peace, and afflict us very sore?

(Is. 63:15–64:12)

44. Abraham's prayer for Ishmael.

Oh, that Ishmael might live before Thee.

(Gen. 17:18)

45. The priestly blessing.

Jehovah bless thee, and keep thee.

---

* The last clause of v. 5 is obscure and has been omitted.

Jehovah make His face to shine upon thee, and be gracious unto thee.

Jehovah lift up His countenance upon thee, and give thee peace.
(Num. 6:24–26)

46. Moses' prayer for a successor.

Let Jehovah, the God of the spirits of all flesh, appoint a man over the congregation, who may go out before them, and who may come in before them, and who may lead them out, and who may bring them in; that the congregation of Jehovah be not as sheep which have no shepherd.
(Num. 27:16, 17)

47. Nehemiah's prayer, when he learns of the evil plight of his countrymen, and of Jerusalem.

I beseech Thee, O Jehovah, God of heaven, the great and terrible God, that keepeth covenant and loving-kindness with them that love Him, and keep His commandments; let Thine ear now be attentive, and Thine eyes open, that Thou mayest hearken unto the prayer of Thy servant, which I pray before Thee at this time day and night, for the children of Israel Thy servants, while I confess the sins of the children of Israel, which we have sinned against Thee. Yea, I and my father's house have sinned: we have dealt very corruptly against Thee, and have not kept the commandments, nor the statutes nor the ordinances, which Thou didst command Thy servant Moses. Remember, I beseech Thee, the word that Thou didst command Thy servant Moses, saying, "If ye trespass, I will scatter you abroad among the peoples: but if ye return unto me, and keep my commandments and do them, though your outcasts were in the uttermost part of the heavens, yet will I gather them from thence and will bring them unto the place that I have chosen, to cause my name to dwell there."

Now these are Thy servants and Thy people whom Thou hast redeemed by Thy great power, and by Thy strong hand. O Lord, I beseech Thee, let now Thine ear be attentive to the prayer of Thy servant, and to the prayer of Thy servants, who delight to fear Thy name; and prosper, I pray Thee, Thy servant, this day, and grant him mercy in the sight of this man. [Artaxerxes I, King of Persia, whose cup-bearer he was.]

(Neh. 1:5–11)

48. Nehemiah's prayer, on hearing how Sanballat and Tobiah derided the efforts of the Jews to rebuild the walls of Jerusalem.

Hear, O our God, for we are despised; and turn back their reproach upon their own head, and give them up for a spoil in a land of captivity; and cover not their iniquity, and let not their sin be blotted out from before Thee; for they have provoked Thee to anger before the builders.

(Neh. 4:4, 5)

49. Nehemiah's prayer, after describing his generous conduct as governor of Judah.

Remember unto me, O my God, for good, all that I have done for this people.

(Neh. 5:19)

50. Nehemiah's prayer when he learns of the intrigues against him.

Now (O God) strengthen Thou my hands.

(Neh. 6:9)

51. Nehemiah's prayer concerning the intriguers.

Remember, O my God, Tobiah and Sanballat according to these their works, and also the prophetess Noadiah, and the rest of the prophets that would have put me in fear.

(Neh. 6:14)

52. Nehemiah's prayer, after describing his zeal for religious reform.

Remember me, O my God, concerning this, and wipe not out my good deeds that I have done for the house of my God, and for the observances thereof.

(Neh. 13:14)

53. Nehemiah's prayer, after describing his zeal for the observance of the Sabbath day.

Remember unto me, O my God, this also, and spare me according to the greatness of Thy loving-kindness.

(Neh. 13:22)

54. Nehemiah's prayer concerning those who have defiled the priesthood by intermarriage with foreign women.

Remember them, O my God, because they have defiled the priesthood, and the covenant of the priesthood, and of the Levites.

(Neh. 13:29)

55. Nehemiah's prayer, after his reorganization of the clergy.

Remember me, O my God, for good. (Neh. 13:31)

56. Prayer of the foreign sailors, before they throw Jonah overboard.

We beseech Thee, O Jehovah, we beseech Thee, let us not perish for this man's life, and lay not upon us innocent blood; for Thou, O Jehovah, hast done as it pleased Thee.

(Jon. 1:14)

57. Jonah's prayer for death, when the Ninevites repent and are saved.

I pray Thee, O Jehovah, was not this what I said, when I was yet in mine own country? That was why I hasted to flee unto Tarshish; for I knew that Thou art a gracious God and merciful, slow to anger, and rich in love, and repentest Thee of the evil. Therefore now, O Jehovah, take, I beseech Thee, my life from me; for it is better for me to die than to live.

(Jon. 4:2, 3)

58. Job's prayer for a speedy death.

Oh, that I might have my request,
And that God would grant me the thing that I long for!
Even that it would please God to crush me,
That He would let loose his hand, and cut me off.
(Job 6:8, 9)

59. Job's prayer for a respite from his sufferings, before he dies.
Let me alone; for my days are vanity.
What is man, that Thou shouldest magnify him,
And that Thou shouldest set Thine heart upon him,[*]
And that Thou shouldest visit him every morning,
And try him every moment?
How long wilt Thou refuse to look away from me,
And to let me alone, till I swallow down my spittle?[†]
If I have sinned, what do I unto Thee, O Thou watcher of men?
Why hast Thou set me as a mark for Thee,
So that I am become a burden unto Thee?
And why dost Thou not pardon my transgression,
And take away mine iniquity?
For now shall I lie down in the dust;
And Thou shalt seek me diligently, but I shall not be.
(Job 7:16b–21)

60. Job's prayer to be hidden in Sheol.
Oh, that Thou wouldest hide me in Sheol.
That Thou wouldest keep me in secret till Thy wrath be past.
That Thou wouldest appoint me a set time and remember me.
(Job 14:13)

61. Prayer of the priests who expect the speedy coming of the great day of Jehovah.
O Jehovah, to Thee do I cry: for the fire hath devoured the pastures of the wilderness, and the flame hath burned all the trees of the field. Yea, the beasts of the field pant unto Thee; for the waterbrooks are dried up, and the fire hath devoured the pastures of the wilderness.
(Joel 1:19, 20)

---

[*] These questions, suggested by Psalm 8:5, are asked by Job in bitter irony.
[†] That is, for a moment.

62. Another prayer of the priests, for mercy.

Spare Thy people, O Jehovah, and give not Thy heritage to reproach, that the heathen mock them not. Why should they say among the peoples, "Where is their God?"

(Joel 2:17)

63. Prayer for the confirmation of peace.

In the path of Thy judgments, O Jehovah, have we waited for Thee: to Thy name, even to Thy memorial name, is the desire of our soul. With my soul have I desired Thee in the night; yea, with my spirit within me do I seek Thee earnestly. Jehovah, Thou wilt ordain peace for us; for Thou hast also wrought all our works for us. O Jehovah our God, other lords besides Thee have had dominion over us, but by Thee only will we celebrate Thy name.

(Is. 26:8, 9, 12, 13)

64. Prayer of Jabez.

Oh, that Thou wouldest bless me indeed, and enlarge my border, and that Thy hand might be with me, and that Thou wouldest keep me from evil, that it be not to my sorrow.

(1 Chr. 4:10)

65. Prayer of Asa before the battle with Zerah.

O Jehovah, there is none besides Thee to help, between the mighty and him that hath no strength. Help us, O Jehovah our God, for we rely on Thee, and in Thy name are we come against this multitude. O Jehovah, Thou art our God; let not man prevail against Thee.

(2 Chr. 14:11)

66. Jehoshaphat's prayer before battle with the combined forces of Moab, Ammon and the Meunim.

O Jehovah, God of our fathers, are not Thou God in heaven? and art not Thou ruler over all the kingdoms of the nations? and in

Thy hand is power and might, so that none is able to withstand Thee. Didst not Thou, O our God, drive out the inhabitants of this land before Thy people Israel, and give it to the seed of Abraham Thy friend forever? And they dwelt therein, and have built Thee a sanctuary therein for Thy name, saying, "If evil come upon us, the sword, judgment, or pestilence or famine, we will stand before this house and before Thee—for Thy name is in this house—and cry unto Thee in our affliction, and Thou wilt hear and serve."

And now, behold, the children of Ammon and Moab and Mount Seir, whom Thou wouldest not let Israel invade, when they came out of the land of Egypt, but they turned aside from them and destroyed them not: behold how they reward us, in that they come to cast us out of Thy possession, which Thou hast given us to inherit. O our God, will not thou judge them? for we have no might against this great company that cometh against us, neither know we what to do, but our eyes are upon Thee.

(2 Chr. 20:6–12)

67. The dying prayer of Zechariah, son of Jehoiada, slain by the command of king Joash.

Jehovah look upon it, and require it.

(2 Chr. 24:22)

68. The prayer of Agur.

Two things have I asked of Thee:
Deny me then not before I die.
Remove far from me falsehood and lies,
Give me neither poverty nor riches.
Feed me with the food that is needful for me;
Lest I be full, and deny Thee, and say, "Who is Jehovah?"
Or lest I be poor and steal,
And use profanely the name of God.
(Prov. 30:7–9)

Intercession

FIRST PERIOD

1. Prayer for the reunion of Judah with Israel.
Hear, O Jehovah, the voice of Judah,
And bring him unto his people.
With his hands he hath contended for it,
And be Thou a help from his adversaries.
(Deut. 33:7)

2. Jacob's prayer for Ephraim and Manasseh.
The God before whom my fathers Abraham and Isaac did walk, the God who hath shepherded me all my life long unto this day, the angel who hath redeemed me from all evil, bless the lads; and let my name be named on them, and the name of my fathers Abraham and Isaac; and let them grow into a multitude in the midst of the earth.
(Gen. 48:15, 16)

3. Moses' prayer for mercy upon the people.
O Jehovah, why doth Thy wrath wax hot against Thy people, which Thou hast brought forth out of the land of Egypt, with great power and with a mighty hand? Wherefore should the Egyptians speak, saying, "For evil did He bring them out to slay them in the mountains, and to consume them from the face of the earth?" Turn from Thy fierce wrath, and repent of this evil against Thy people.

Remember Abraham, Isaac and Israel, Thy servants, to whom Thou swarest by Thine own self, and saidst unto them, "I will multiply your seed as the stars of heaven, and all this land that I have spoken of will I give unto your seed, and they shall inherit it forever."
(Ex. 32:11–13; cf. Deut. 9:26–29)

4. Moses' prayer that the guilty people be forgiven.

Oh, this people have sinned a great sin, and have made them gods of gold. Yet now, if Thou wilt forgive their sin–; and if not, blot me, I pray Thee, out of Thy book which Thou hast written.
(Ex. 32:31, 32)

5. Another prayer of Moses that the people be forgiven.

If now I have found favor in Thy sight, O my Lord, let my Lord, I pray Thee, go in the midst of us, for it is a stiff-necked people; and pardon our iniquity and our sin, and take us for Thine inheritance.
(Ex. 34:9)

6. Moses' prayer for the leprous Miriam.

Heal her, O God, I beseech Thee.
(Num. 12:13)

7. Moses' prayer that the murmuring people be spared.

Now, I pray thee, let the power of the Lord be great, according as Thou hast spoken, saying, "Jehovah is slow to anger and rich in love, forgiving iniquity and transgression, although He does not leave the guilty unpunished, visiting the iniquity of the fathers upon the children, upon the third and upon the fourth generation." Pardon, I beseech Thee, the iniquity of this people, according to Thy great loving-kindness, and according as Thou hast forgiven this people, from Egypt until now.
(Num. 14:17–19)

8. David's prayer for the people who were smitten by the pestilence.

Lo, it is I that have sinned, and it is I that have done perversely, but these sheep, what have they done? let Thine hand, I pray Thee, be against me and against my father's house.

(2 Sam. 24:17; 1 Chr. 21:17)

9. Elijah's prayer for the dead child of the widow of Zarephath.

O Jehovah, my God, I pray Thee, let this child's soul come into him again.

(1 Kgs. 17:21)

10. Elisha's prayer for his servant, who is terrified by the sight of the hosts that beleaguer the city.

O Jehovah, I pray Thee, open his eyes that he may see.

(1 Kgs. 6:17)

11. Amos's prayer that the impending judgment may be stayed.

O Lord Jehovah, forgive, I beseech Thee; how shall Jacob stand? for he is small.

(Amos 7:2, 5)

12. Abraham's intercession for Sodom.

Wilt Thou consume the righteous with the wicked? Peradventure there be fifty righteous within the city; wilt Thou consume and not spare the place for the fifty righteous that are therein? That be far from Thee to do after this manner, to slay the righteous with the wicked, that so the righteous should be as the wicked; that be far from Thee. Shall not the Judge of all the earth do right?

Behold now. I have taken upon me to speak unto the Lord, who am but dust and ashes: peradventure there shall lack five of the fifty righteous: wilt Thou destroy all the city for lack of five?

Peradventure there shall be forty found there.

Oh, let not the Lord be angry, and I will speak: peradventure there shall thirty be found there.

Behold now, I have taken upon me to speak unto the Lord; peradventure there shall be twenty found there.

Oh, let not the Lord be angry, and I will speak yet but this once: peradventure ten shall be found there.

(Gen. 18:23–31)

13. Ezekiel's prayer, when, in his vision, he sees the sinners in Jerusalem slain by supernatural executioners.

Oh, Lord Jehovah! wilt Thou destroy all the residue of Israel, in Thy pouring out of Thy wrath upon Jerusalem?

(Ezek. 9:8)

14. Ezekiel's prayer, on the death of Pelatiah.

Oh, Lord Jehovah! wilt Thou make a full end of the remnant of Israel?

(Ezek. 11:13)

SECOND PERIOD

15. Hezekiah's prayer for those who were ceremonially unclean at the celebration of the Passover.

May Jehovah the good pardon everyone that setteth his heart to seek God, Jehovah, the God of his fathers, though he be not cleansed according to the purification of the sanctuary.

(2 Chr. 30:18, 19)

Thanksgiving

FIRST PERIOD

1. Prayer of Abraham's servant after he has been successfully guided to a wife for Isaac.

Blessed be Jehovah the God of my master Abraham, who hath not forsaken His loving-kindness and His faithfulness towards my master: as for me, Jehovah hath led me in the way to the house of my master's brethren.

(Gen. 24:27)

2. Prayer of thanksgiving on the occasion of the annual presentation of the first-fruits at the sanctuary.

A wandering Aramean was my father; and he went down into Egypt and sojourned there, few in number; and he became there a nation, great, mighty, and populous. And the Egyptians dealt ill with us and afflicted us, and laid upon us hard bondage; and we cried unto Jehovah, the God of our fathers, and Jehovah heard our voice, and saw our affliction and our toil and our oppression, and Jehovah brought us forth out of Egypt with a mighty hand and with an outstretched arm, and with great terribleness, and with signs and with wonders, and He hath brought us into this place and hath given us this land, a land that floweth with milk and honey.

And now, behold, I have brought the first of the fruit of the ground, which Thou, O Jehovah, hast given me.

(Deut. 26:5–10)

3. David's prayer, on hearing Nathan's prophecy that his kingdom would be everlasting.

Who am I, O Lord Jehovah, and what is my house, that Thou hast brought me thus far? And this was yet a small thing in Thine eyes, O Lord Jehovah, but Thou hast spoken also of Thy servant's house for a great while to come.* And what can David say more unto Thee? for Thou knowest Thy servant, O Lord Jehovah. For Thy word's sake, and according to Thine own heart, hast Thou wrought all this greatness, to make Thy servant know it.

Wherefore Thou art great, O Jehovah God; for there is none like Thee, neither is there any God besides Thee, according to all that we have heard with our ears. And what one nation in the earth is like Thy people, even like Israel, whom God went to redeem unto Himself for a people, and to make Him a name and to do for them great and terrible things, in driving another people and its god before His people.† And Thou didst establish to Thyself Thy people Israel to be a people unto Thee forever; and Thou, Jehovah, didst become their God.

And now, O Jehovah God, the word that Thou hast spoken concerning Thy servant and concerning his house, confirm Thou it forever, and do as Thou hast spoken. And let Thy name be magnified forever, saying, "Jehovah of hosts is God over Israel," and the house of Thy servant David shall be established before Thee. For Thou, O Jehovah of hosts, the God of Israel, hast revealed to Thy servant, saying, "I will build thee a house"; therefore hath Thy servant found in his heart to pray this prayer unto Thee.

And now, O Lord Jehovah, Thou art God, and Thy words are truth, and Thou hast promised this good thing unto Thy servant. Now therefore let it please Thee to bless the house of Thy servant, that it may continue forever before Thee; for Thou, O Lord

---

* The last clause of v. 19 is obscure, and has been omitted.

† This is a plausible reconstruction of v. 23, which can hardly be correct as it stands (cf. 1 Chr. 17:21).

Jehovah, hast spoken it; and with Thy blessing let the house of Thy servant be blessed forever.

    (2 Sam. 7:18–29; 1 Chr. 17:16–27)

4. A prayer of gratitude for some deliverance.
    I called upon Thy name, O Jehovah,
    Out of the lowest dungeon
    Thou didst hear my voice: hide not
    Thine ear at my cry for help.
    Thou drewest near in the day that I called upon Thee;
    Thou saidst, "Fear not."
    Thou hast pleaded the causes of my soul,
    Thou hast redeemed my life.
    (Lam. 3:55–58)

SECOND PERIOD

5. A prayer of gratitude.

I will give thanks unto Thee, O Jehovah,
For, though Thou wast angry with me,
Thine anger is turned away,
And Thou didst comfort me.
Behold, God is my salvation;
I will trust and not be afraid.
For Jehovah is my strength and song,
And He is become my salvation.
(Is. 12:1, 2)

6. Ezra's prayer, which immediately follows his account of Artaxerxes' very generous decree.

Blessed be Jehovah, the God of our fathers, who hath put such a thing as this in the king's heart, to beautify the house of Jehovah which is in Jerusalem; and hath extended loving-kindness unto me before the king, and his counselors, and before all the king's mighty princes.
(Ezra 7:27, 28)

7. Melchizedek's prayer after the victory of Abraham.

Blessed be Abram of God Most High, possessor of heaven and earth; and blessed be God Most High who hath delivered thine enemies into thy hand.
(Gen. 14:19, 20)

8. A prayer of thanksgiving for deliverance.

Out of my affliction I called to Jehovah,
And He answered me.
Out of the belly of Sheol I cried,
And Thou heardest my voice,
Thou didst cast me into the depth, in the heart of the seas,
And the flood was round about me.
All Thy waves and Thy billows passed over me.

I said, "I am cast out from before Thine eyes,
How shall I look again to Thy holy temple?"
The waters compassed me about, even to the soul;
The deep was round about me,
The weeds were wrapped about my head.
Down I went to the bottoms of the mountains,
The earth with her bars closed upon me forever.
Yet Thou hast brought up my life from the pit, O Jehovah my God.
When my soul fainted within me, I remembered Jehovah.
And my prayer came in unto Thee, into Thy holy temple.
They that regard lying vanities
Forsake their own good.
But I will sacrifice unto Thee with the voice of thanksgiving:
I will pay that which I have vowed,
Salvation is of Jehovah.
(Jon. 2:2–9)

9. *A song of salvation.*
    I have sinned and perverted that which was right,
    And He hath not requited it unto me,
    He hath redeemed my soul from going into the pit,
    And my life shall behold the light.
    (Job 33:27, 28)

10. *Prayer of gratitude, possibly on the news of the victories of Alexander the Great.*
    O Jehovah, Thou art my God;
    I will exalt Thee, I will praise Thy name.
    For Thou hast done wonderful things,
    Which were truly and surely purposed of old.
    Thou hast made of a city a heap,
    Of a fortified city a ruin,
    The palace of the proud to be no city,
    It shall never more be built.
    Therefore shall a strong people glorify Thee,
    And tyrants shall fear Thee.

For Thou hast been a stronghold to the poor,
A stronghold to the needy in distress,
A refuge from the storm, a shade from the heat.
But the insolence of the proud Thou layest low.
(Is. 25:1–5)

11. David's prayer, after the presentation of the free-will offerings of the people towards the building of the temple.

Blessed be Thou, O Jehovah, the God of Israel our father, forever and ever.

Thine, O Jehovah, is the greatness, and the power, and the glory, and the victory, and the majesty: for all that is in the heavens and in the earth is Thine. Thine is the kingdom, O Jehovah, and Thou art exalted as head above all. Both riches and honor come of Thee, and Thou reignest over all; and in Thy hand is power and might, and in Thy hand it is to make great, and to give strength unto all. Now, therefore, our God, we thank Thee and praise Thy glorious name.

But who am I, and what is my people, that we should be able to offer so willingly after this sort? for all things come of Thee, and of Thine own have we given Thee. For we are strangers before Thee, and sojourners, as all our fathers were; our days on the earth are as a shadow, and there is no abiding. O Jehovah, our God, all this store that we have prepared to build Thee a house for Thy holy name, cometh of Thy hand, and is all Thine own.

I know also, my God, that Thou triest the heart, and hast pleasure in uprightness. As for me, in the uprightness of my heart I have willingly offered all these things; and now have I seen with joy Thy people, that are present here, offer willingly unto Thee.

O Jehovah, God of Abraham, of Isaac, and of Israel, our fathers, keep this forever as the purpose in the thoughts of the hearts of Thy people, and direct their hearts toward Thee; and give unto Solomon my son a perfect heart, to keep Thy commandments, Thy testimonies, and Thy statutes, and to do all these things, and to build the palace, for which I have made provision.
(1 Chr. 29:10–19)

12. Daniel's prayer for gratitude, after Nebuchadnezzar's dream has been divinely revealed to him.

Blessed be the name of God forever and ever, for wisdom and might are His. He changeth the times and the seasons, He removeth kings and setteth up kings; He giveth wisdom unto the wise, and knowledge to them that have understanding. He revealeth the deep and secret things; He knoweth what is in the darkness, and the light dwelleth with Him.

I thank Thee and praise Thee, O Thou God of my fathers, who hast given me wisdom and might and hast now made known unto me what we desired of Thee; for Thou hast made known unto us the king's matter.

(Dan. 2:20–23)

Confession

FIRST PERIOD

1. Confession of Israel, when assailed by the Ammonites.

We have sinned against Thee, because we have forsaken our God and served the Baalim.

(Judg. 10:10)

2. Another confession and prayer.

We have sinned. Do Thou unto us whatsoever seemeth good unto Thee; only deliver us, we pray Thee, this day.

(Judg. 10:15)

3. Confession of Israel at Mizpah.

We have sinned against Jehovah.

(1 Sam. 7:6)

4. David's confession after numbering the people.

I have sinned greatly in that which I have done. But now, O Jehovah, put away, I beseech Thee, the iniquity of Thy servant, for I have done very foolishly.

(2 Sam. 24:10)

5. Ideal confession of penitent Israel.

Take away (our) iniquity altogether, and let us receive good* (at Thy hands); so will we render Thee the fruit of our lips.

---

* The text here is somewhat uncertain.

Assyria shall not save us, we will not ride upon horses,* neither will we say any more to the work of our hands, "Ye are our gods"; for in Thee the fatherless findeth mercy.

(Hos. 14:2, 3)

6. Jeremiah's confession, at his call.

Oh, Lord Jehovah! behold, I know not how to speak; for I am a child.

(Jer. 1:6)

7. Ideal confession of penitent Israel.

Behold, we are come unto Thee, for Thou art Jehovah our God. Truly the hills, the noise upon the mountains,† is deceitful; truly in Jehovah our God is the salvation of Israel. But the shameful thing** hath devoured the labor of our fathers from our youth, their flocks and their herds, their sons and their daughters. Let us lie down in our shame, and let our confusion cover us; for we have sinned against Jehovah our God, we and our fathers, from our youth even unto this day, and we have not obeyed the voice of Jehovah our God.

(Jer. 3:22b–25)

8. Confession of the heathen that idolatry is vain.

Our fathers have inherited nought but lies, vanities among which there is none that can help.

(Jer. 16:19)

---

* That is, we will make no league with Egypt (any more than with Assyria). They forswear foreign help and idolatry.

† The text is somewhat uncertain, but the reference is apparently to the worship in the sanctuaries on the high places.

** That is, idolatry.

SECOND PERIOD

9. Praise of Jehovah and confession of national disobedience.

Oh, Lord Jehovah! behold, Thou hast made the heavens and the earth by Thy great power and by Thine outstretched arm. There is nothing too hard for Thee. Thou showest loving-kindness unto thousands and dost recompense the iniquity of the fathers into the bosom of their children after them—the great, the mighty God, Jehovah of hosts is His name; great in counsel, and mighty in work, whose eyes are open upon all the ways of the sons of men, to give everyone according to his ways and according to the fruit of his doings; who didst set signs and wonders in the land of Egypt even unto this day, both in Israel and among other men, and didst make Thee a name, as at this day, and didst bring forth Thy people out of the land of Egypt with signs, and with wonders, and with a strong hand, and with an outstretched arm, and with great terror, and didst give them this land which Thou didst swear to their fathers to give them, a land flowing with milk and honey; and they came in, and possessed it, but they obeyed not Thy voice, neither walked in Thy law. They have done nothing of all that Thou didst command them to do; therefore Thou hast caused all this evil to come upon them.

(Jer. 32:17–23)

10. Ezra's prayer, on hearing that the Jews had intermarried with their heathen neighbors.

O my God, I am ashamed and blush to lift up my face to Thee, my God; for our iniquities are increased over our head, and our guiltiness is grown up unto the heavens. Since the days of our fathers we have been exceeding guilty unto this day; and for our iniquities have we, our kings, and our priests, been delivered into the hand of the kings of the lands, to the sword, to captivity, and to plunder, and to confusion of face, as it is this day.

And now, for a little moment, grace hath been shown from Jehovah our God, to leave us a remnant to escape, and to give us a nail in His holy place, that our God may lighten our eyes, and give us a little reviving in our bondage. For we are bondmen; yet our God hath not forsaken us in our bondage, but hath extended loving-kindness unto us in the sight of the kings of Persia, to give us a re-viving, to set up the house of our God, and to repair the ruins thereof, and to give us a wall in Judah and in Jerusalem.

And now, O our God, what shall we say after this? for we have forsaken Thy commandments, which Thou hast commanded by Thy servants the prophets, saying, "The land, unto which ye go to possess it, is an unclean land, through the uncleanness of the peoples of the lands, through their abominations, which have filled it from one end to another with their filthiness. Now therefore give not your daughters unto their sons, neither take their daughters unto your sons, nor seek their peace or their prosperity forever; that ye may be strong, and eat the good of the land, and leave it for an inheritance to your children forever."

And after all that is come upon us for our evil deeds, and for our great guilt, seeing that Thou, our God, hast punished us less than our iniquities deserve, and hast given us such a remnant as this, shall we again break Thy commandments, and join in affinity with the peoples that do these abominations? Wouldest not Thou be angry with us till Thou hadst consumed us, so that there should be no remnant, nor any to escape?

O Jehovah, God of Israel, Thou art righteous; for we are left a remnant that is escaped, as it is this day. Behold, we are before Thee in our guiltiness, for none can stand before Thee because of this.

(Ezra 9:6–15)

*11. Ezra's prayer, after the people had confessed their sins.**

Thou art Jehovah, even Thou alone. Thou hast made heaven, the heaven of heavens, with all their host, the earth and all things that are thereon, the seas and all that is therein, and Thou preser-vest them all; and the host of heaven worshipeth Thee.

Thou art Jehovah, the God who didst choose Abram and bring him forth out of Ur of the Chaldees, and didst give him the name

---

* This prayer is introduced in the Greek version by the words, "And Ezra said."

of Abraham, and Thou didst find his heart faithful before Thee, and didst make a covenant with him to give the land of the Canaanite, the Hittite, the Amorite, and the Perizzite, and the Jebusite, and the Girgashite, to give it unto his seed; and Thou hast performed Thy words, for Thou art righteous.

Thou didst see the affliction of our fathers in Egypt, and didst hear their cry by the Red Sea, and show signs and wonders upon Pharaoh, and on all his servants, and on all the people of his land; for Thou knewest that they dealt proudly against them, and didst get Thee a name, as it is this day. And Thou didst divide the sea before them, so that they went through the midst of the sea on the dry land; and their pursuers Thou didst cast into the depths, as a stone into the mighty waters.

Moreover, by a pillar of cloud Thou didst lead them by day, and by a pillar of fire by night, to give them light in the way wherein they should go. Thou didst come down also upon Mount Sinai, and speak with them from heaven, and Thou didst give them right ordinances and true laws, good statutes and commandments, and make known unto them Thy holy Sabbath, and give them commandments, and statutes, and a law, by Moses Thy servant. Thou didst give them bread from heaven, for their hunger, and didst bring forth water for them out of the rock for their thirst, and didst command them that they should go in to possess the land which Thou hadst sworn to give them.

But they and our fathers dealt proudly and hardened their neck, and hearkened not to Thy commandments, and refused to obey, neither were they mindful of Thy wonders that Thou didst among them, but hardened their neck, and set their head to return to their bondage in Egypt. But Thou art a God ready to pardon, gracious and merciful, slow to anger and rich in love, and Thou didst not forsake them. Yea, when they had made them a molten calf and said, "This is thy God that brought thee up out of Egypt," and had wrought great provocations, yet Thou, in Thy manifold mercy, didst not forsake them in the wilderness: the pillar of cloud departed not from them by day, to lead them in the way, neither the pillar of fire by night, to show them light and the way wherein they should go. Thou didst also give Thy good spirit to instruct them, and didst not withhold Thy manna from their mouth, and didst give them water for their thirst. Yea, forty years didst Thou sustain them in the wilderness, and they lacked nothing; their clothes did not wax old, nor did their feet swell.

Moreover, Thou didst give them kingdoms and peoples, which Thou didst allot; so they possessed the land of Sihon, King of Heshbon, and the land of Og, King of Bashan. Their children also didst Thou multiply as the stars of heaven, and Thou didst bring them into the land concerning which Thou didst say to their fathers that they should go in to possess it. So the children went in and possessed the land, and Thou didst subdue before them the inhabitants of the land, the Canaanites, and didst give them into their hands, with their kings, and the peoples of the land, that they might do with them as they would. And they took fortified cities, and a fat land, and took possession of houses full of all good things, cisterns hewn out, vineyards, and olive yards, and fruit trees in abundance; so they ate and were filled, and became fat and delighted themselves in Thy great goodness.

Nevertheless, they were disobedient, and rebelled against Thee, and cast Thy law behind their backs, and slew Thy prophets that testified against them to turn them again unto Thee, and they wrought great provocations. Therefore Thou didst deliver them into the hand of their adversaries, who distressed them; and in the time of their trouble, when they cried unto Thee, Thou didst hear from heaven, and, according to Thy manifold mercies, Thou didst give them saviors who saved them out of the hand of their adversaries.

But after they had rest, they did evil again before Thee; therefore Thou didst leave them in the hand of their enemies, so that they had the dominion over them; yet, when they returned, and cried unto Thee, Thou didst hear from heaven, and many times didst Thou deliver them according to Thy mercies, and testify against them, that Thou mightest bring them again unto Thy law. Yet they dealt proudly and hearkened not unto Thy commandments, but sinned against Thine ordinances—which, if a man do, he shall live—and withdrew the shoulder, and hardened their neck, and would not hear. Yet many years didst Thou bear with them, and testify against them by Thy spirit through Thy prophets, yet they would not give ear; therefore Thou didst give them into the hand of the peoples of the lands. Nevertheless in Thy manifold mercies Thou didst not make a full end of them, nor forsake them; for Thou art a gracious and merciful God.

Now therefore, O our God, the great, the mighty, and the terrible God, who keepest covenant and loving-kindness, let not all the travail seem little before Thee that hath come upon us, on our kings, on our princes, and on our priests, and on our prophets, and on our fathers, and on all Thy people, since the time of the kings of Assyria unto this day. Howbeit Thou art just in all that is come upon us, for Thou hast dealt truly, but we have done wickedly; neither have our kings, our princes, our priests, nor our fathers, kept Thy law, nor hearkened unto Thy commandments and Thy testimonies wherewith Thou didst testify against them. For they have not served Thee in the time of their kingly rule, and despite Thy great goodness which Thou didst show them, and the large and fat land which Thou gavest them, they have not turned from their wicked deeds.

Behold, we are servants this day, and as for the land that Thou didst give unto our fathers, to eat the fruit thereof and the good thereof, behold, we are servants in it; and it yieldeth much increase unto the kings whom Thou hast set over us because of our sins. Also they have power over our bodies, and over our cattle, at their pleasure, and we are in great distress.[*]

(Neh. 9:6–37)

12. Confession of Job, after hearing the speech of the Almighty.
Behold, I am of small account; what shall I answer Thee?
I lay my hand upon my mouth.
Once have I spoken, but I will not repeat it;

---

[*] The conclusion of this prayer seems to have been lost. It is natural to expect at this point a petition for the restoration of Israel.

Yea, twice, but I will do so no more.
(Job 40:4, 5)

13. Another confession of Job.
I know that Thou canst do all things,
And that no purpose of Thine can be restrained.
I had heard of Thee by the hearing of the ear,
But now mine eye hath seen Thee;
Wherefore I retract and repent
In dust and ashes.
(Job 42:2, 5, 6)

14. Daniel's prayer after reading Jeremiah's prophecy of the seventy years' desolation of Jerusalem (Jer. 25:11; 29:10).

Oh, Lord, the great and dreadful God, who keepeth covenant and loving-kindness with them that love Him and keep His commandments, we have sinned, and have dealt perversely, and have done wickedly, and have rebelled, even turning aside from Thy precepts and from Thine ordinances. Neither have we hearkened unto Thy servants the prophets, that spake in Thy name to our kings, our princes, and our fathers, and to all the people of the land.

O Lord, righteousness belongeth unto Thee, but unto us confusion of face, as it is this day—to the men of Judah, and to the inhabitants of Jerusalem, and unto all Israel that are near and that are far off, through all the countries whither Thou hast driven them, because of their trespass that they have trespassed against Thee. O Lord, to us belongeth confusion of face, to our kings, to our princes, and to our fathers, because we have sinned against Thee. To the Lord our God belong mercies and forgiveness, for we have rebelled against Him, neither have we obeyed the voice of Jehovah our God, to walk in His laws, which He set before us by His servants the prophets.

Yea, all Israel have transgressed Thy law, even turning aside that they should not obey Thy voice; therefore hath the curse been poured out upon us, and the oath that is written in the law of

Moses, the servant of God; for we have sinned against Him. And He hath confirmed His words which He spake against us, and against our judges that judged us, by bringing upon us a great evil; for under the whole heaven hath not been done as hath been done upon Jerusalem. As it is written in the law of Moses, all this evil is come upon us, yet have we not entreated the favor of Jehovah our God, that we should turn from our iniquities, and have discernment in Thy truth. Therefore hath Jehovah watched over the evil, and brought it upon us; for Jehovah our God is righteous in all His works which He doeth, and we have not obeyed His voice.

And now, O Lord our God, that hast brought Thy people forth out of the land of Egypt with a mighty hand, and hast gotten Thee renown, as at this day; we have sinned, we have done wickedly. O Lord, according to all Thy righteousness, let Thine anger and Thy wrath, I pray Thee, be turned away from Thy city Jerusalem, Thy holy mountain because for our sins and for the iniquities of our fathers, Jerusalem and Thy people are become a reproach to all that are round about us.

Now therefore, O our God, hearken unto the prayer of Thy servant, and to his supplications, and cause Thy face to shine upon Thy sanctuary that is desolate, for the Lord's sake. O my God, incline Thine ear, and hear; open Thine eyes, and behold our desolations, and the city which is called by Thy name. For we do not present our supplications before Thee for our righteousness, but for Thy great mercies' sake.

O Lord, hear; O Lord, forgive; O Lord, hearken and do. Defer not, for Thine own sake, O my God, because Thy city and Thy people are called by Thy name.

(Dan. 9:4–19)

Vows

1. Jacob's vow at Bethel.

If God will be with me, and will keep me in the way that I go, and will give me bread to eat and raiment to put on, so that I come again to my father's house in peace, and Jehovah will be my God, then this stone, which I have set up for a pillar, shall be God's house; and of all that Thou shalt give me I will surely give the tenth unto Thee.

(Gen. 28:20–22)

2. Israel's vow on approaching Canaan.

If Thou wilt indeed deliver this people into my hand, then I will devote their cities to utter destruction.

(Num. 21:2)

3. Jephthah's vow, before his assault upon the Ammonites.

If Thou wilt indeed deliver the children of Ammon into my hand, then it shall be that, whatsoever cometh forth from the doors of my house to meet me, when I return in peace from the children of Ammon, it shall be Jehovah's, and I will offer it up for a burnt-offering.

(Judg. 11:30, 31)

4. Hannah's vow as she prayed for a child.

O Jehovah of hosts, if Thou wilt indeed look upon the affliction of Thine handmaid, and remember me, and not forget Thine

231

handmaid, but wilt give unto Thine handmaid a man-child, then I will give him unto Jehovah all the days of his life, and there shall no razor come upon his head.

(1 Sam. 1:11)

5. *Absalom's vow in Geshur.*

If Jehovah shall indeed bring me again to Jerusalem, then I will serve Jehovah.

(2 Sam. 15:8)

Complaints

FIRST PERIOD

1. Samson, at Ramath-lehi, after the slaughter of the Philistines.

Thou hast given this great deliverance by the hand of Thy servant; and now shall I die for thirst, and fall into the hand of the uncircumcised?

(Judg. 15:18)

2. Moses' complaint, when a still harder service is imposed upon Israel by Pharaoh.

Lord, wherefore hast Thou dealt ill with this people? Why is it that Thou hast sent me? For since I came to Pharaoh to speak in Thy name, he hath dealt ill with this people: neither hast Thou delivered Thy people at all.

(Ex. 5:22, 23)

3. Moses complaint, when the people, weary of the manna, long for flesh.

Wherefore hast Thou dealt ill with Thy servant? and wherefore have I not found favor in Thy sight, that Thou layest the burden of all this people upon me? Have I conceived all this people, have I brought them forth, that Thou shouldest say unto me, "Carry them in thy bosom as a nursing-father carrieth the sucking child," unto the land which Thou swarest unto their fathers? Whence should I have flesh to give unto all this people? for they weep unto me, saying, "Give us flesh, that we may eat." I am not able to bear all this people alone, because it is too heavy for me. And if Thou deal thus with me, kill me, I pray Thee, out of hand, if I have found favor in Thy sight, and let me not see my wretchedness.

(Numbers 11:11–15)

4. Prayer of Moses and Aaron at the rebellion of Korah.

O God, the God of the spirits of all flesh, shall one man sin, and wilt Thou be wroth with all the congregation?

(Numbers 16:22)*

5. Joshua's prayer after the defeat of Israel at Ai.

Alas, O Lord Jehovah, wherefore hast Thou at all brought this people over the Jordan, to deliver us into the hand of the Amorites, to cause us to perish? Would that we had been content and stayed beyond the Jordan! Oh, Lord, what shall I say, after that Israel hath turned their backs before their enemies? For the Canaanites and all the inhabitants of the land will hear of it, and will compass us round, and cut off our name from the earth; and what wilt Thou do for Thy great name?

(Josh. 7:7–9)

6. Elijah's prayer, after the death of the widow's son.

O Jehovah, my God, hast Thou also brought evil upon the widow, whose guest I am, by slaying her son?

(1 Kgs. 17:20)

7. Jeremiah's lament.

O Jehovah, Thou knowest. Remember me and visit me, and avenge me of my persecutors. Take me not away in Thy long-suffering, know that for Thy sake I have suffered reproach.

Thy words were found, and I did eat them, and Thy words were unto me a joy and the rejoicing of my heart; for I am called by Thy name, O Jehovah, God of hosts.

---

* This passage, though its documentary source is late, may not inappropriately be placed here.

I sat not in the assembly of them that make merry, nor did I rejoice. I sat alone because of Thy hand upon me, for Thou hast filled me with (Thine own) indignation.

Why is my pain perpetual, and my wound incurable, refusing to be healed? Hast Thou indeed become unto me as a deceitful brook, and as waters that fail?

(Jer. 15:15–18)

8. Jeremiah's lament, as he thinks of his ill success.

O Jehovah, Thou hast beguiled me, and I was beguiled. Thou art stronger than I, and hast prevailed. I am become a laughing-stock all the day; everyone mocketh me.

(Jer. 20:7)

9. Habakkuk's lament.

O Jehovah, how long shall I cry, and Thou wilt not hear?—cry unto Thee of wrong, and Thou wilt not save? and why dost Thou cause me to look upon wrong?

(Hab. 1:2)

10. Another lament.

Art Thou not from everlasting, O Jehovah my God, my Holy One? O Thou that art of purer eyes than to behold evil, and that canst not look upon iniquity, wherefore dost Thou look (silently) on, while traitors deal treacherously, and holdest Thy peace, when the wicked swalloweth up the man that is more righteous than he?

(Hab. 1:12, 13)

11. Prayer from the siege of Jerusalem.

See, O Jehovah, and behold
To whom Thou hast done thus.
Shall the women eat their fruit,
The children that they fondled?
Shall priest and prophet be slain
In the sanctuary of the Lord?
On the ground in the streets there lie

Youths and old men.
My virgins and my young men
Are fallen by the sword.
Thou hast slain them in the day of Thine anger,
Thou hast slaughtered without pity.
(Lam. 2:20, 21)

12. Prayer of sorrowful Jerusalem.
We have transgressed and rebelled,
Thou hast not pardoned.
Thou hast wrapped Thyself in anger, and pursued us,
Thou hast slain without pity.
Thou hast wrapped Thyself in a cloud,
So that prayer passed not through.
Thou hast made us an offscouring and refuse
In the midst of the peoples.
All our enemies have opened
Their mouth wide against us.
Fear and the pit are come upon us,
Devastation and destruction.
(Lam. 3:42–47)

SECOND PERIOD

13. Job's lament over the injustice of his lot.

Do not condemn me.

Show me why Thou contendest with me.

Is it good unto Thee that Thou shouldest oppress,

That Thou shouldest despise the work of Thy hands?

Hast Thou eyes of flesh?

Or seest Thou as man seeth?

Are Thy days as the days of man?

Or Thy years as man's days?

For Thou inquirest after mine iniquity,

And searchest after my sin,

Though Thou knowest that I am not guilty,

And that there is not falseness in my hand.

Thy hands have framed me and fashioned me,

And now wilt Thou turn and destroy me?

Remember, I beseech Thee, that Thou hast fashioned me as a clay,

And wilt Thou bring me into dust again?

Hast Thou not poured me out as milk,

And curdled me like cheese?

Thou hast clothed me with skin and flesh,

And knit me together with bones and sinews.

Thou hast granted me life and loving-kindness,

And Thy visitation hath preserved my spirit.

Yet this is what Thou didst hide in Thy heart,

Now I know that this was Thy purpose.*

If I sinned, then Thou wouldest mark me,

And wouldest not acquit me of mine iniquity.

If I were wicked, woe unto me;

And were I righteous, yet must I not lift up mine head.

I am filled with shame, and drunk with sorrow.

And if my head be lifted up, Thou dost hunt me as a lion.

---

* That is, to torment and destroy him.

And again Thou showest Thyself marvelous against me.
Thou renewest Thy witnesses against me.
And dost increase Thine indignation upon me.
An ever-changing host (of foes) is with me.
Why then didst Thou bring me forth out of the womb?
I should have given up the ghost, and no eye had seen me.
I should have been as though I had not been.
I should have been carried from the womb to the grave.
Are not the days of my life few?
Leave me alone, that I may brighten a little,
Before I go whence I shall not return,
Even to the land of darkness and of the deep shadow.
(Job 10:2–21)

14. *Job's lament over the pathos of his fate.*
Why dost Thou hide Thy face,
And hold me for Thine enemy?
Wilt Thou harass a driven leaf?
And wilt Thou pursue the dry stubble?
For Thou writest bitter things against me,
And makest me to inherit the iniquities of my youth.
Thou puttest my feet in the stocks,
And markest all my paths.
Thou drawest a line around the soles of my feet.
Man that is born of a woman,
Is of few days, and full of trouble.
He cometh forth like a flower, and withereth.
He fleeth also as a shadow, and abideth not.
And dost Thou open Thine eyes upon such a one,
And bringest me into judgment with Thee?
Who can bring a clean thing out of an unclean? not one.
Seeing his days are determined,
And the number of his months is with Thee,
Look away from him that he may have peace,
That he may enjoy, as a hireling, his day.
(Job 13:24–14:6)

The Prayers of the
New Testament

The Prayers of Jesus

1. *The Lord's Prayer.*

(a) Our Father who art in heaven, hallowed be Thy name. Thy kingdom come. Thy will be done, as in heaven, so on earth.

Give us this day our daily bread. And forgive us our debts, as we also have forgiven our debtors. And bring us not into temptation, but deliver us from evil.*

(Matt. 6:9–13)

(b) Father, hallowed be Thy name, Thy kingdom come.

Give us day by day our daily bread. And forgive us our sins; for we ourselves also forgive everyone that is indebted to us. And bring us not into temptation.

(Luke 11:2–4)

2. *Thanksgiving*

I praise Thee, O Father, Lord of heaven and earth, that Thou didst hide these things from the wise and understanding, and didst reveal them unto babes; yea, Father, for so it was well-pleasing in Thy sight.

(Matt. 11:25, 26; Luke 10:21)

---

* In the original, this is probably to be regarded personally–the evil one. But to a modern and western ear, the familiar translation better represents the essential idea, and may even be correct: it finds considerable support in Romans 12:9, "abhorring *that which is evil,*" where the word is unambiguously neuter (cf. John 17:15).

3. Prayer in Gethsemane.

(a) My Father, if it be possible, let this cup pass away from me: nevertheless not as I will, but as Thou wilt.

(Matt. 26:39)

(b) My Father, if this cannot pass away, except I drink it, Thy will be done.

(Matt. 26:42)

(c) Abba, Father, all things are possible unto Thee; take away this cup from me. Nevertheless not what I will, but what Thou wilt.

(Mark 14:36)

(d) Father, if Thou be willing, remove this cup from me; nevertheless not my will, but Thine be done.

(Luke 22:42)

4. Prayer upon the Cross.

Father, forgive them; for they know not what they do.
(Luke 23:34)

5. Another prayer upon the Cross.

My God, my God, why hast Thou forsaken me?
(Matt. 27:46; Mark 15:34)

6. The last prayer upon the Cross.

Father, into Thy hands I commend my spirit.
(Luke 23:46)

7. At the grave of Lazarus.

Father, I thank thee that Thou heardest me. And I know that Thou hearest me always, but because of the multitude that standeth around, I said it, that they may believe that Thou hast sent me.

(John 11:41, 42)

8. Now is my soul troubled.

Father, save me from this hour.[*] But for this cause came I unto this hour. Father, glorify Thy name.

(John 12:27)

9. Intercessory Prayer.

Father, the hour is come; glorify Thy Son, that the Son may glorify Thee; even as Thou gavest Him authority over all flesh, that, to as many as Thou hast given Him, He should give eternal life. I glorified Thee on the earth, having accomplished the work which Thou hast given me to do; and now, Father, glorify Thou me with Thine own self with the glory which I had with Thee before the world was.

I manifested Thy name unto the men whom Thou gavest me out of the world. Thine they were, and Thou gavest them to me; and they have kept Thy word. Now they know that all things whatsoever Thou hast given me are from Thee; for the words which Thou gavest me I have given unto them, and they received them, and knew of a truth that I came forth from Thee, and they believed that Thou didst send me. I pray for them: I pray not for the world, but for those whom Thou hast given me, for they are Thine; and all things that are mine are Thine, and Thine are mine, and I am glorified in them. And I am no more in the world, and these are in the world, and I come to Thee. Holy Father, keep them in Thy name which Thou hast given me, that they may be one, even as we.

While I was with them, I kept them in Thy name which Thou hast given me; and I guarded them, and not one of them perished but the son of perdition, that the scripture might be fulfilled. But now I come to Thee; and these things I speak in the world, that they may have my joy fulfilled in themselves. I have given them

---

[*] Or this clause may be read interrogatively; "Shall I say, 'Father save me from this hour'?" In that case, this is a prayer which Jesus refuses to pray.

Thy word; and the world hated them, because they are not of the world, even as I am not of the world. I pray not that Thou shouldest take them out of the world, but that Thou shouldest keep them from the evil. They are not of the world, even as I am not of the world. Sanctify them in the truth; Thy word is truth. As Thou didst send me into the world, even so send I them into the world. And for their sakes I sanctify myself, that they themselves also may be sanctified in truth.

Neither for these only do I pray, but for them also that believe on me through their word; that they all may be one—even as Thou, Father, art in me, and I in Thee, that they also may be in us, that the world may believe that Thou didst send me. And the glory which Thou hast given me I have given unto them, that they may be one, even as we are one; I in them and Thou in me—that they may be perfected into one: that the world may know that Thou didst send me, and didst love them as even Thou didst love me.

Father, I desire that they also, whom Thou hast given me, be with me where I am, that they may behold my glory which Thou hast given me; for Thou didst love me before the foundation of the world. O righteous Father, the world knew Thee not, but I knew Thee, and these knew that Thou didst send me, and I made known unto them Thy name, and will make it known, that the love wherewith Thou didst love me may be in them, and I in them.

(John 17)

The Other Prayers of the New Testament

PETITION

1. The publican's prayer.
God, be Thou merciful to me, the sinner.
(Luke 18:13)

2. Prayer of the dying thief.
Jesus, remember me, when Thou comest in* Thy kingdom.
(Luke 23:42)

3. Prayer for a successor to Judas.
Thou, Lord, who knowest the hearts of all men, show which of these two Thou hast chosen to take the place in this ministry and apostleship from which Judas fell away, that he might go to his own place.
(Acts 1:24, 25)

4. Prayer of the friends of Peter and John, after the latter, on their release, had told all that the chief priests and elders had said to them.
O Master, Thou that didst make the heaven and the earth and the sea, and all that in them is, Thou who, by the Holy Spirit, by the mouth of our father David Thy servant, didst say,

---

* Or *into.*

> Why did the Gentiles rage,
> And the peoples imagine vain things?
> The kings of the earth set themselves,
> And the rulers were gathered together
> Against the Lord, and against his Anointed:

for of a truth in this city against Thy holy servant Jesus whom Thou didst anoint, both Herod and Pontius Pilate, with the Gentiles and the peoples of Israel, were gathered together, to do whatsoever Thy hand and Thy counsel foreordained to come to pass.

And now, Lord, look upon their threatenings, and grant unto Thy servants to speak Thy word with all boldness, while Thou stretchest forth Thy hand to heal; and that signs and wonders may be done through the name of Thy holy servant Jesus.
(Acts 4:24–30)

5. *Stephen's dying prayer.*
    Lord Jesus, receive my spirit.
    (Acts 7:59)

6. *Stephen's last words.*
    Lord, lay not this sin to their charge.
    (Acts 7:60)

7. *Prayer of the martyred souls from underneath the altar.*
    How long, O Master, the holy and true, doest Thou not judge and avenge our blood on them that dwell on the earth?
    (Rev. 6:10)

8. *Prayer for the coming of Jesus.*
    Amen. Come, Lord Jesus.
    (Rev. 22:20)

9. *Paul's prayer for the Ephesian Church.*
    O Father, from whom every family in heaven and on earth is named! Grant, according to the riches of Thy glory, that they may

be strengthened with power through Thy spirit in the inward man: that Christ may dwell in their hearts through faith–to the end that, being rooted and grounded in love, they may be strong to apprehend with all the saints what is the breadth and length and height and depth, and to know the love of Christ which passeth knowledge, that they may be filled unto all the fullness of God.

(Eph. 3:15–19)

THANKSGIVING

1. Prayer of the aged Simeon, after taking the infant Jesus in his arms.
Now lettest Thou Thy servant depart, Master,
According to Thy word, in peace:
For mine eyes have seen Thy salvation,
Which Thou hast prepared before the face of all peoples–
A light for revelation to the Gentiles,
And the glory of Thy people Israel.
(Luke 2:29–32)

2. The Pharisee's prayer.
God, I thank Thee that I am not as the rest of men, extortioners, unjust, adulterers, or even as this publican. I fast twice in the week, I give tithes of all that I get.
(Luke 18:11, 12)

PRAISE

1. Praise of the heavenly host.
Glory to God in the highest,
And on earth peace among men in whom He is well pleased.
(Luke 2:14)

2. Praise of the four living creatures.
Holy, holy, holy, is the Lord God, the Almighty, who was and is and is to come.
(Rev. 4:8)

3. Praise of the four and twenty elders.

Worthy art Thou, our Lord and our God, to receive the glory and the honor and the power; for Thou didst create all things, and because of Thy will they were, and were created.

(Rev. 4:11)

4. The voice of many angels round about the throne.

Worthy is the Lamb that hath been slain to receive the power, and riches, and wisdom, and might, and honor, and glory, and blessing.

(Rev. 5:12)

5. The praise of all creation.

Unto Him that sitteth on the throne, and unto the Lamb, be the blessing, and the honor, and the glory, and the dominion, forever and ever.

(Rev. 5:13)

6. The voice of an innumerable multitude.

Salvation unto our God who sitteth on the throne, and unto the Lamb.

(Rev. 7:10)

7. Praise of the angels round about the throne.

Amen. Blessing, and glory, and wisdom, and thanksgiving, and honor, and power, and might, be unto our God forever and ever. Amen.

(Rev. 7:12)

8. The sound of great voices in heaven.

The kingdom of the world is become the kingdom of our Lord, and of His Christ; and He shall reign forever and ever.

(Rev. 11:15)

9. Praise of the four and twenty elders.

We give Thee thanks, O Lord God, the Almighty, who art and who wast because Thou hast taken Thy great power, and didst reign. And the nations were wroth, and Thy wrath came, and the time of the dead to be judged, and the time to give their reward to Thy servants the prophets, and to the saints, and to them that fear Thy name, the small and the great; and to destroy them that destroy the earth.

(Rev. 11:17, 18)

10. The song of Moses and the Lamb.

Great and marvelous are Thy works, O Lord God, the Almighty. Righteous and true are Thy ways, Thou King of the ages. Who shall fear Thee, O Lord, and glorify Thy name? for Thou only art holy; for all the nations shall come and worship before Thee, for Thy righteous acts have been made manifest.

(Rev. 15:3, 4)

11. The voice of the angel of the waters.

Righteous art Thou, who art and who wast, Thou Holy One, because Thou didst thus judge: for they poured out the blood of saints and prophets, and blood hast Thou given them to drink: they deserve it.

(Rev. 16:5, 6)

12. Voice of the altar.

Yea, O Lord God, the Almighty, true and righteous are Thy judgments.

(Rev. 16:7)

13. Voice of the four and twenty elders and of the four living creatures, when the blood of the martyrs has been avenged.

Amen. Hallelujah.

(Rev. 19:4)

14. Voice of a great multitude.

Hallelujah; for the Lord God, the Almighty, reigneth.

(Rev. 19:6)

Benedictions and Doxologies

1. The God of peace be with you all.
(Rom. 15:33)

2. Grace be with you (all).
(1 Tim. 6:21; Tit. 3:15; Heb. 13:25)

3. The Lord be with thy spirit.
(2 Tim. 4:22)

4. Grace be to you and peace.
(1 Thess. 1:1)

5. Grace be to you and peace from God our Father.
(Col. 1:2)

6. Grace be to you and peace from God our Father and the Lord Jesus Christ.
(1 Cor. 1:3; 2 Cor. 1:2; Eph. 1:2; Phil. 1:2; 2 Thess. 1:2; Phile. 1:3)

7. Grace and peace from God the Father and Christ Jesus our Savior.
(Titus 1:4)

8. Grace to you and peace be multiplied.
(1 Pet. 1:2)

9. Grace to you and peace be multiplied in the knowledge of God and of Jesus our Lord.
(2 Pet. 1:2)

10. Peace be unto you all that are in Christ.
(1 Pet. 5:14)

11. The grace of our Lord Jesus Christ be with you (all).
(Rom. 16:20; 1 Cor. 16:23; 1 Thess. 5:28; 2 Thess. 3:18)

12. The grace of our Lord Jesus Christ be with your spirit.
(Gal. 6:18; Phile. 1:25)

13. The grace of the Lord Jesus be with the saints.
(Rev. 22:21)

14. The Lord of peace Himself give you peace at all times in all ways. The Lord be with you all.
(2 Thess. 3:16)

15. The Lord direct your hearts into the love of God and into the patience of Christ.
(2 Thess. 3:5)

16. Mercy unto you and peace and love be multiplied.
(Jude 1:2)

17. Grace, mercy, peace, from God the Father and Christ Jesus our Lord.
(1 Tim. 1:2; 2 Tim 1:2)

18. The grace of the Lord Jesus Christ, and the love of God, and the communion of the Holy Spirit, be with you all.
(2 Cor. 13:14)

19. Grace to you and peace from God the Father, and our Lord Jesus Christ, who gave Himself for our sins, that He might deliver

us out of the present evil world, according to the will of our God and Father; to whom be the glory forever and ever. Amen.
(Gal. 1:3–5)

20. Now to Him that is able to establish you according to my gospel and the preaching of Jesus Christ, according to the revelation of the mystery which hath been kept in silence through times eternal, but not is manifested, and by the Scriptures of the prophets, according to the commandment of the eternal God, is made known unto all the nations unto obedience of faith, to the only wise God, through Jesus Christ, be the glory forever. Amen.
(Rom. 16:25–27)

21. Now unto Him that is able to do exceeding abundantly above all that we ask or think, according to the power that worketh in us, unto Him be the glory in the Church and in Christ Jesus unto all generations forever and ever. Amen.
(Eph. 3:20, 21)

22. Now our Lord Jesus Christ Himself, and God our Father who loved us and gave us eternal comfort and good hope, through grace, comfort your hearts and establish them in every good work and word.
(2 Thess. 2:16, 17)

23. Now unto the King eternal, immortal, invisible, the only God, be honor and glory forever and ever. Amen.
(1 Tim. 1:17)

24. Now the God of peace, who brought again from the dead the great Shepherd of the sheep with the blood of an eternal covenant, even our Lord Jesus, make you perfect in every good thing to do His will, working in you that which is well pleasing in His sight, through Jesus Christ; to whom be the glory forever and ever. Amen.
(Heb. 13:20, 21)

25. Now unto Him that is able to keep you from stumbling, and to set you before the presence of His glory without blemish in exceeding joy, to the only God our Savior, through Jesus Christ our Lord, be glory, majesty, dominion, and power, before all time, and now, and forevermore. Amen.

(Jude 1:24, 25)

26. Grace to you and peace, from Him who is and who was and who is to come, and from the seven spirits that are before His throne, and from Jesus Christ, who is the faithful witness, the first-born of the dead, and the ruler of the kings of the earth. Unto Him that loveth us, and loosed us from our sins by His blood, and made us to be a kingdom, priests unto His God and Father; to Him be the glory and the dominion forever and ever. Amen.

(Rev. 1:4–6)

Part 4

Biblical Prayers for Modern Use

Petition

1. Strengthen Thou my hands.
(Neh. 6:9)

2. Lord Jesus, receive my spirit.
(Acts 7:59)

3. I pray Thee, show me Thy glory.
(Ex. 33:18)

4. Remember me, O my God, for good.
(Neh. 13:31)

5. Father, into Thy hands I commend my Spirit.
(Luke 23:46)

6. If Thy presence go not with us, carry us not up hence.
(Ex. 33:15)

7. Give us help against the adversary, for vain is the help of man.
(Ps. 60:11; 108:12)

8. Let Thy mercy, O Lord, be upon us, according as we hope in Thee.
(Ps. 33:22)

9. O Lord, grant unto Thy servants to speak Thy word with all boldness.
(Acts 4:29)

10. Hear Thou in heaven Thy dwelling-place; and when Thou hearest, forgive.

(1 Kgs. 8:30)

11. O Lord God, remember me, I pray Thee, and strengthen me, I pray Thee.

(Judg. 16:28)

12. O Lord, pardon our iniquity and our sin, and take us for Thine inheritance.

(Ex. 34:9)

13. My Father, if this cup cannot pass away except I drink it, Thy will be done.

(Matt. 26:42)

14. O Lord, I pray Thee, teach us what we shall do unto the child that shall be born.

(Judg. 13:8)

15. Turn us again, O God of hosts, and cause Thy face to shine, and we shall be saved.

(Ps. 80:7)

16. Thou, O Lord, art in the midst of us, and we are called by Thy name. Leave us not.

(Jer. 14:9)

17. Help, Lord, for the godly man ceaseth; for the faithful fail from among the children of men.

(Ps. 12:1)

18. Remember me, O my God, and spare me according to the greatness of Thy loving-kindness.

(Neh. 13:29)

19. I pray Thee, if I have found favor in Thy sight, show me now Thy ways, that I may know Thee.

(Ex. 33:13)

20. May the good Lord pardon everyone that setteth his heart to seek the Lord God of his fathers.

(2 Chr. 30:18, 19)

21. Father, if Thou be willing, remove this cup from me; nevertheless not my will, but Thine be done.

(Luke 22:42)

22. My Father, if it be possible, let this cup pass away from me; nevertheless not as I will, but as Thou wilt.

(Matt. 26:39)

23. Abba, Father, all things are possible unto Thee; take away this cup from me. Nevertheless not what I will, but what Thou wilt.

(Mark 14:36)

24. O Lord, revive Thy work in the midst of the years, in the midst of the years make Thyself known: in wrath remember mercy.

(Hab. 3:2)

25. O Lord, be gracious unto us; we have waited for Thee. Be Thou our arm every morning, our salvation also in the time of trouble.

(Is. 33:2)

26. Heal me, O Lord, and I shall be healed; save me, and I shall be saved; for Thou art my praise. Thou art my refuge in the day of evil.

(Jer. 17:14, 17)

27. Search me, O God, and know my heart; try me and know my thoughts. And see if there be any wicked way in me, and lead me in the way everlasting.

(Ps. 139:23, 24)

28. Thou, O Lord, abidest forever, Thy throne is from generation to generation. Turn us unto Thee, O Lord, and we shall be

turned. Renew our days as of old.
(Lam. 5:19, 21)

29. God be merciful unto us, and bless us, and cause His face to shine upon us: that Thy way may be known upon earth, Thy saving health among all nations.
(Ps. 67:1, 2)

30. Be merciful unto me, O God, be merciful unto me. For my soul trusteth in Thee. Yea, in the shadow of Thy wings I take refuge, until these calamities be overpast.
(Ps. 57:1)

31. Hear my voice, O God, in my complaint: preserve my life from fear of the enemy. Hide me from the secret counsel of the wicked, from the tumult of the workers of iniquity.
(Ps. 64:1, 2)

32. O Lord, I know that the way of man is not in himself: it is not in man that walketh to direct his steps. O Lord, correct me, but in measure; not in Thine anger, lest Thou bring me to nothing.
(Jer. 10:23, 24)

33. O Lord, I beseech Thee, let now Thine ear be attentive to the prayer of Thy servant, who delights to fear Thy name; and prosper, I pray Thee, Thy servant this day, and grant him mercy.
(Neh. 1:11)

34. Be graciously pleased, O God, to deliver me; make haste to help me, O Lord. I am poor and needy, make haste unto me, O God. Thou art my help and my deliverer. O Lord, make no tarrying.
(Ps. 40:13, 17; 70:1, 5)

35. O Lord, there is none besides Thee to help, between the mighty and him that hath no strength. Help us, O Lord our God, for we rely on Thee. O Lord, Thou art our God; let not man prevail against Thee.
(2 Chr. 14:11)

36. Save me, O God, by Thy name, and judge me by Thy strength. Hear my prayer, O God, give ear to the words of my mouth. For strangers are risen up against me, and violent men have sought after my soul.

(Ps. 54:1–3)

37. Let the Lord, the God of the spirits of all flesh, set a man over the congregation, who may go out before them and who may come in before them, that the congregation of the Lord be not as sheep which have no shepherd.

(Num. 27:16, 17)

38. Thou, O Lord, art a God full of compassion and gracious, slow to anger, and abundant in mercy and truth. O turn unto me, and have mercy upon me. Give Thy strength unto Thy servant, and save the son of Thine handmaid.

(Ps. 86:15, 16)

39. How long shall I have trouble in my soul, and sorrow in my heart all the day? Consider and hear me, O Lord my God; lighten mine eyes, lest I sleep the sleep of death. I have trusted in Thy mercy, my heart shall rejoice in Thy salvation.

(Ps. 13:2, 3, 5)

40. Thou art my refuge, my portion in the land of the living. Attend unto my cry, for I am brought very low. Deliver me from my persecutors, for they are stronger than I. Bring my soul out of prison, that I may praise Thy name.

(Ps. 142:5–7)

41. Remember me, O Lord, with the favor that Thou bearest unto Thy people. O visit me with Thy salvation, that I may see the good of Thy chosen, that I may rejoice in the gladness of Thy nation, that I may glory with Thine inheritance.

(Ps. 106:4, 5)

42. Turn us, O God of our salvation, and cause Thine anger towards us to cease. Wilt Thou be angry with us forever? Wilt Thou

not revive us again, that Thy people may rejoice in Thee? Show us Thy mercy, O Lord, and grant us Thy salvation.
(Ps. 85:4–7)

43. Lord, my heart is not naughty nor mine eyes lofty, neither do I exercise myself in great matters, or in things too wonderful for me. Surely I have stilled and quieted my soul; like a weaned child with his mother, like a weaned child is my soul within me.
(Ps. 131:1, 2)

44. Be merciful unto me, O God; for man would swallow me up, all the day long he fighting oppresseth me. Mine enemies would swallow me up all the day long, for they be many that fight proudly against me. What time I am afraid, I will trust in Thee.
(Ps. 56:1–3)

45. O Lord my God, I am but a little child. I know not how to go out or come in. And Thy servant is in the midst of this people which Thou hast chosen. Give therefore Thy servant an understanding heart to judge Thy people, that I may discern between good and evil.
(1 Kgs. 8:7–9)

46. Our Father who art in heaven, hallowed be Thy name. Thy kingdom come. Thy will be done in earth, as it is in heaven. Give us this day our daily bread; and forgive us our debts, as we forgive our debtors. And lead us not into temptation, but deliver us from evil.
(Matt. 6:9–13)

47. Out of the depths have I cried unto Thee, O Lord. Lord, hear my voice; let Thine ears be attentive to the voice of my supplications. If Thou, Lord, shouldest mark iniquities, O Lord, who could stand? But there is forgiveness with Thee, that Thou mayest be feared.
(Ps. 130:1–4)

48. O Lord God of our fathers, art not Thou God in heaven? and art not Thou ruler over all the kingdoms of the nations? and in

Thy hand is power and might, so that none is able to withstand
Thee. We have no might, neither know we what to do, but our
eyes are upon Thee.

(2 Chr. 20:6, 12)

49. Deliver me from mine enemies, O my God; defend me from
them that rise up against me. Deliver me from the workers of iniquity, and save me from blood-thirsty men. For, lo, they lie in wait
for my soul: the mighty are gathered against me—not for my transgression, nor for my sin, O Lord.

(Ps. 59:1–3)

50. Unto Thee do I lift up mine eyes, O Thou that dwellest in
the heavens. Behold, as the eyes of servants look unto the hand of
their masters, and as the eyes of a maiden unto the hand of her
mistress, so our eyes look unto the Lord our God, until that He
have mercy upon us. O Lord, have mercy upon us.

(Ps. 123:1–3)

51. Deal Thou with me, O Lord, for Thy name's sake because
Thy loving-kindness is good, deliver Thou me. For I am poor and
needy, and my heart is wounded within me. I am gone, like the
shadow, when it declineth. Help me, O Lord my God. O save me
according to Thy loving-kindness.

(Ps. 109:21–23, 26)

52. When the people are smitten down before the enemy, because they have sinned against Thee; if they turn again to Thee
and confess Thy name and pray and make supplication unto
Thee, then hear Thou in heaven, and forgive the sin of Thy people and bring them again unto the land which Thou gavest to their
fathers.

(1 Kgs. 8:33, 34)

53. O Lord, rebuke me not in Thine anger, neither chasten me
in Thy hot displeasure. Have mercy upon me, O Lord, for I am
withered away. O Lord, heal me, for my bones are troubled. My

soul also is sore vexed: but Thou, O Lord, how long? Return, O Lord, deliver my soul. O save me for Thy mercies' sake.
(Ps. 6:1–4)

54. Hear my cry, O God, attend unto my prayer. From the end of the earth will I cry unto Thee, when my heart is overwhelmed; lead me to the rock that is higher than I. For Thou hast been a shelter to me, and a strong tower from the enemy. I will abide in Thy tabernacle forever, I will take refuge in the covert of Thy wings.
(Ps. 61:1–4)

55. Thou art holy, O Thou that inhabitest the praises of Israel. Our fathers trusted in Thee: they trusted and Thou didst deliver them. They cried unto Thee, and were delivered: they trusted in Thee, and were not put to shame. Be not far from me; for trouble is near, and there is none to help. Be not Thou far off, O Lord; O my strength, haste Thee to help me.
(Ps. 22:3–5, 11, 19)

56. Look down from heaven, and behold from Thy holy and glorious habitation. Restrain not Thy pity; for Thou art our Father. Thou, O Lord, art our Father; our Redeemer is Thy name from of old. Thou, O Lord, art our Father. We are the clay, and Thou our potter, and we all are the work of Thy hand. Be not wroth very sore, O Lord, neither remember iniquity forever.
(Is. 63:15, 16; 64:8, 9)

57. Remember not against us the iniquities of our forefathers; let Thy tender mercies meet us speedily, for we are brought very low. Help us, O God of our salvation, for the glory of Thy name, and deliver us, and forgive our sins, for Thy name's sake. Let the sighing of the prisoner come before Thee; according to the greatness of Thy power, preserve Thou those that are appointed to death.
(Ps. 79:8, 9, 11)

58. Unto Thee will I cry, O Lord, my rock. Be not silent unto me; lest, if Thou be silent unto me, I become like them that go

down into the pit. Hear the voice of my supplications, when I cry unto Thee, when I lift up my hands towards Thy holy oracle. Draw me not away with the wicked, and with the workers of iniquity, that speak peace with their neighbors, but mischief is in their hearts.

(Ps. 28:1–3)

59. Hear, O Lord, when I cry with my voice; have mercy also upon me, and answer me. When Thou saidst, "Seek ye my face," my heart made answer, "Thy face, Lord, will I seek." Hide not Thy face from me, put not Thy servant away in anger. Thou hast been my help. Leave me not, nor forsake me, O God of my salvation. Teach me Thy way, O Lord, and lead me in a plain path.

(Ps. 27:7–9, 11)

60. When heaven is shut up, and there is no rain, because the people have sinned against Thee; if they pray, and confess Thy name, and turn from their sin, when Thou dost afflict them; then hear Thou in heaven, and forgive the sin of Thy servants, when Thou teachest them the good way wherein they should walk, and send rain upon the land which Thou hast given to the people for an inheritance.

(1 Kgs. 8:35, 36)

61. In Thee, O Lord, do I put my trust; let me never be put to shame: deliver me in Thy righteousness. Bow down Thine ear unto me, deliver me speedily. Be Thou my strong rock, a house of defense to save me. For Thou art my rock and my fortress, therefore for Thy name's sake lead me and guide me. Pull me out of the net that they have laid privily for me, for Thou art my stronghold.

(Ps. 31:1–4)

62. O satisfy us early with Thy mercy, that we may rejoice and be glad all our days. Make us glad according to the days wherein Thou hast afflicted us, and the years wherein we have seen evil. Let Thy work appear unto Thy servants, and Thy glory upon

their children. And let the beauty of the Lord our God be upon us; and establish Thou the work of our hands, yea, the work of our hands establish Thou it.
(Ps. 90:14–17)

63. Examine me, O Lord, and prove me; try my heart and my mind. For Thy loving-kindness is before mine eyes, and I have walked in Thy truth. I will wash my hands in innocency; so will I compass Thine altar, O Lord. Lord, I love the habitation of Thy house, and the place where Thy glory dwelleth. Gather not my soul with sinners, nor my life with men of blood. As for me, I will walk in mine integrity. Redeem me and be merciful unto me.
(Ps. 26:2, 3, 6, 8, 9, 11)

64. Give ear to my words, O Lord, consider my meditation. Hearken unto the voice of my cry, my king and my God; for unto Thee do I pray. My voice shalt Thou hear in the morning, O Lord, in the morning will I direct my prayer unto Thee, and keep watch. As for me, I will come into Thy house in the multitude of Thy mercy; in Thy fear will I worship toward Thy holy temple. Lead me, O Lord, in Thy righteousness: make Thy way straight before my face.
(Ps. 5:1–3, 7, 8)

65. Hear the right, O Lord, attend unto my cry; give ear unto my prayer that goeth not out of feigned lips. Thou hast proved my heart, Thou hast visited me in the night; Thou hast tried me, and findest no evil purpose in me. Incline Thine ear unto me, and hear my speech. Show Thy marvelous loving-kindness, O Thou that savest by Thy right hand them that put their trust in Thee. Keep me as the apple of the eye; hide me under the shadow of Thy wings.
(Ps. 17:1, 3, 6–8)

66. Lord, I have called upon Thee, make haste unto me; give ear unto my voice, when I call unto Thee. Let my prayer be set forth as incense before Thee, and the lifting up of my hands as the evening sacrifice. Set a watch, O Lord, before my mouth; keep the

door of my lips. Incline not my heart to any evil thing, to practice deeds of wickedness with them that work iniquity. Mine eyes are unto Thee, O God the Lord. In Thee do I take refuge, leave not my soul destitute.

(Ps. 141:1–4, 8)

67. Give ear to my prayer, O God, and hide not Thyself from my supplication. Attend unto me and hear me; I am restless in my complaint and moan. My heart is sore pained within me, and the terrors of death are fallen upon me. Fearfulness and trembling are come upon me, and horror hath overwhelmed me. As for me, I will call upon God, and the Lord will save me. Evening, and morning, and at noon will I complain and moan; and He will hear my voice. God will hear, even He that abideth of old.

(Ps. 55:1, 2, 4, 5, 16, 17, 19)

68. O Lord, God of my salvation, I have cried day and night before Thee. Let my prayer enter into Thy presence, incline Thine ear unto my cry. For my soul is full of troubles, and my life draweth nigh to the grave. I am become as a man that hath no strength. Thou hast laid me in the lowest pit, in dark places, in the deeps. Thou hast put mine acquaintance far from me. I have called daily upon Thee, I have spread forth my hands unto Thee. Unto Thee, O Lord, do I cry, and in the morning my prayer comes before Thee.

(Ps. 88:1–3, 6, 8, 9, 13)

69. Behold, heaven and the heaven of heavens cannot contain Thee; how much less this house! Yet have Thou respect unto the prayer of Thy servant, and to his supplication, to hearken unto the cry and the prayer which Thy servant prayeth before Thee this day, that Thine eyes may be open to this house night and day, even toward the place of which Thou hast said, "My name shall be there." Hearken Thou to the supplication of Thy servant and of Thy people; yea, hear Thou in heaven Thy dwelling-place and, when Thou hearest, forgive.

(1 Kgs. 8:27–30)

70. Bow down Thine ear, O Lord, and answer me; for I am poor and needy. Preserve my soul; O Thou my God, save Thy servant that trusteth in Thee. Be merciful unto me, O Lord, for unto Thee do I cry all the day long. Rejoice the soul of Thy servant, for unto Thee, O Lord, do I lift up my soul. For Thou, Lord, art good and ready to forgive, and plenteous in mercy unto all them that call upon Thee. Give ear, O Lord, unto my prayer, and attend to the voice of my supplications. In the day of my trouble I will call upon Thee, for Thou wilt answer me.

(Ps. 86:1–7)

71. Have mercy upon me, O Lord, for I am in trouble; mine eye is consumed with grief, yea, my soul and my body. My life is spent with grief and my years with sighing, my strength faileth. I am forgotten as a dead man out of mind, I am like a broken vessel. For I hear the backbiting of many, cause for terror is on every side. But I have trusted in Thee, O Lord: I have said, "Thou art my God." My times are in Thy hand. Make Thy face to shine upon Thy servant; save me for Thy mercies' sake. Let me not be put to shame, O Lord, for I have called upon Thee.

(Ps. 31:9, 10, 12–17)

72. Lord, make me to know mine end, and the measure of my days, what it is; let me know how frail I am. Behold, Thou hast made my days as a handbreadth, and my lifetime is as nothing before Thee. And now, Lord, what wait I for? my hope is in Thee. Deliver me from all my transgressions. Remove Thy stroke away from me, I am consumed by the blow of Thine hand. Hear my prayer, O Lord, and give ear unto my cry. Hold not Thy peace at my tears; for I am a stranger with Thee and a sojourner, as all my fathers were. Oh, spare me that I may smile again, before I go hence, and be no more.

(Ps. 39: 4, 5, 7, 8, 10, 12, 13)

73. Save me, O my God, for the waters are come in unto my soul. I sink in deep mire, where there is no standing; I am come

into deep waters, where the floods overflow me. I am weary with my crying, my throat is dried; mine eyes fail while I wait for my God. O God, Thou knowest my foolishness, and my sins are not hid from Thee. Deliver me out of the mire, and let me not sink, let me be delivered out of the deep waters. Answer me, O Lord, for Thy loving-kindness is good; turn unto me according to the multitude of Thy tender mercies. And hide not Thy face from Thy servant, for I am in trouble; hear me speedily. Draw nigh unto my soul, and redeem it.

(Ps. 69:1–3, 5, 14, 16–18)

74. In Thee, O Lord, do I put my trust, let me never be put to shame. Deliver me in Thy righteousness, and rescue me; bow down Thine ear unto me and save me. Be Thou to me a strong habitation, whereunto I may continually resort. Thou art my rock and my fortress. Thou art my hope, O Lord God; Thou art my trust from my youth. Cast me not off in the time of old age, forsake me not when my strength faileth. O God, be not far from me; O my God, make haste for my help. I will hope continually and will praise Thee yet more and more. O God, Thou hast taught me from my youth. Yea, even when I am old and gray-headed, O God, forsake me not.

(Ps. 71:1–3, 5, 9, 12, 14, 17, 18)

75. O Lord, rebuke me not in Thy wrath, neither chasten me in Thy hot displeasure. I am bent, I am bowed down greatly, I go mourning all the day long. Lord, all my desire is before Thee, and my groaning is not hid from Thee. My heart throbbeth, my strength faileth me; as for the light of mine eyes, it also is gone from me. My lovers and my friends stand aloof, and my kinsmen stand afar off. In Thee, O Lord, do I hope; Thou wilt answer, O Lord my God. I am ready to fall, and my sorrow is continually before me. I have to confess my guilt, I am sorry because of my sin. Forsake me not, O Lord; O my God, be not far from me. Make haste to help me, O Lord, my salvation.

(Ps. 38:1, 6, 9, 11, 15, 17, 18, 21, 22)

76. Hear my prayer, O Lord; give ear to my supplications; in Thy faithfulness answer me and in Thy righteousness. And enter not into judgment with Thy servant, for in Thy sight no man living is righteous. My spirit is overwhelmed within me, my heart within me is desolate. I remember the days of old, I meditate on all Thy doings, I muse on the work of Thy hands. I spread forth my hands unto Thee, my soul thirsteth after Thee. Cause me to hear Thy loving-kindness in the morning, for in Thee do I trust. Cause me to know the way wherein I should walk, for I lift up my soul to Thee. I flee unto Thee to hide me. Teach me to do Thy will, for Thou art my God. Let Thy good spirit lead me in an even path. Quicken me, O God, for Thy name's sake. In Thy righteousness, O bring my soul out of trouble.

(Ps. 143:1, 2, 4–11)

77. Hear my prayer, O Lord, and let my cry come unto Thee. Hide not Thy face from me in the day when I am in trouble. Incline thine ear unto me; in the day when I call answer me speedily. My days are like a shadow that declineth, and I am withered like grass. But Thou, O Lord, dost abide forever, and Thy memorial name unto all generations. Thou wilt arise and have mercy upon Zion; for it is time to have pity upon her, yea, the set time is come. O my God, take me not away in the midst of my days; Thy years are throughout all generations. Of old hast Thou laid the foundations of the earth, and the heavens are the work of Thy hands. They shall perish, but Thou shalt endure; yea, all of them shall wax old like a garment; as a vesture shalt Thou change them, and they shall be changed. But Thou art the same, and Thy years shall have no end.

(Ps. 102:1, 2, 11–13, 24–27)

78. Unto Thee, O Lord, do I lift up my soul. O my God, in Thee have I trusted, let me not be put to shame. Show me Thy ways, O Lord, teach me Thy paths. Guide me in Thy truth, and teach me, for Thou art the God of my salvation; for Thee do I wait all the day. Remember, O Lord Thy tender mercies and Thy loving-

kindnesses, for they have been ever of old. Remember not the sins of my youth, nor my transgressions; according to Thy loving-kindness remember Thou me, for Thy goodness' sake, O Lord. For Thy name's sake, O Lord, pardon mine iniquity, for it is great. Turn Thee unto me, and have mercy upon me, for I am desolate and afflicted. O bring me out of my distresses. Look upon mine affliction and my travail, and forgive all my sins. O keep my soul and deliver me, let me not be put to shame, for in Thee do I take refuge.

(Ps. 25:1, 2, 4–7, 11, 16–18, 20)

Intercession

1. Lord, lay not this sin to their charge.
(Acts 7:60)

2. Do good in Thy good pleasure unto Zion.
(Ps. 51:18)

3. Father, forgive them, for they know not what they do.
(Luke 23:34)

4. May the good Lord pardon everyone that setteth his heart to seek the Lord God of his fathers.
(2 Chr. 30:18, 19)

5. Save Thy people, and bless Thine inheritance. Shepherd them also, and bear them up forever.
(Ps. 28:9)

6. Look down from Thy holy habitation, from heaven, and bless Thy people and the land which Thou hast given us.
(Deut. 26:15)

7. I pray, not that Thou shouldest take them out of the world, but that Thou shouldest keep them from the evil. Sanctify them in the truth; Thy word is truth.
(John 17:15, 17)

8. O Father, from whom every family in heaven and on earth is named! Grant, according to the riches of Thy glory, that they may

273

be strengthened with might through Thy spirit in the inward man: that Christ may dwell in their hearts by faith—to the end that, being rooted and grounded in love, they may be strong to apprehend with all the saints what is the breadth and length and height and depth, and to know the love of Christ, which passeth knowledge, that they may be filled unto all the fullness of God.

(Eph. 3:15–19)

9. If the people sin against Thee—for there is no man that sinneth not—and Thou be angry with them, and deliver them to the enemy, so that they carry them away captive unto the land of the enemy, far or near; yet, if they shall bethink themselves in the land whither they are carried captive, and turn again, and make supplication unto Thee in the land of them that carried them captive, and say, "We have sinned, we have done perversely and wickedly"; if they return to Thee with all their heart and with all their soul in the land of their enemies who carried them captive, and pray unto Thee, then hear Thou their prayer and their supplication in heaven Thy dwelling-place, and forgive the people who have sinned against Thee, and all their transgressions wherein they have transgressed against Thee, and give them compassion before those who carried them captive, that they may have compassion on them.

(1 Kgs. 8:46–50)

Thanksgiving

1. Thou hast preserved my soul from the pit of destruction; Thou hast cast all my sins behind Thy back.
   (Is. 38:17)

2. Behold, now, Thy servant hath found favor in Thy sight, and Thou hast magnified Thy loving-kindness which Thou hast showed unto me in saving my life.
   (Gen. 19:19)

3. I have sinned and perverted that which was right, and He hath not requited it unto me. He hath redeemed my soul from going into the pit, and my life shall behold the light.
   (Job 33:27, 28)

4. Thou, O Lord, art a shield about me; my glory, and the lifter up of my head. I cry unto the Lord with my voice, and He answers me out of His holy hill. I laid me down, and slept; I awaked; for the Lord sustaineth me.
   (Ps. 3:3–5)

5. Many, O Lord my God, are Thy wonderful works which Thou hast done, and Thy thoughts which are to us-ward. There is none to be compared to Thee. Were I to declare and speak of them, they are more than can be numbered.
   (Ps. 40:5)

6. I called upon Thy name, O Lord, out of the lowest dungeon. Thou didst hear my voice. Thou drewest near in the day that I called upon Thee; Thou saidst, "Fear not." Thou hast pleaded the causes of my soul. Thou hast redeemed my life.
(Lam. 3:55–58)

7. Lord, now lettest Thou Thy servant depart in peace, according to Thy word; for mine eyes have seen Thy salvation, which Thou hast prepared before the face of all peoples—a light to lighten the Gentiles, and the glory of Thy people Israel.
(Luke 2:29–32)

8. Into thy hand I commend my spirit; Thou hast redeemed me, O Lord God of truth. I will be glad and rejoice in Thy loving-kindness; for Thou hast seen my affliction, Thou hast known my soul in adversities. Thou hast set my feet in a large place.
(Ps. 31:5, 7, 8)

9. Though I walk through the valley of the shadow of death, I will fear no evil, for Thou art with me: Thy rod and Thy staff, they comfort me. Thou preparest a table before me in the presence of mine enemies. Thou hast anointed my head with oil; my cup runneth over.
(Ps. 23:4, 5)

10. I will sing of Thy power; yea, I will sing aloud of Thy loving-kindness in the morning. For Thou hast been my high tower, and a refuge in the day of my distress. Unto Thee, O my strength, will I sing praises; for God is my high tower, the God of my mercy.
(Ps. 59:16, 17)

11. O Lord, I will give thanks unto Thee; for, though Thou wast angry with me, Thine anger is turned away, and Thou didst comfort me. Behold, God is my salvation; I will trust, and not be afraid. For Jehovah is my strength and song, and He is become my salvation.
(Is. 12:1, 2)

12. In God have I put my trust, I will not be afraid. What can man do unto me? Thy vows are upon me, O God; I will render thank offerings unto Thee. For Thou hast delivered my soul from death, and my feet from falling, that I may walk before God in the light of the living.
(Ps. 56:11–13)

13. I will praise Thee, O Lord, with my whole heart: I will show forth all Thy marvelous works. I will be glad and rejoice in Thee, I will sing praise to Thy name, O Thou Most High. For Thou hast maintained my right and my cause: Thou art seated on the throne, judging righteously.
(Ps. 9:1, 2, 4)

14. O Lord, Thou art my God, I will exalt Thee, I will praise Thy name; for Thou hast done wonderful things which were truly and surely purposed of old. Thou hast been a stronghold to the poor, a stronghold to the needy in distress, a refuge from the storm, a shade from the heat.
(Is. 25:1, 4)

15. I am continually with Thee, Thou hast holden my right hand. Thou wilt guide me with Thy counsel and afterward receive me to glory. Whom have I in heaven but Thee? and there is none upon earth that I desire beside Thee. My flesh and my heart faileth, but God is my portion forever.
(Ps. 73:23–26)

16. Out of my affliction, I called to the Lord and He answered me. The waters compassed me about even to the soul, the deep was round about me. Yet hast Thou brought up my life from the pit, O Lord my God. When my soul fainted within me, I remembered the Lord, and my prayer came in unto Thee.
(Jon. 2:1, 5–7)

17. Thou visitest the earth and waterest it, Thou greatly enrichest it. Thou providest them corn, when Thou hast so prepared it,

Thou waterest its furrows abundantly, Thou dost settle the ridges thereof, Thou makest it soft with showers, Thou blessest the springing thereof. Thou crownest the year with thy goodness.
(Ps. 65:11–13)

18. Thou art great, and doest wonders, Thou art God alone. Teach me Thy way, O Lord; I will walk in Thy truth: unite my heart to fear Thy name. I will praise Thee, O Lord my God, with all my heart, and I will glorify Thy name forevermore. For great is Thy mercy toward me, and Thou hast delivered my soul from the lowest depths.
(Ps. 86:10–13)

19. Thou hast set me at large when I was in distress. Many there be that say, "Who will show us any good?" Lord, lift Thou up the light of Thy countenance upon us. Thou hast put gladness in my heart, more than is theirs when their corn and wine are increased. In peace will I both lay me down and sleep; for Thou, Lord, makest me to dwell alone in safety.
(Ps. 4:1, 6–8)

20. Oh, how great is Thy goodness which Thou hast laid up for them that fear Thee, which Thou hast wrought for them that take refuge in Thee before the sons of men. In the covert of Thy presence Thou wilt hide them. Thou wilt keep them secretly. Blessed be the Lord, for He hath showed me His marvelous loving-kindness. Thou didst hear the voice of my supplications when I cried unto Thee.
(Ps. 31:19–22)

21. Thou, O God, hast proved us; Thou hast tried us as silver is tried. Thou didst bring us into the net, Thou didst lay a sore burden upon us. Thou didst cause men to ride over our heads; we went through fire and through water, but Thou broughtest us out into a wealthy place; I will go into Thy house and pay Thee my vows, which my lips have uttered and my mouth spake, when I was in trouble.
(Ps. 66:10–14)

22. Who am I, O Lord, and what is my house, that Thou hast brought me thus far? Thou art great, O Lord; there is none like Thee, neither is there any God besides Thee, according to all that we have heard with our ears. And now, O Lord, the word that Thou hast spoken concerning Thy servant and concerning his house, confirm Thou it forever, and do as Thou hast spoken; and let Thy name be magnified forever.

(2 Sam. 7:18, 22, 25, 26)

23. O Lord my God, I cried unto Thee, and Thou hast healed me. O Lord, Thou hast brought up my soul from the grave, Thou hast kept me alive, that I should not go down to the pit. I cried unto Thee, O Lord, and unto the Lord I made supplication: "Hear, O Lord, and have mercy upon me. Lord, be Thou my helper." Thou hast turned for me my mourning into dancing, Thou hast girded me with gladness; to the end that I may sing praise to Thee and not be silent. O Lord my God, I will give thanks unto Thee forever.

(Ps. 30:2, 3, 8, 10–12)

24. The Lord is the portion of mine inheritance and of my cup— my lot continually. The lines are fallen unto me in pleasant places; yea, I have a goodly heritage. I will bless the Lord, who hath given me counsel; yea, my heart instructeth me in the night seasons. I have set the Lord always before me because He is at my right hand, I shall not be moved. Therefore my heart is glad. For Thou wilt not leave my soul to the grave. Thou wilt show me the path of life, in Thy presence is fullness of joy. In Thy right hand there are pleasures forevermore.

(Ps. 16:2, 5–11)

25. O God, Thou art my God; I will seek Thee earnestly. My soul thirsteth for Thee, my flesh longeth for Thee, in a dry and weary land where no water is. Because Thy loving-kindness is better than life, my lips shall praise Thee. So will I bless Thee while I live, I will lift up my hands in Thy name. My soul shall be satisfied and my mouth shall praise Thee with joyful lips, when I remember

Thee upon my bed, and meditate on Thee in the night watches. For Thou hast been my help, and in the shadow of Thy wings will I rejoice. My soul followeth hard after Thee: Thy right hand upholdeth me.

(Ps. 63:1, 3–8)

Confession

1. Our backslidings are many; we have sinned against Thee.
(Jer. 14:7)

2. Father, I have sinned against heaven, and in Thy sight: I am no more worthy to be called Thy son.
(Luke 15:18, 19)

3. I am not worthy of the least of all the mercies, and of all the faithfulness, which Thou hast showed unto Thy servant.
(Gen. 32:10)

4. I have sinned greatly in that which I have done. But now, I beseech Thee, O Lord, take away the iniquity of Thy servant; for I have done very foolishly.
(2 Sam. 24:10)

5. I acknowledged my sin unto Thee, and mine iniquity did I not hide. I said, "I will confess my transgressions unto the Lord"; and Thou forgavest the iniquity of my sin.
(Ps. 32:5)

6. We looked for peace, but no good came; and for a time of healing; and behold! dismay. We acknowledge, O Lord, our wickedness, and the iniquity of our fathers; for we have sinned against Thee.
 (Jer. 14:19, 20)

7. O Thou that hearest prayer, unto Thee shall all flesh come. Iniquities prevail against me; as for our transgressions, Thou wilt purge them away. Blessed is the man whom Thou choosest and causest to approach unto Thee.

(Ps. 65:2–4)

8. We are all become as one that is unclean, and all our righteousnesses are as a polluted garment, and we all do fade as a leaf, and our iniquities, like the wind, have taken us away, and there is none that calleth upon Thy name, that stirreth up himself to take hold of Thee.

(Is. 64:6, 7)

9. I beseech Thee, O Lord, God of heaven, the great and terrible God, that keepeth covenant and loving-kindness with them that love Him, and keep His commandments; let Thine ear now be attentive and Thine eyes open, that Thou mayest hearken unto the prayer of Thy servant, which I offer before Thee at this time for Thy servants, while I confess the sins which we have committed against Thee. We have dealt very corruptly against Thee, and have not kept the commandments, nor the statutes, nor the ordinances which Thou didst command.

(Neh. 1:5–7)

10. O my God, I am ashamed and blush to lift up my face to Thee, my God; for our iniquities are increased over our head, and our guiltiness is grown up unto the heavens. Since the days of our fathers, we have been exceeding guilty unto this day, and for our iniquities have we been delivered to confusion of face. And now, O our God, what shall we say after this? for we have forsaken Thy commandments. And after all that is come upon us for our evil deeds, and for our great guilt, seeing that Thou, our God, hast punished us less than our iniquities deserve, shall we again break Thy commandments? Wouldest not Thou be angry with us till Thou hadst consumed us? Behold, we are before Thee in our guiltiness, for none can stand before Thee because of this.

(Ezra 9:6, 7, 10, 13, 15)

11. Have mercy upon me, O God, according to Thy loving-kindness; according to the multitude of Thy tender mercies blot out my transgressions. Wash me thoroughly from mine iniquity and cleanse me from my sin. For I acknowledge my transgressions, and my sin is ever before me. Against Thee have I sinned, and done that which is evil in Thy sight. Wash me, and I shall be whiter than snow. Make me to hear joy and gladness, that the bones which Thou hast broken may rejoice. Hide Thy face from my sins, and blot out all mine iniquities. Create in me a clean heart, O God, and renew a right spirit within me. Cast me not away from Thy presence, and take not Thy holy spirit from me. Restore unto me the joy of Thy salvation. O Lord, open Thou my lips; and my mouth shall show forth Thy praise.
(Ps. 51:1–4, 7–12, 15)

12. O Lord, the great and dreadful God, who keepeth covenant and loving-kindness with them that love Him and keep His commandments, we have sinned and have dealt perversely and have done wickedly, and have rebelled, even turning aside from Thy precepts and from Thine ordinances. O Lord, righteousness belongeth unto Thee, but unto us confusion of face. To the Lord our God belong mercies and forgiveness, for we have rebelled against Him, neither have we obeyed His voice, to walk in His laws. Therefore hath the curse been poured out upon us, for we have sinned against Him. The Lord our God is righteous in all His works which He doeth, and we have not obeyed His voice. And now, O Lord our God, we have sinned, we have done wickedly. O Lord, according to all Thy righteousness, let Thine anger, I pray Thee, be turned away. Hearken, O our God, unto the prayer of Thy servant, and to his supplications, and cause Thy face to shine upon us. For we do not present our supplications before Thee for our righteousness, but for Thy great mercies' sake. O Lord, hear; O Lord, forgive; O Lord, hearken and do.
(Dan. 9:4–10, 15–19)

Praise

1. Blessing, and glory, and wisdom, and thanksgiving, and honor, and power, and might, be unto our God forever and ever.
   (Rev. 7:12)

2. Worthy art Thou, our Lord and our God, to receive the glory and the honor and the power; for Thou didst create all things, and because of Thy will they were and were created.
   (Rev. 4:11)

3. Great and marvelous are Thy works, Lord God Almighty. Just and true are Thy ways, Thou everlasting King. Who shall not fear Thee, O Lord, and glorify Thy name? for Thou only art holy.
   (Rev. 15:3, 4)

4. Thou art Lord, even Thou alone. Thou hast made heaven the heaven of heavens, with all their host, the earth, and all things that are thereon, the seas, and all that is therein, and Thou preservest them all; and the host of heaven worshipeth Thee.
   (Neh. 9:6)

5. Blessed be the name of God forever and ever, for wisdom and might are His. He giveth wisdom unto the wise, and knowledge to them that have understanding. He revealeth the deep and secret things; He knoweth what is in the darkness, and the light dwelleth with Him.
   (Dan. 2:20, 22)

6. Ah, Lord God! behold, Thou hast made the heavens and the earth by Thy great power and by Thine outstretched arm, and there is nothing too hard for Thee. Thou showest loving-kindness unto thousands—the great, the mighty God, the Lord of hosts is His name, great in counsel and mighty in work.
(Jer. 32:17–19)

7. Thy mercy, O Lord, is in the heavens, and Thy faithfulness reacheth unto the clouds. Thy righteousness is like the mountains of God, Thy judgments are a great deep. O Lord, Thou preservest man and beast. How excellent is Thy loving-kindness, O God, and the children of men put their trust under the shadow of Thy wings. They shall be abundantly satisfied with the fatness of Thy house, and Thou shalt make them drink of the river of Thy pleasures. For with Thee is the fountain of life, in Thy light shall we see light. O continue Thy loving-kindness unto them that know Thee, and Thy righteousness to the upright in heart.
(Ps. 36:5–10)

8. Blessed be Thou, O Lord God, forever and ever. Thine, O Lord, is the greatness and the power and the glory and the victory, and the majesty; for all that is in the heavens and the earth is Thine. Thine is the kingdom, O Lord, and Thou art exalted as head above all. Both riches and honor come from Thee, and Thou reignest over all; and in Thy hand is power and might and in Thy hand it is to make great, and to give strength unto all. Now therefore, O our God, we thank Thee and praise Thy glorious name. We are strangers before Thee and sojourners, as all our fathers were; our days on the earth are as a shadow, and there is no abiding.
(1 Chr. 29:10–13, 15)

Benedictions and Doxologies

1. Now unto the King, eternal, immortal, invisible, the only God, be honor and glory, forever and ever. Amen.
(1 Tim. 1:17)

2. The grace of the Lord Jesus Christ, and the love of God, and the communion of the Holy Spirit, be with you all.
(2 Cor. 13:14)

3. The Lord bless thee and keep thee, the Lord make His face shine upon thee, and be gracious unto thee, the Lord lift up His countenance upon thee, and give thee peace.
(Num. 6:24–26)

4. Now unto Him that is able to keep you from falling and to present you faultless before the presence of His glory, with exceeding joy, to the only God our Savior, be glory and majesty, dominion and power, both now and ever. Amen.
(Jude 1:24, 25)

5. Now unto Him that is able to do exceeding abundantly above all that we ask or think, according to the power that worketh in us, unto Him be the glory in the Church and in Christ Jesus, throughout all ages, world without end. Amen.
(Eph. 3:20, 21)

6. Now the God of peace, who brought again from the dead our Lord Jesus, that great Shepherd of the sheep, through the blood of an everlasting covenant, make you perfect in every good work to do His will, working in you that which is well-pleasing in His sight, through Jesus Christ; to whom be glory forever and ever. Amen.

(Heb. 13:20, 21)

Sentences Introductory to Public Worship

Oh magnify the Lord with me, and let us exalt His name together. (Ps. 34:3)

Oh come, let us worship and bow down: let us kneel before the Lord our maker. For He is our God, and we are the people of His pasture and the sheep of His hand.
(Ps. 95:6, 7)

Serve the Lord with gladness, come before His presence with singing. Enter into his gates with thanksgiving, and into His courts with praise: give thanks unto Him and bless His name. For the Lord is good, His loving-kindness endureth forever, and His faithfulness unto all generations.
(Ps. 100:2, 4, 5)

Oh, send out Thy light and Thy truth. Let them lead us, let them bring us unto Thy holy hill.
(Ps. 43:3)

It is a good thing to give thanks unto the Lord, and to sing praises unto Thy name, O most High: to show forth Thy loving-kindness in the morning, and Thy faithfulness every night.
(Ps. 92:1, 2)

How amiable are Thy tabernacles, O Lord of hosts! My soul longeth, yea, even fainteth for the courts of the Lord: my heart and my flesh cry out unto the living God. Blessed are they that dwell in Thy house, they will praise Thee evermore.

(Ps. 84:1, 2, 4)

Praise waiteth for Thee, O God, in Zion, and unto Thee shall the vow be performed. O Thou that hearest prayer, unto Thee shall all flesh come.

(Ps. 65:1, 2)

Blessed is the man whom Thou choosest, and causest to approach unto Thee, that he may dwell in Thy courts. We shall be satisfied with the goodness of Thy house, even of Thy holy temple.

(Ps. 65:4)

Who shall ascend into the hill of the Lord? and who shall stand in His holy place? He that hath clean hands and a pure heart; who hath not lifted up his soul unto vanity, nor sworn deceitfully. He shall receive a blessing from the Lord, and righteousness from the God of his salvation.

(Ps. 24:3–5)

Lord, who shall abide in Thy tabernacle? Who shall dwell in Thy holy hill? He that walketh uprightly, and worketh righteousness, and speaketh truth in his heart.

(Ps. 15:1, 2)

I was glad when they said unto me, "Let us go unto the house of the Lord." Our feet are standing within Thy gates, O Jerusalem.

(Ps. 122:1, 2)

I will lift up mine eyes to the hills: from whence cometh my help? My help cometh from the Lord, who made heaven and earth.

(Ps. 121:1, 2)

O God, Thou art my God, early will I seek Thee: my soul thirsteth for Thee, my flesh longeth for Thee. Because Thy loving-

kindness is better than life, my lips shall praise Thee.
(Ps. 63:1, 3)

O Lord, open Thou my lips, and my mouth shall show forth Thy praise. For Thou delightest not in sacrifice, else would I give it Thee: Thou hast no pleasure in burnt offering. The sacrifices of God are a broken spirit: a broken and a contrite heart, O God, Thou wilt not despise.
(Ps. 51:15–17)

Behold, bless ye the Lord, all ye servants of the Lord, that stand by night in the courts of the Lord.
(Ps. 134:1)

Praise ye the name of the Lord: praise Him, O ye servants of the Lord. Ye that stand in the house of the Lord, in the courts of the house of our God. Praise the Lord, for the Lord is good: sing praises unto His name, for it is pleasant.
(Ps. 135:1–3)

This is the day which the Lord hath made: we will rejoice and be glad in it.
(Ps. 118:24)

Blessed is the people that know the joyful sound: they shall walk, O Lord, in the light of Thy countenance. In Thy name shall they rejoice all the day.
(Ps. 89:16)

As for me, in the abundance of Thy loving-kindness will I come into Thy house: in Thy fear will I worship toward Thy holy temple.
(Ps. 5:7)

O ye servants of the Lord, praise the name of the Lord. From the rising of the sun unto the going down of the same the Lord's name is to be praised.
(Ps. 113:1, 3)

Give praise to our God, all ye his servants, ye that fear Him, the small and the great.

(Rev. 19:5)

Oh, taste and see that the Lord is good. Blessed is the man that trusteth in Him.

(Ps. 34:8)

Wherewithal shall I come before the Lord, and bow myself before the high God? What doth the Lord require but to do justly and to love mercy, and to walk humbly with thy God.

(Mic. 6:6, 8)

The hour cometh, and now is, when the true worshipers shall worship the Father in spirit and truth: for such doth the Father seek to be His worshipers. God is spirit, and they that worship Him must worship Him in spirit and in truth.

(John 4:23, 24)

Draw nigh unto God, and He will draw nigh unto you. Cleanse your hands and purify your hearts.

(James 4:8)

Let us draw near with a true heart in fullness of faith, having our hearts sprinkled from an evil conscience.

(Heb. 10:22)

Let us draw near with boldness unto the throne of grace, that we may receive mercy and find grace to help in time of need.

(Heb. 4:16)

Ye are come unto Mount Zion, and unto the city of the living God, the heavenly Jerusalem, and to Jesus the mediator of a new covenant.

(Heb. 12:22, 24)

Where two or three are gathered together in My name, there am I in the midst of them.

(Matt. 18:20)

From the rising of the sun even unto the going down of the same, My name is great among the nations: for I am a great King, saith the Lord of hosts.

(Mal. 1:11, 14)

Great is the Lord, and greatly to be praised. Honor and majesty are before Him: strength and beauty are in His sanctuary.

(Ps. 96:4, 6)

The eyes of all wait upon Thee. Thou openest Thine hand and satisfiest the desire of every living thing. The Lord is nigh unto all them that call upon Him, to all that call upon Him in truth.

(Ps. 145:15, 16, 18)

Seek ye the Lord, while He may be found; call ye upon Him while He is near; for as the heavens are higher than the earth, so are my ways higher than your ways, and my thoughts than your thoughts, saith the Lord.

(Is. 55:6, 9)

God is our refuge and strength, a very present help in trouble. Therefore we will not fear, though the earth be moved, and though the mountains be shaken into the heart of the seas.

(Ps. 46:1, 2)

Thy mercy, O Lord, is in the heavens, and Thy faithfulness reacheth unto the skies. Thy righteousness is like the mountains of God, Thy judgments are a great deep. O Lord, Thou preservest man and beast.

(Ps. 36;5, 6)

How excellent is Thy loving-kindness, O God. Therefore the children of men take refuge under the shadow of Thy wings. Thou wilt make them to drink of the river of Thy pleasures. For with Thee is the fountain of life: in Thy light shall we see light.

(Ps. 36:7–9)

Bow down Thine ear, O Lord, and answer us; for we are poor and needy. Rejoice the soul of Thy servants; for unto Thee, O Lord, do we lift up our soul.

(Ps. 86:1, 4)

As the hart panteth after the waterbrooks, so panteth our soul after Thee, O God.

(Ps. 42:1)

Cause us to hear Thy loving-kindness in the morning, for in Thee do we trust. Cause us to know the way wherein we should walk, for we lift up our soul unto Thee.

(Ps. 143:8)

Great is the Lord, and greatly to be praised, and His greatness is unsearchable. We will meditate on the glorious honor of Thy majesty, and of Thy wondrous works.

(Ps. 145:3, 5)

They that trust in the Lord shall be as Mount Zion, which cannot be moved, but abideth forever. As the mountains are round about Jerusalem, so the Lord is round about His people from this time forth and forevermore.

(Ps. 125:1, 2)

My soul waiteth for the Lord, more than they that watch for the morning. Hope ye in the Lord; for with the Lord there is mercy and plenteous redemption.

(Ps. 130:6, 7)

Behold, the eye of the Lord is upon them that fear Him, upon them that hope in His mercy. Our soul waiteth for the Lord: He is our help and our shield.

(Ps. 33:18, 20)

The eyes of the Lord are toward the righteous, and His ears are open unto their cry. The Lord is nigh unto them that are of a broken heart, and saveth such as are of a contrite spirit.

(Ps. 34:15, 18)

The eternal God is our refuge, and underneath are the everlasting arms.

(Deut. 33:27)

Ask, and it shall be given you; seek, and ye shall find; knock, and it shall be opened unto you. For everyone that asketh receiveth, and he that seeketh findeth, and to him that knocketh it shall be opened.

(Matt. 7:7, 8)

This is the boldness which we have toward Him, that, if we ask anything according to His will, He heareth us.

(1 John 5:14)

Trust in the Lord, and do good; rest in the Lord, and wait patiently for Him.

(Ps. 37:3, 7)

There is none like unto Thee, O Lord. Thou art great and Thy name is great in might. Who should not fear Thee, O King of the nations?

(Jer. 10:6, 7)

Let the words of our mouth and the meditations of our heart be acceptable in Thy sight, O Lord, our rock and our redeemer.

(Ps. 19:14)

General Index

Spiritual things, prayer for, 38, 39, 42, 48, 99, 133, 147
Standing at prayer, 85, 86
Stephen, 9, 85, 87, 120, 127, 133
Stevenson, 149, 154
Sympathy, 74, 75, 107

Tabitha, 48, 78
Temple, 91
Thanksgiving, 9, 10, 48–51, 133–135, 149, 150, 213–219, 247
of Jesus, 97
in Paul, 10, 112–114
Theological prayers, 166
Third person in prayer, 161, 162
Time of prayer, 89, 90, 95
Transfiguration, 109, 144, 145

Transition from second to third person, 62, 161
Tyre, Paul at, 9

Unanswered prayer, 77, 78, 80, 106, 117, 143

Vengeance, prayer for, 27, 28, 40, 108, 133
Vows, 82

Weeping, 83
Will of God, 78, 108
Wisdom, prayer for, 28
Women praying, 12, 13, 87
Work accompanying prayer, 82, 83

Zacharias, 20
Zedekiah, 29, 32, 47

Scripture Index

28:9	30	8:35, 36	265
28:15	30	8:38	86
30:7, 8	31	8:39	65, 166
30:8	31	8:41	147
		8:41–43	14
2 Samuel		8:46	42, 166
2:1	31	8:46–50	274
5:19	31	8:47	44, 90
7:18	86, 279	8:48	36
7:18–29	67, 215	8:51–53	23
7:19	214	8:54	85, 87
7:22	279	8:56–60	199
7:23	140, 214	8:60	76
7:25, 26	279	10:9	14
7:25–27	72	13:6	46, 81
15:8	82, 232	17:20	234
15:31	188	17:20, 21	87
16:12	55	17:21	47, 80, 88, 211
19:19, 20	25	17:21, 22	80
19:20	161	ch. 18	80
21:1	7	18:1	20
24:10	281	18:26	88, 191
24:17	43, 59, 211	18:26, 28	84
24:25	59	18:28	87
		18:33, 34	75
1 Kings		18:36	66, 89
3:5–14	20	18:36, 37	88, 164, 191
3:7–9	192	18:42	60, 85
3:11	36, 38	19:4	23, 191
3:13	36	19:9, 13	20
6:17	211	22:5	8
ch. 8	36, 160	22:6	31
8:3	14	22:7	31
8:7–9	262	22:32	59
8:14, 22	85		
8:22	86	**2 Kings**	
8:22, 54	86	2:24	80
8:23–53	198	3:11	8, 31
8:27	64, 161	3:27	84
8:27–30	267	4:33	90
8:28–53	164	4:35	80, 81
8:30	258	5:15	25
8:31, 32	165	5:23	25
8:33, 34	263	6:17	80